THE
AMERICAN
CHURCH
IN CRISIS

GROUNDBREAKING RESEARCH BASED ON A NATIONAL
DATABASE OF OVER 200,000 CHURCHES

THE AMERICAN CHURCH IN CRISIS

DAVID T. OLSON

FOREWORD BY CRAIG GROESCHEL

ZONDERVAN®

ZONDERVAN.com/
AUTHORTRACKER
follow your favorite authors

 ZONDERVAN®

The American Church in Crisis
Copyright © 2008 by David T. Olson

Requests for information should be addressed to:
Zondervan, *Grand Rapids, Michigan* 49530

Library of Congress Cataloging-in-Publication Data

Olson, David T., 1953-
    The American church in crisis : groundbreaking research based on a national database
of over 200,000 churches / David T. Olson ; foreword by Craig Groeschel.
      p. cm.
    Includes bibliographical references.
    ISBN-13: 978-0-310-27713-2 (hardcover)
    ISBN-10: 0-310-27713-2 (hardcover)
    1. Church attendance – United States – Statistics. I. Title.
BV652.5.O47 2008
277.3'.083 – dc22

                        2007049134

Interior design by Mark Sheeres

Printed in the United States of America

---

08 09 10 11 12 13 14 15 • 12 11 10 9 8 7 6 5 4 3 2 1

To Shelly,
the love of my life

CONTENTS

FOREWORD

Sitting on my back porch last Sunday afternoon, I asked myself the same question I have posed hundreds of times before: *Is our church* really *making a difference?*

Sometimes when I get together with my close pastor friends, we are optimistic, full of hope for the future of our churches. Other times, we have more sobering conversations. *Do the people we lead* really *care about the Gospel? Are they* really *growing closer to Christ? Is the world any better because our churches exist?*

Certainly, God is using most ministries to make some sort of difference. Marriages are healed. Teens are mentored. People of all ages are baptized. But just how much of a difference are we making? Is the American church gaining ground? Or losing it?

Dave Olson sheds invaluable insight on the condition, direction, and immediate needs of the American church. Dave writes with a rare combination of pastoral experience and denominational leadership backed up by rich church research. His meaningful findings answer most of the questions I've been asking ... and dozens I didn't know I *should* have been asking.

If you listen closely, you can hear the alarm. It's blaring. And its tone is growing louder by the second. The American church is in trouble. We are clearly losing ground we can't afford to lose.

What's at stake is not the future of denominations, church buildings, or the jobs of pastors. What's at stake are the souls of thousands of people who don't see any need for Christ, much less his church.

Dave is calling out a warning that all of our churches need to hear. Thankfully, his message is not the typical, fatalistic, doom-filled prophecy about the imminent demise of the American church. Instead, this book is packed with valuable insight, priceless research, and years of wisdom, all pointing toward practical answers about how to renew Christ's church.

If you have ever wondered, *Are we making a difference?* you are not alone. This book will equip you and motivate you to better communicate the life, love, and truth of Jesus Christ.

CRAIG GROESCHEL
Senior pastor of LifeChurch.tv

ACKNOWLEDGMENTS

Who I am, what I believe, and how I view the world was shaped by many people.

I am particularly indebted to the influence of my mother and father, both recently in the presence of the Lord. My father had a Ph.D in New Testament and helped shape how I view Scripture and hermeneutics. My mother bequeathed to me activistic energy.

I am thankful to the two denominations who hired me to help lead church planting. The Baptist General Conference hired Steve Johnson, Paul Johnson, and me when we were 34, 35, and 36 years old respectively, and soon after that, Erwin McManus, who was younger still, to lead their church planting movement. It was a risk that paid great dividends for me personally and professionally, through working with these great colleagues and thinkers as well as the learning and adventure it brought.

I began working for the Evangelical Covenant Church in 1993. The Covenant ethos has been formative in my personal and theological development, as in their history they have lived out parts of the Gospel that were underdeveloped in my understanding. I am particularly indebted to Gary Walter and John Notehelfer for their wisdom and spirituality. A host of church planters, CG & E staff, and regional church planting directors have been great friends, three of which have been pastor of the new churches our family attended—Ray Johnston, Efrem Smith, and Jan Bros. Special thanks to Craig Groeschel for his generosity in writing the foreword.

Bob Smietana was a Godsend to me by injecting more stories and better structure into the manuscript.

The writings of N. T. Wright, C. S. Lewis, J. R. R. Tolkien, Dorothy Sayers, and Lionel Basney enriched my thoughts about the Gospel and its communication—thank you.

I am grateful to Zondervan for taking a risk on a new author and for the help of Paul Engle and Jim Ruark.

Most of all, I wish to thank my wife Shelly, daughter Erica, and son John for their insightful suggestions and help with the manuscript. Daughters Andrea and Katie were also a great source of encouragement and ideas. Together they have helped create the great family of which I am privileged to be a part.

LIST OF FIGURES

Chapter 5. "Poor, Uneducated, and Easy to Command"

Chapter 6. Denominational Winners and Losers

Chapter 7. The Survival of the Species

Chapter 8. Why Established Churches Thrive or Decline

LIST OF ABBREVIATIONS

ABC	American Baptist Churches USA
AG	Assemblies of God
BGC	Baptist General Conference
C&MA	Christian and Missionary Alliance
COGTN	Church of God (Cleveland, TN)
COTN	Church of the Nazarene
CRC	Christian Reformed Church
DC	Christian Church (Disciples of Christ)
EC	Episcopal Church
ECC	Evangelical Covenant Church
EFCA	Evangelical Free Church of America
ELCA	Evangelical Lutheran Church in America
IPHC	International Pentecostal Holiness Church
LCMS	Lutheran Church–Missouri Synod
PCUSA	Presbyterian Church (U.S.A.)
PCA	Presbyterian Church in America
RCA	Reformed Church in America
SBC	Southern Baptist Convention
UCC	United Church of Christ
UMC	United Methodist Church
WELS	Wisconsin Evangelical Lutheran Synod

Division into "mainline" and "evangelical" is based on the Glenmary Religious Congregations and Membership Study. Further information is in chapter 1, note 17.

INTRODUCTION: WHY EXAMINE THE AMERICAN CHURCH?

Is the American Church Booming?

The American church is in crisis. At first glance this may not be apparent, but while many signs of its evident success and growth abound, in reality the American church is losing ground as the population continues to surge.

To the casual observer, the American church appears to be booming. Drive along Algonquin Road in South Barrington, Illinois, on a Sunday morning, and you will find uniformed police officers directing traffic into Willow Creek Community Church's vast parking lot. Volunteers in matching vests coordinate the parking, creating the feeling that you are attending a major league baseball game rather than a church service. In Willow Creek's massive lobby, an army of greeters welcomes visitors, points parents to the Promiseland children's program, and directs worshipers to the main auditorium. Inside the 7,000-seat auditorium, a praise band leads the congregation in spirited, high-energy singing, followed by a message delivered by a pastor whose image is projected on two massive video screens. The church and its satellite campuses draw more than 20,000 people each weekend. A similar scene is repeated each Sunday in hundreds of megachurches across the United States. While few reach the size of Willow Creek, more than 1,200 Protestant megachurches average more than 2,000 in weekly attendance, according to Scott Thumma, a sociologist of religion at Hartford Seminary.[1]

I received the same positive impression while thumbing through a copy of *Outreach Magazine* that ran an article titled "The 100 Fastest-Growing U.S. Churches." Willow Creek is on the list, as is Saddleback Community Church in Orange County, California; the Potter's House in Dallas; Lakewood Church in Houston; Salem Baptist Church in Chicago; and Life Church in Oklahoma City. The combined weekly attendance of the 10 fastest-growing churches in America, according to this issue of *Outreach*, is 153,232 people. The top 100 fastest-growing Protestant churches increased by 141,148 attendees last year. Lakewood Church in Houston is the fastest-growing church, expanding by a remarkable 12,000 people in attendance in one year. Cleveland Community Church in Clayton, North Carolina, is last on the list, increasing by 627 worshipers. These megachurches present a fabulously optimistic picture of the American church.[2]

The latest polls seem to confirm this glowing picture of the American church. The Gallup Organization reports that more than 40 percent of Americans say that in the last week they attended a house of worship. The Barna Group, in a study released in May 2007, reports even better numbers: 43 percent of Americans attend each week. If these poll numbers reflected reality, between 120 and 129 million Americans should be in a worship service on any given weekend. However, these numbers do not reflect reality. When you start to do the math, the vision of a booming American church unravels. As we will see, the actual attendance is less than half of what polls suggest.

In reality the church in America is not booming. It is in crisis. On any given Sunday, the vast majority of Americans are absent from church. Even more troublesome, as the American population continues to grow, the church falls further and further behind. If trends continue, by 2050 the percentage of Americans attending church will be half the 1990 figure.

For the past twenty years, The American Church Research Project (TACRP) has compiled comprehensive data on the state of the church in the United States. This research provides reliable attendance numbers for each of the 3,141 U.S. counties, for each state, and for the nation as a whole. The database includes attendance figures for more than 200,000 individual Christian churches, as reported from head counts conducted by each church. It also includes the zip code and founding date of most of these churches. In addition, for the 60,000 churches that do not report attendance, their membership was multiplied by the denomination's attendance-to-membership ratio. For the remaining 45,000 Christian churches that report neither membership nor attendance,[3] a realistic estimate was developed by using a statistical model that factored in the population, growth rate, and average attendance of the churches' counties. The research includes all historically orthodox Christian churches but does not include nonorthodox Christian churches or non-Christian religions.[4]

Throughout this book we will examine that data to acquire an in-depth perspective of the present reality of the church in America, not the church as we would wish—a booming church with a bright future—but the church as it truly is, with all of its challenges and possibilities. In a sense, a comprehensive physical will be performed, to check the vital signs of the American church and to determine its true condition.

Here are some of the questions that will be asked:

- How many people actually attend church on a weekend in the United States?
- Has the church kept pace with the 68 million new births and the 23 million new immigrants who have arrived in the United States since 1990?
- How have the recent shifts in American culture affected the church, and how is the church responding to those changes?
- Considering the growth of large churches, is the megachurch trend adversely affecting small and midsized churches?
- How does the age of a church affect its growth rate? Does aging negatively affect churches in the same way that aging affects human bodies?
- Are churches growing faster in affluent communities or underprivileged neighborhoods?
- Has the growth rate of evangelical churches increased or declined in recent years?
- Membership in mainline denominations has declined for the past 40 years. Is their attendance declining as well?
- While Roman Catholic churches are growing substantially in membership, what about attendance at Mass?

The answers to these questions will unfold throughout the book. My goal is not to be alarmist, but rather to paint an accurate picture of the church's current reality and then suggest a constructive path forward for the American church.

Building, Decaying, Restoring

In his poem "The Rock," T. S. Eliot wrote eloquently about the church's challenges and potential:

> And the Church must be forever building,
> And always decaying,
> And always being restored.[5]

Eliot employed three phrases to capture the ebb and flow of the life of Christ's church. "Always decaying" indicates that every organic entity diminishes and decays over time. In fact, in the biological world, decay is often necessary for new growth to appear. "Forever building" depicts the pattern of creative initiatives that promote life and vitality. Building may be unplanned or strategic, and that choice will usually determine the level of its influence and its longevity. "Always being restored" describes a spiritual and supernatural act of God. Restoration takes place when God acts through the power of the gospel story and the movement of the Holy Spirit, breathing new life into his church. The combined process of building and restoration unite human and divine efforts to fashion the house of God. "For we are God's co-workers; you are God's field, God's building" (1 Cor. 3:9).

This book will guide us on a comprehensive journey to reveal the simultaneous decay and building occurring in American Christianity. Churches cannot wisely build or be restored until they first discern the changes taking place.

Camp Meetings and Societal Change

The goal of moving from decay to restoration is not simply for the church to grow numerically, not simply to have more churches with more people sitting in them. Instead, the goal is to move the church into more fruitful ministry so that the church can transform culture with the love and grace of God. Spiritual transformation gives rise to both personal and societal change. The late poet and scholar Lionel Basney's deeply insightful essay "Immanuel's Ground" illustrates this transformation. Awarded Best Essay in the 1999 American Scholar Awards, Basney's essay describes the connection between the Second Great Awakening and the abolitionist movement. The "Jerusalem" of camp meeting Pentecost was Cane Ridge, Kentucky, where the original small log chapel today sits "restored and quiet, encased in a stone basilica" to protect the church from outside elements.

Tens of thousands attended these revivals and were transformed by encounters with God. As both slave and free worshiped together, the experience changed the manner in which white Christians perceived slavery. The experience of worship alerted them to the incongruity between their social and spiritual reality.

In the electric atmosphere of the camp meetings, Basney wrote, "the rules of normal culture vanished. The little church had a slave balcony, but outside, slaves and masters marched side by side and women and children preached." The Great Awakening helped spark popular interest in abolitionist politics. Biblical images of the Promised Land called forth, in both slave and free Christians, the hope of a restored community.

> Crossing over Jordan into campground, tenting there, the "hundred circling camps" with their altars and their "righteous sentence" read out in torch light: such images are not chosen or designed—rather, exuded, almost, from intense experience—but they made war over slavery plausible and therefore possible.[6]

Basney projected these powerful camp meeting experiences forward to the present day, using them to envision religion's potential influence on culture.

A new iconography is a new history, a set of conditions to which unprecedented things can be deliberatively done. Any intensely religious event is an intensely worldly event. It remakes the world itself by affecting the meanings of the most comprehensive, least avoidable conditions. A religious event that does not change the meaning of light and dark, food and drink, field and city, war and peace, birth and death, slavery and freedom, has too superficial a connection with us. One that does can create culture. Not a new mind, but a new world.[7]

A new hope, a new reality, a new world—that is the dream of the church, a dream in which God powerfully transforms our lives, our communities, our culture, and our world through the message and mission of Jesus.

Ultimately, the new world for which we long can be birthed only through an ancient story. This story is an epic drama about a God who created people for an intimate love relationship with himself and with each other, a God who created a world of wondrous beauty, peace, and harmony. But paradise was lost. Sin entered God's perfect world and infected every particle of creation. Decay, corruption, strife, and turmoil afflict our world. Self and pride reign supreme. Everyone has felt the sharp sting of sin, hatred, guilt, alienation, and conflict—as inflictor as well as recipient. As a result, each of us will one day face death and God's ultimate judgment.

But the good news of the Christian faith is that God has intervened. Jesus became flesh to bring about a dramatic act of redemption, restoration, and re-creation. Through his life, death, resurrection, and ascension, the inexorable path toward decay, degeneration, and destruction has turned a sharp corner. New life in Christ provides a taste of the fullness of life as God intended.

Just as Jesus did not come to us disembodied, today's telling of the gospel requires hands, feet, and words to translate love from intangible idea to personal touch. This story requires a committed community seeking God's reign on earth as in heaven. That committed community is Christ's church. Devoted yet imperfect followers of Christ are asked to do the extraordinary: to love as Christ loved, to serve as Christ served, and to live as Christ's community for the world. Sorrowfully, the church often fails, yet it often has acted as a powerful agent to preserve hope in times of despair, righteousness in times of iniquity, and justice in times of oppression. Christ's church can make a unique contribution to our culture, challenging the aspects of our society that destroy God's good creation and helping to birth a new world. Restoration can happen within each of us and within the church, giving a taste of heaven on earth.

The following chapters present a snapshot of American Christianity, showing where decay is occurring, where building is happening, and where restoration might break forth. Only when Christians know the true state of the American church and why foundational changes are transpiring can they then understand how to rebuild and restore the church.

My desire is simple: to help the people of God faithfully serve Christ and their neighbors. With this book my intention is to objectively observe reality and then suggest productive pathways that will produce health and growth, consistent with the gospel of Christ. My prayer is that by discovering the contours of the spiritual terrain of the American church, Christ's church may, in the midst of decay, begin the invigorating and rejuvenating journey of "forever building and always being restored."

Part I

OBSERVATION

If you want to know whether a man is religious, don't ask him, observe him.

Ludwig Wittgenstein[1]

The story of Joshua and Caleb's reconnaissance of the Promised Land provides a model for facing change in the church and culture today. This narrative is an early chapter in the grand overarching story of salvation, a saga inaugurated by the patriarchs, culminating in the coming of the Messiah. Before the people of Israel entered the Promised Land, they scouted the territory. God spoke to Moses, saying, "Send some men to explore the land of Canaan, which I am giving to the Israelites" (Num. 13:2). So Moses chose twelve for the scouting party.

Understanding any situation requires accurate onsite observation. All effective observation begins with perceptive questions. Before the Israelites marched into Canaan or even developed a strategy, Moses asked his scouting party to find the answers to a series of questions:

> "See what the land is like and whether the people who live there are strong or weak, few or many. What kind of land do they live in? Is it good or bad? What kind of towns do they live in? Are they unwalled or fortified? How is the soil? Is it fertile or poor? Are there trees in it or not? Do your best to bring back some of the fruit of the land." (Num. 13:18–20)

These questions required detailed research. This would not be a daylong cursory survey. The mission of the scouts would involve extensive travel and take forty days to complete.

Before determining a strategy for change, church leaders must first understand the shifts occurring within church and culture. The church needs explorers to delve into the demographic and spiritual topography of our country. This book will ask a series of explorative questions similar in nature to Moses' questions above. This scrutiny is necessary, because little academic research has examined the attendance trajectory of the church in America. No single source paints an entirely clear picture.

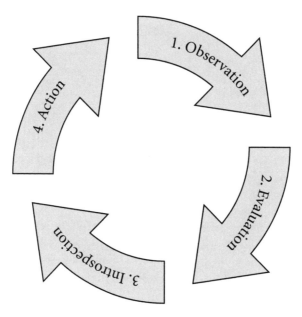

Fig. I.1. The four-stage assessment process.

The book of Numbers suggests a four-stage process for assessing America's spiritual terrain. *Observation,* the first stage, involves *asking questions and collecting data.* The American church is a complex image in need of greater clarity. Its picture is richly hued, with unique regional themes and religious histories and practices. In the first six chapters, these observations paint a portrait of the American church. The first chapter asks the foundational question, "How many people really attend a Christian church on any given weekend?"

Chapter 1

HOW MANY PEOPLE REALLY ATTEND CHURCH?

"Where is she? She was right here! How will we find her?"

Our family flew overnight to England, drove directly to downtown London, and caught a taxi to Westminster Abbey and the Houses of Parliament. When we finished our sightseeing, the family began to walk eastward toward our car. At the incredibly busy intersection of Parliament and Bridge streets, we all agreed that we desperately needed food, as we had eaten our last meal somewhere over the Atlantic.

Our youngest daughter, Katie, believed that we were all following her as she headed into the crowd in search of a restaurant. Two minutes later, she looked back and noticed that no one was following her. Her heart began to beat rapidly, and tears welled up.

At the same moment, the rest of the family noticed that Katie had disappeared. Our daughter was lost in a city of 15 million people. Our London

excursion had become every parent's nightmare. We divided up to search for our lost Katie. In the meantime, realizing her plight, Katie had reversed direction and began retracing her steps. Not long afterward, her older brother, John, became the hero by finding Katie and bringing her back to the appointed rendezvous site.

I remember our London experience when pondering the challenges the church faces. My daughter, thinking we were following her, looked behind and discovered that no one was there. If Christians were to look around, they would find that far fewer Americans are following their lead and authentically connecting to a local church than they might think. In a spiritual sense, so many Americans are lost.

That sense of "lost" haunts American culture. In spite of our technological advances and scientific certainty, our prosperity and abundant possessions, many people are miserable. In the 1990s a PBS documentary labeled this condition "affluenza," which was defined as both "the bloated, sluggish and unfulfilled feeling that results from efforts to keep up with the Joneses" and "an epidemic of stress, overwork, waste and indebtedness caused by dogged pursuit of the American Dream."[1] Greg Easterbrook, a senior editor of the *New Republic*, called this the "progress paradox," or "how life gets better while people feel worse."[2]

Perhaps the most recent sign of this discontent in American culture is the success of *The Secret*, a get-rich-quick guide that debuted in December 2006. By March 2007, with 1.75 million copies already in print, the book's publisher announced plans for an additional 2 million copies, the largest print order in the company's history, according to *Publishers Weekly*. Sara Nelson, editor of *Publishers Weekly*, described *The Secret*'s success, saying, "Nobody ever went broke overestimating the desperate unhappiness of the American public."[3]

However, most people know there is more to life than making money or achieving success. Christianity addresses the quest for meaningful answers to life's deepest longings and questions such as "Is there a God?" "What is my destiny?" "Is there a place for me in this world?"

Orthodox Christianity confesses that an experience with the true God and belief in Jesus as Savior and Lord brings salvation — moving people from the category of lost to that of found. Lionel Basney described this Christian experience:

> For it is finally a matter of how belief is born in the new believer. That it occurs is plain; how it occurs may be told, and the narratives can, within a given community, be formalized, but finally we will have no evidence but the narrative. I once was lost, but now am found.
>
> "Those who are awakened to the light," Tillich wrote, "ask passionately the question of ultimate reality. They are different from those who do not." ... The truth is that religious believers are always asking themselves this question ... and that if there is a subjective answer in devotion, *the objective evidence is the persistence of the community that believes.*[4]

Don't Ask; Observe

This chapter asks, "How many people belong to 'the community that believes'?" This complex question is best answered by looking at four categories of belief expressed through behavior:

1. How many people attend an orthodox Christian church on any given weekend?
2. How many people regularly participate in the life of that community? (Not all are present every week.)
3. How many people have some level of occasional connection to a Christian community?
4. How many people report belonging to a particular church tradition, even though they have no authentic connection as shown by their actions?

A growing number of religious researchers believe that weekend church attendance is the most helpful indicator of America's spiritual climate. Attendance gives a more accurate picture of a person's religious commitment than membership. As the philosopher Ludwig Wittgenstein said, "If you want to know whether a man is religious, don't ask him, observe him."

Attendance is a real-time indicator, a weekly appraisal of commitment. Membership reflects a commitment to a church made in the past but may not be reflective of current actions. The value of membership also differs by generation. The builder generation (born 1920–45) loved to join organizations. The boomer cohort (born 1946–64) resists institutional commitment. Looking at attendance rather than membership diminishes the effect of this generational difference.

Should church attendance numbers matter to Christians? Yes, they should. When church attendance declines, fewer people hear the gospel for the first time, take the sacraments, or hear of God's love for them. Fewer marriages are restored. Fewer teenagers find a listening ear. The question "How many people attend church?" matters deeply because people matter.

Recently, a pastor sent me an email asking about the importance of church attendance. He attended a presentation in which I pointed out that church attendance lagged behind population growth. He asked me why that mattered. I compared the dramatic growth in the number of children in his home state, Arizona, with the more modest increase in church attendance. The church in Arizona grew in attendance by 1.4 percent each year from 2000 to 2005, while the general population grew by 3 percent each year. During that five-year period, 22,000 additional children and teenagers began to attend church regularly. Yet from 2000 to 2005, the under 18 population of Arizona grew by 207,000.

In the short span of five years, 185,000 children and youth were born in or moved to Arizona who had no consistent connection to a church. Does that matter? Attendance numbers are significant because they represent people who are loved by God.

What Percentage Attend?

How many people attend church each week? This remains a surprisingly controversial question. Since 1939 Gallup pollsters have asked Americans if they went to church in the last week. In February 1939 Gallup asked, "Did you happen to go to church last Sunday?" and 41 percent of people said yes. And every year since, while the question has changed to "Did you yourself happen to attend church or synagogue in the last seven days?" the answer has remained the same. Around 40 percent of people say yes, they went to church this week. From 2002 to 2005, the yes answer to Gallup polls ranged from 40 to 44 percent. During that same period, the Barna Research Group reported similar findings: 43 to 47 percent of American adults surveyed said that they attended church on the past weekend. Clearly, both polls accurately describe what people *say* about their church attendance pattern. Whether the answers accurately describe people's actual behavior is another story.

As well as reporting poll numbers, both Barna and Gallup comment on changes in church attendance patterns. George Barna writes,

> From the mid-eighties to the mid-nineties, church attendance was on a roller coaster ride. In 1986, 42 percent of adults attended a church service during a typical week in January. Attendance rose steadily, reaching a peak of 49 percent in 1991, before beginning a very slow but steady descent back to 43 percent in January 2002.[5]

Barna often microanalyzes the polling data for each year. In 1997 he made this comment:

> The escalation of interest in religion and spirituality has brought about a significant influx of adults back to the church. These gains have been steadily increasing since last January, when just 37 percent of adults were attending religious services during a typical week. Since that time attendance has consistently grown, reaching 43 percent in January of this year.[6]

If the American church grew in attendance by 6 percent in one year, then 16 million additional people began to attend church in that year. With that sort of growth, worship attendance at every church in America would have increased by an average of 54 people. Since the average size of a Protestant church in America is 124, most churches would have noticed such a large increase. However, no reports surfaced of churches swamped by new attendees.

In 2004 George H. Gallup Jr. reported on changes in the polling numbers for Roman Catholic church attendance. He wrote, "Weekly church attendance among U.S. Catholics appears to be on the rebound from an all-time low of 35 percent last February (2003).... The November 2003 data show that 45 percent of Catholics and 48 percent of Protestants say they attend church services weekly."[7] According to Gallup, 6.5 million absent Catholics returned to weekly Mass attendance in a nine-month period in 2003.[8] The average parish would have grown in attendance by 325 in those nine months. That would be an astounding increase, considering that Catholic parishes average 792 in attendance.

Instead of Roman Catholic churches being filled with the returning faithful, attendance counts actually dwindled. Two of the nation's most prominent archdioceses illustrate the significant decline during this period. In early 2004 the *Boston Globe* reported that in the Archdiocese of Boston, weekly Mass attendance had dropped 15 percent in the wake of the clergy sexual-abuse crisis. According to archdiocese figures, Mass attendance in October of 2003 was 304,000, down 15 percent from October 2001.[9] The Archdiocese of Chicago reported a 5.9 percent decline in Mass attendance from October 2002 to October 2003.[10] Mass attendance counts throughout the country showed a significant decline during this period rather than a strong recovery.

Attendance polls can also be internally inconsistent with other polling information collected by the same organization. In 2005 Barna reported that 47 percent of Americans went to church each weekend. With the U.S. population then at 296 million, church attendance would have reached 140 million people each week. However, Barna also reported that the average attendance at a Protestant church service was 90 adults.[11] When adjusted for children and multiplied by the number of Protestant churches in America, and Catholic Mass attendance is accounted for, this calculation would show that 52 million people attended a Christian church each weekend in 2005. Which number is correct: 140 million or 52 million?

In 2006 Frank Newport, editor in chief of the Gallup Poll, told *Christianity Today* that the results of their poll "should not be taken as a precise indicator of actual churchgoing behavior." Why? Because the question about church attendance is part of a larger opinion survey, not part of a specific study to determine actual churchgoing behavior. To obtain a "more precise" figure, *Christianity Today* reported, Gallup "would have to approach the problem differently — using multiple surveys, having respondents keep track of actual churchgoing behavior, and doing follow-up calls." Newport also wondered, according to *Christianity Today*, "if people tell pollsters what they usually do, rather than reporting actual behavior for a given week."[12]

The Halo Effect

Pollsters call this overreporting the "halo effect." The U.S. presidential election in 1996 provides an example of overreporting. Polls after the election reported that 58 percent of adults claimed they voted, when the official election count showed that only 49 percent voted. The halo effect occurs when people want to show themselves engaged in socially acceptable behavior. Three subjects typically generate a halo effect: sex, politics, and religion.

In the early 1990s, researchers began to question the accuracy of church attendance polls. In 1993 sociologist Penny Long Marler, C. Kirk Hadaway, and Mark Chaves examined church attendance counts and found them much lower than expected. In a follow-up study in 1999, published in *Sociology of Religion*, they noted: "Religious behavior was found to be misreported, even by the members of a conservative, Bible-belt church. Most of the misreporting was by church members who considered themselves to be among the most active members of the congregation. Americans overreport socially desirable behavior and underreport socially undesirable behavior."[13]

Sociologists Stanley Presser and Linda Stinson published results from a study of notes in personal diaries written from the mid-1960s to the 1990s. They found that many Americans were not at church when they claimed to be. They estimated that church attendance was about 26 percent during that interval.[14]

In recent studies of selected counties in the United States and Canada, individuals were counted as they went into houses of worship. The researchers later interviewed a random sampling of adults in these counties. They found that the survey results were inflated by about 100 percent from the actual attendance figures. Although about 40 percent of the American adults said that they attended church, around 20 percent actually attended. Canadians overreported their attendance by the same percentage.[15]

More recently, Kirk Hadaway and Penny Long Marler published another study, "How Many Americans Attend Worship Each Week? An Alternative Approach to Measurement," in the *Journal for the Scientific Study of Religion*.[16] They compiled data from more than 300,000 Christian congregations in the United States and found that the churches totaled 52 million people in attendance, or 17.7 percent of the American population in 2004.

These studies indicate a rather large halo effect for self-reported church attendance. How much higher are the polls than the actual attendance count? The research of the American Church Research Project shows that 17.5 percent of the population attended an orthodox Christian church on any given weekend in 2005. Nonorthodox Christian churches and non-Christian religions[17] add an additional 35,000 houses of worship while increasing the 2005 attendance percentage to 19.5 percent.

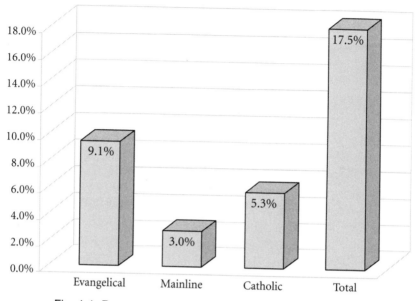

Fig. 1.1. Percentage of population attending a Christian church on any given weekend in 2005.

Thus, actual attendance counts weighed against poll results indicate that many people do not tell the truth in these surveys. While virtually all Christians occasionally miss church because of vacation, sickness, or other obligations, those things do not account for most of the variance. According to Marler and Hadaway, "Misreporting apparently is not caused by memory lapses, but instead results from active church members reporting behavior that is consistent with their perceptions of themselves as active churchgoers."[18]

How Many Participate?

While the most helpful category is weekly attendance, a second valuable question is "How many people are regular participants in the life of a church community?" A regular participant attends a Christian church on a consistent basis. A simple definition used by The American Church Research Project for "regular participant" is a person who attends church at least three out of every eight Sundays—another way of saying more than once a month. By using statistical modeling to calculate the frequency of attenders in the typical American congregation, the results show that 23 percent of Americans are "regular participants."[19]

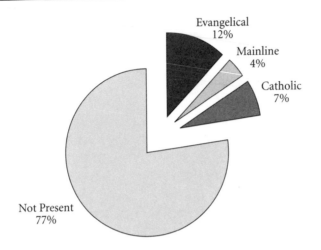

Fig. 1.2. 2005 "regular participants" by category.

"Regular participant" is a helpful designation to discern commitment in American Christianity. These 23 percent of Americans not only profess faith in Christ, but also live out their faith through active participation in the life of a church.

The converse is also true. Seventy-seven percent of Americans do not meet this definition. Seventy-seven percent of Americans do not have a consistent, life-giving connection with a local church. Is an authentic connection to the life of a church an integral part of Christianity? The late Henri Nouwen answered that question well:

> Listen to the Church. I know that isn't a popular bit of advice at a time and in a country where the Church is frequently seen more as an "obstacle" in the way rather than as the "way" to Jesus. Nevertheless, I'm profoundly convinced that the greatest spiritual danger for our times is the separation of Jesus from the Church. The Church is the body of the Lord. Without Jesus, there can be no Church; and without the Church, we cannot stay united with Jesus. I've yet to meet anyone who has come closer to Jesus by forsaking the Church. To listen to the Church is to listen to the Lord of the Church.[20]

How Many Are Connected?

The third category asks, "How many people have some level of occasional connection to a believing community?" How many people attend church once a month or less and occasionally contribute money to that church? An additional 14 percent of Americans belong to this group.[21] These first three categories together comprise 37 percent of Americans and are considered "active members."

How Many Claim Membership but Never Attend?

The fourth category is defined by the final question, "How many people report belonging to a particular church tradition, even though they have no authentic connection, particularly as shown by their actions?" Fifteen percent is the best estimate for this group.[22] All four categories comprise 52 percent of Americans and are considered "inclusive members." These four categories are shown in figure 1.3.

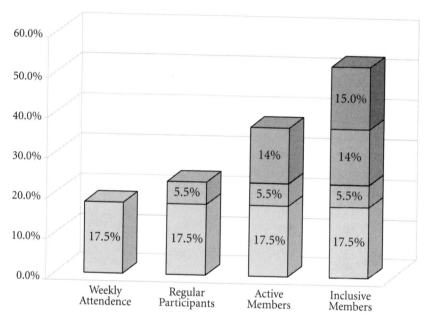

Fig. 1.3. Four categories of attendees and members.

Implications for the Church

Christians have always claimed that the gospel at its core is a rescue project initiated by God. Jesus emphasized this in the three parables of Luke 15—the lost sheep, the lost coin, and the lost son. Luke 19:10 makes clear that "the Son of Man came to seek and to save what was lost." Jesus came to find lost people. He came to reconcile us to God, creating within us new hearts, new lives, and new stories. Still, all of us have neighbors who have never heard the message of Jesus in a clear and compelling manner.

Our family helped start a new church in 1995. The congregation initially met in Greenhills Elementary School in Granite Bay, California, a 1960s facility with a small parking lot embedded in a neighborhood of ranch houses. As the church began to grow, the lot filled up and attendees began to park on neighborhood streets. Church member Steve Gall, realizing that some neighbors were unhappy with the extra Sunday morning traffic, organized a bagels and orange juice delivery to each home, using red Radio Flyer wagons.

A young mother who lived across the street from the school noticed the new church and was motivated by the gift to attend the following week. The next Sunday she dressed up and stood ready to set out through her front door, but she could not find the courage to make that hundred-yard walk to the school's front door. Fear of the unknown held her back. She repeated the ritual the following week. On the third Sunday she finally overcame her fear, crossed the street, and entered the auditorium. As the service progressed, she began to cry. She did not know why the music, the message, and the people touched such a deep part of her being, but she returned weekly. A month later she attended the church's Welcome Class—an introduction to the Christian life and the church. As the group talked about the gospel and what becoming a follower of Jesus would mean, she made the decision to say yes to God and became a Christian.

When this mother shared her story with the class a few weeks later, she concluded, "God knew I would never attend a church on my own, but he loved me so very much, he started a church right across the street from my house. He knew that was the only way I would ever find my way to him."

> I once was lost but now am found,
> Was blind, but now I see.

Questions for Reflection and Discussion

1. Are you surprised at the church attendance percentage in the United States? Why do you think the percentage is so low?
2. Do you think a vital and consistent connection with a local church is important for a Christian? Why or why not?
3. What activities could your church engage in to move people from the "inclusive member" category to the "regular attendee" category in their commitment? (See fig. 1.3.)
4. What changes would your church have to make to connect better with people who have no Christian heritage or memory?

Please go to www.theamericanchurch.org/TACIC/Chapter1.htm
for updates and additional information and resources for this chapter.

Chapter 2

THE TRAJECTORY OF THE AMERICAN CHURCH

The record for the fastest roller coaster in the world belongs to Kingda Ka at Six Flags Great Adventure in New Jersey. Riders are conveyed on a 90-degree ascent to the top of a 456-foot tower, then hurtled earthward, reaching a top speed of 128 miles per hour. Roller coaster fanatic Arthur Levine commented, "I can't imagine a more thrilling ride. Insane acceleration, speed, height, and drop. The launch scared me silly—and I'm a fairly seasoned coaster vet."[1]

For many of us, the mere thought of boarding a roller coaster scares us silly. Do you remember your feelings as the roller coaster ascends the first *clickity-clack* incline and then begins to hurtle earthward? My daughter Andrea loves the excitement and anticipation and raises her hands aloft in a display of sheer glee. For me, the sudden descent produces a sense of fear and even terror, causing my courage to melt away. My stomach rises to my throat, and in my mind's eye the possibility of a crash or even death seems imminent. I try to raise my hands, but find them permanently locked in a death grip on the safety bar.

The trajectory of the American church can create similar feelings for people—exhilaration in some cases, fear and anxiety in others. Psalm 107:26–27 describes the descending feeling:

> They mounted up to the heavens and went down to the depths;
> > in their peril their courage melted away.
> They reeled and staggered like drunkards.
> > they were at their wits' end.

This chapter takes a look at the overall trajectory of the American church in light of national population growth. Is the church ascending or descending with respect to size and influence? Is the church emerging or submerging? Is growth important, necessary, or even desirable? What does numeric decline say about health, vitality, and energy? If a church's attendance plateaus, should that be called "stagnation" or "equilibrium"?

The answers to these questions matter. Over the past forty years, the United States' population has grown dramatically. The trajectory of the church affects the church's capability to share the gospel with America's many new people. People like Alyzandra Marcella Ruiz.

Alyzandra Marcella Ruiz

Alyzandra, or "Aly" as her parents nicknamed her, was born in Chicago on October 18, 2006, just before six o'clock in the morning — near the exact time the Census Bureau predicted that the U.S. population would reach 300 million. While the *Chicago Sun Times* admitted that no one knows exactly who the 300 millionth American is, Aly was her hometown's best bet. Minutes later Emanuel Plata and Zoë Emille Hudson were born in Manhattan and Kiyah Lanaé Boyd in Atlanta — they too were top candidates for this demographic honor.[2]

Whoever was the 300 millionth American, his or her arrival made one thing perfectly clear — at a time when the populations of most developed nations were stagnant or declining, the United States was growing at unprecedented numbers. In just under 40 years, the U.S. population expanded by 100 million people — from 200 million in 1967 to 300 million in 2006. According to the *Economist*, that trend will likely continue. "Such robust growth is unique among rich countries," the *Economist* reported in October 2006. "As America adds 100 million people over the next four decades, Japan and the European Union are expected to lose almost 15 million."[3]

How Many New Americans Have Arrived Since 1990?

Chapter 1 revealed that 52 million people attend a Christian church on any given weekend in the United States. At the same time, population growth from 1990 to 2006 has created an unusual anomaly with that attendance figure.

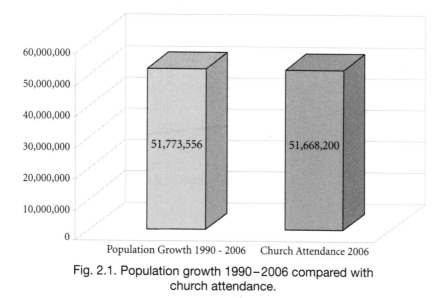

Fig. 2.1. Population growth 1990–2006 compared with church attendance.

As figure 2.1 shows, the population of the United States has grown by 52 million people from 1990 to 2006, which happens to be the same number that attend church on any given weekend. Among those new arrivals are 68,510,978 newborn babies and 22,873,578 immigrants—a total of 91 million additional people. Accounting for the 39,611,000 who died in that time period produces the net population growth of 52 million people.

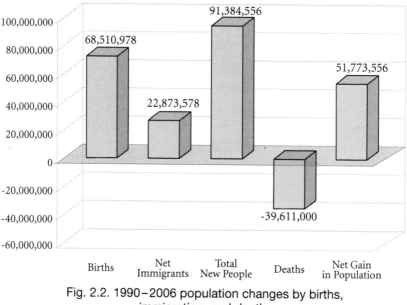

Fig. 2.2. 1990–2006 population changes by births, immigration, and death.

Let those numbers sink into your head and heart. More than 91 million people live in the United States today who did not live here 16 years ago.

Is the American Church Keeping Up with Population Growth?

While this robust growth in the number of Americans has taken place, no growth in church attendance has occurred! In 1990, 52 million people attended worship each week—in 2006 the number remained unchanged. However, because of the sizable population growth, the percentage of Americans who attend church is declining. Figure 2.3 documents the decline in overall attendance percentage from 1990 to 2000 and finally to 2005. The graph also presents the changes in the attendance percentage at evangelical, mainline, and Roman Catholic churches.

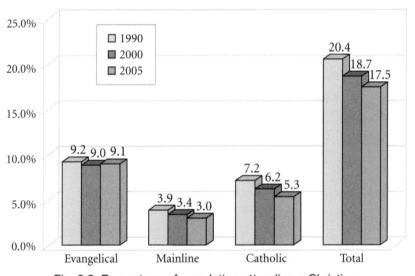

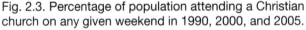

Fig. 2.3. Percentage of population attending a Christian church on any given weekend in 1990, 2000, and 2005.

The percentage of Americans who attended a Christian church on any given weekend declined from 20.4 percent in 1990 to 17.5 percent in 2005. Evangelical churches nearly kept up with population growth, declining from 9.2 percent to 9.1 percent. Mainline church attendance declined from 3.9 percent to 3.0 percent over that 15-year period, a 24 percent loss. Roman Catholic Church attendance fell from 7.2 percent to 5.3 percent, a loss of 26 percent. Chapter 3 will investigate why mainline and Roman Catholic churches are experiencing accelerated attendance decline in this decade.

Population Growth versus Church Attendance Growth

America's population is growing at dissimilar rates throughout the nation. The Sunbelt states (the southernmost states from Virginia to Southern California) continue to grow most rapidly in population, while the Great Plains region and the Rust Belt (the industrial cities bordering the Great Lakes) have stagnant growth rates. The rate of population growth creates a major impact on whether the church can keep up with the increase in the population. In Arizona, for example, church attendance grew 7.3 percent from 2000 to 2005, robust growth by any standard. However, the population grew by 15.3 percent during that same period, producing a net attendance percentage decline of 7 percent. Typically, the faster a region's rate of population growth, the more difficult task the church faces in keeping up with those increasing numbers.[4] Figure 2.4 shows each state's growth or decline from 2000 to 2005 in the percentage of the population attending church on a weekend. The shaded states declined, while the white states grew. In how many states did the church attendance grow faster than population growth?

In no single state did church attendance keep up with population growth! Of the 50 states, Hawaii's church attendance came closest to keeping up with population growth, missing that goal by the narrowest of margins — .02 of one percentage point! However, when the attendance data range was expanded to 1990 – 2005, Hawaii was the only state in the nation to witness church attendance growth outstripping population growth during that period, brought about by Hawaii's rapid church growth in the 1990s. That has led many Christian researchers, including myself, to desire to visit Hawaii to discover whether the soil, the water, or the sun causes such vibrant growth. In three other states, the church nearly kept up with population growth from 2000 to 2005 — Oklahoma, Arkansas, and Alabama. The states with the greatest decline were in the New England region.

Despite the uniformity of decline in all 50 states, a somewhat more optimistic picture appears when attendance percentage growth is viewed by county. Figure 2.5 shows that 2,303 counties experienced decline, while 795 counties witnessed their church attendance increasing faster than the population growth.

Roman Catholic Growth and Decline

As shown in figure 2.6, the Roman Catholic Church grew faster than population growth in six states from 2000 to 2005, while declining in 44 states. The largest declines were in the Northeast and the Midwest. In many of the

Southern states, Roman Catholic attendance grew faster than the population. In states such as Georgia and Florida, although Roman Catholic
attendance increased considerably, the church's growth could not keep up
with the rapidly expanding population.

Mainline Growth and Decline

From 2000 to 2005, mainline church attendance did not grow faster than
the population in any state. Nevada, Utah, Wyoming, Arizona, and New
Hampshire had the greatest percentage decline as each state experienced
strong population growth. Mainline churches declined the least in the
more conservative portions of the country. Alabama, Kentucky, Tennessee, Louisiana, and Delaware had the lowest percentage of decline. Nine of
the 10 states with the least decline were Southern states.

Evangelical Growth and Decline

From 2000 to 2005, the evangelical church grew in 28 states and declined
in 22 states. New Mexico, Delaware, Nebraska, North Carolina, and Alaska
had the greatest percentage of decline. Vermont, Rhode Island, Massachusetts, Minnesota, and Nevada had the greatest attendance percentage
increase. Most interesting was the uniform decline in the 10 Southern
states from Texas to North Carolina, often known as the Bible Belt. These
10 states experienced a combined numerical growth in evangelical attendance of 5 percent, but the population grew by 8 percent, producing an
attendance percentage decline in each state.

How Did the Church in the First Three Centuries Respond to Its Growth Challenge?

The challenge facing the American church can seem insurmountable.
Millions of people in the United States have no connection to a Christian
church, and nothing short of a miracle will keep the church growing at the
rate of population growth.

The early Christian church faced a similar challenge. In AD 40 the Roman
Empire had a population of 60 million people with a very small Christian
population. By AD 350 there were as many as 31 million Christians — more
than half of the population.[5] Many historians believe that mass conversions
caused such astounding growth, such as when 3,000 people converted on the
day of Pentecost. In his book *The Cities of God*, Rodney Stark quotes from the
famed historian Adolph von Harnack, who argued, "Christianity must have
reproduced itself by means of miracles."[6] That idea troubled Stark, who spent
much of his career studying how conversion takes place and how religious

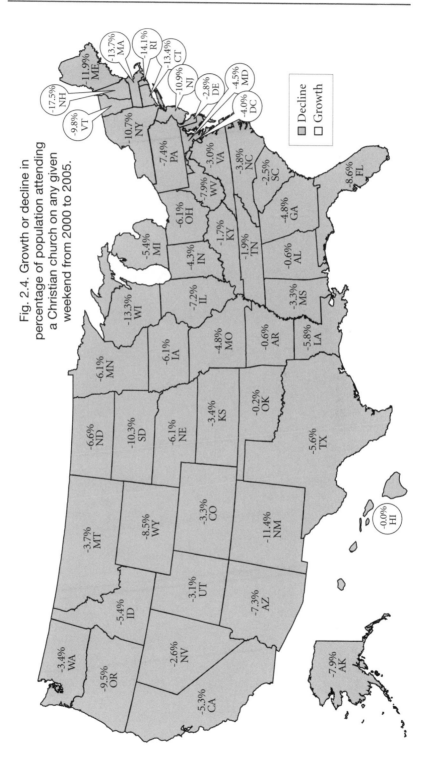

Fig. 2.4. Growth or decline in percentage of population attending a Christian church on any given weekend from 2000 to 2005.

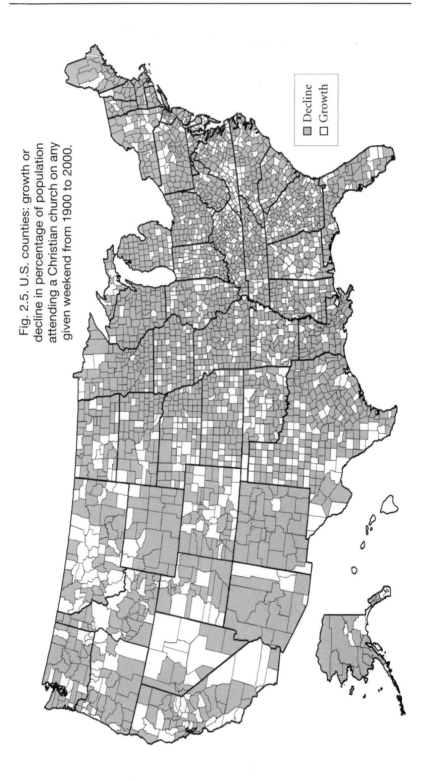

Fig. 2.5. U.S. counties: growth or decline in percentage of population attending a Christian church on any given weekend from 1900 to 2000.

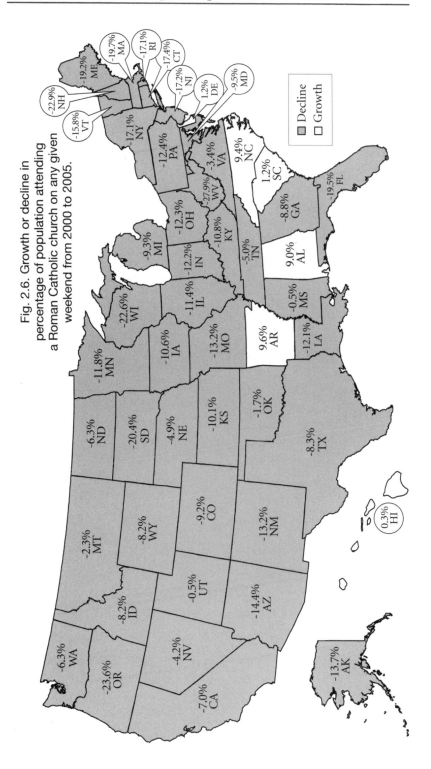

Fig. 2.6. Growth or decline in percentage of population attending a Roman Catholic church on any given weekend from 2000 to 2005.

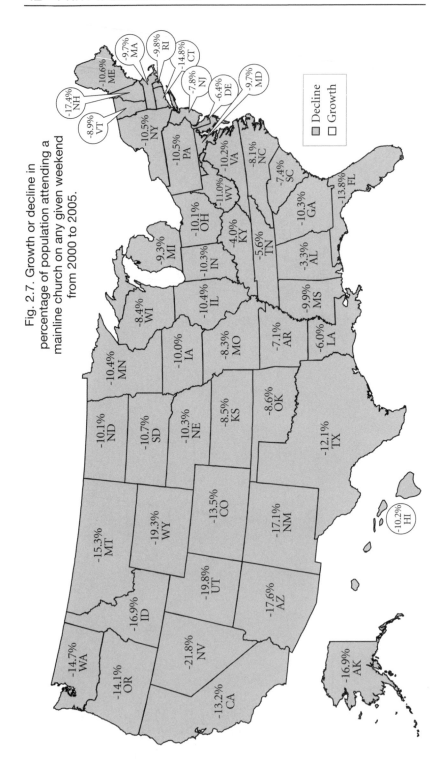

Fig. 2.7. Growth or decline in percentage of population attending a mainline church on any given weekend from 2000 to 2005.

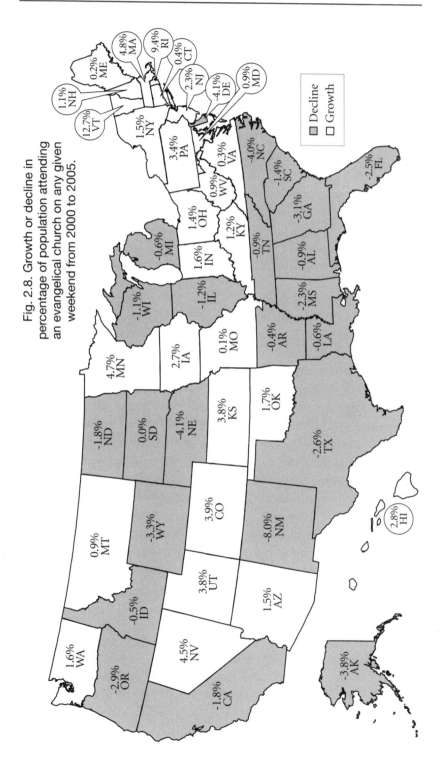

Fig. 2.8. Growth or decline in percentage of population attending an evangelical church on any given weekend from 2000 to 2005.

groups grow. As Stark began to examine the growth of early Christianity in detail, he discovered something quite remarkable. In a 1995 *Sociology of Religion* article, he wrote, "Fortunately, the 'facts' justifying the miraculous assumption [of Harnack] were wrong. The only reason people believed in an arithmetic need for mass conversion was because no one ever bothered to do the actual arithmetic."[7] When Stark did the math, he discovered that the church growing by as little as 3.42 percent a year would account for the remarkable growth of Christianity in the first three centuries.

Given the recent struggles of the church, growing by 3.42 percent each year seems no easy task, but when consistent growth takes place over an extended period of time, something revolutionary can happen. The early church teaches us that solid, moderate growth year after year can indeed produce a revolution. We will discover in chapter 11 what changes would be necessary for the American church to keep up with population growth.

Reflection

As I reflect on this chapter, I cannot stop thinking about those 91 million new people who live in our country. Over 70 million of them are under the age of 17 (births plus immigrant children). Try to imagine looking out over a sea of humanity of that size. A scene from the book of Revelation comes to mind: "I looked, and there before me was a great multitude that no one could count, from every nation, tribe, people and language, standing before the throne and in front of the Lamb" (Rev. 7:9). How many of those 70 million new Americans will be in that great throng in heaven? Or consider just the 23 million new immigrants to the United States. God is truly bringing the nations to America. Imagine looking out over such a group, stretching for mile upon mile. How many of those 23 million will stand before God's throne?

A friend of mine who pastors a new bilingual church in California told me this story of one of the 91 million new Americans:

> I was invited by a rancher to speak at a farm employees' retreat in May. The event was not religious per se. This year I spoke of God's purpose for their lives. At the beginning of the retreat, I gave each person a small tool. Most did not know its function. I asked them, "If we don't know its purpose, who would we ask?" They all responded, "The creator." I responded, "Do you know your purpose? If not, why not seek the Creator?" My invitation was that during the weekend, if they had a desire to seek God, they could just walk up to me, hand me the little tool, and I would pray with them.
>
> The next morning, after I'd had the last bite of a delicious sausage, a gentleman came up behind me and tossed his tool on the table in front of

my plate and sat down. I turned to look at him and could see the hunger and pain in his eyes. "I want to know this God, and I want to know the truth." We spent the rest of the morning talking and praying. When we returned home, I spent about two months in discipleship with him and his wife. He attended his first service that next Sunday in May and has not stopped since.

Will the American church ascend or descend? How can the church step off the treadmill of stagnation and experience genuine growth and vitality? How will we connect with the 68 million born since 1990 and the 23 million immigrants? The challenge ultimately becomes an issue of the heart, a question of love. The late Sam Shoemaker, one of the founders of Alcoholics Anonymous, expressed his own call to bring others into relationship with God through his poem, "I Stand by the Door."

> I stand by the door.
> I neither go too far in, nor stay too far out,
> The door is the most important door in the world—
> It is the door through which people walk when they find God.
>
> The most tremendous thing in the world
> Is for people to find that door—the door to God.
> The most important thing any person can do
> Is to take hold of one of those blind, groping hands,
> And put it on the latch—the latch that only clicks
> And opens to the person's own touch.
> People die outside that door, as starving beggars die
> On cold nights in cruel cities in the dead of winter—
> Die for want of what is within their grasp.
> They live, on the other side of it—live because they have not found it.
> Nothing else matters compared to helping them find it,
> And open it, and walk in, and find Him....
> So I stand by the door.[8]

As we face the challenges of the church in America, we may feel like riders disembarking from a roller coaster ride, "reeling and staggering like drunkards at our wits' end." If so, remember the psalmist's words of hope that immediately follow: "They cried out to the LORD in their trouble, and he brought them out of their distress" (Ps. 107:28). There is hope for a brighter future, grounded in God's abiding desire for all people everywhere to hear the gospel, turn, and enter into the family of God. First, though, the church needs to come to grips with the dramatic changes that have happened to the American church since the beginning of the new millennium. That is the subject of the next chapter of this story.

Questions for Reflection and Discussion

1. Based on your experience, do you sense that the American church is emerging or submerging? What do you see that confirms your instincts?
2. What is your reaction to the U.S. population growth from 1990 to 2006 being equivalent to the total church attendance?
3. Look at the map of your branch of Christianity and its growth or decline by state. What does the map tell you about the vitality of Christianity in your branch and in your part of the country?
4. What are ways that your church can better connect with the 91 million new Americans?

Please go to www.theamericanchurch.org/TACIC/Chapter2.htm for updates and additional information and resources for this chapter.

Chapter 3

THE MILLENNIUM EFFECT

Marin County, California, appears to be the Promised Land. The stately symmetry of the Golden Gate Bridge leads north to the Marin Peninsula, bordered on the west by the Pacific Ocean and on the east by San Francisco Bay. Sitting on the deck of a harborside restaurant in Sausalito, one can watch the waters of the bay shimmer in the sunlight, an exquisite setting to show off "The City," San Francisco, in the distance. Alcatraz sits in the bay midway between Marin County and San Francisco, a reminder of the blending in our world of the beauty of creation and the destruction of sin.

Marin County is the most affluent county in America.[1] In 2003 Sausalito had the highest median home value of any American city. Marin County leads the nation with the highest level of household expenditures, the highest percentage of BMWs, and the highest per capita income in the nation.[2] Here the bewitching sirens of this world call so strongly. Money (and all of its trappings), power, and social status are cultural necessities. Experimentation with new forms of religious experience is common, promising to create peace in overstressed lives. Marin County is called the affluent epicenter of the self-obsessed. Author Anne Lamott describes her home county this way:

> None of the adults in our circle believed. Believing meant that you were stupid. Ignorant people believed, uncouth people believed, and we were heavily couth. My dad was a writer and my parents were intellectuals who went to the Newport Jazz festival every year for their vacation and listened to Monk and Mozart and Modern Jazz Quartet.... [My father] worshiped at the church of Allen Ginsburg, at the Roger Tory Peterson Holiness Temple, the Tabernacle of Miles Davis.[3]

Why choose Marin County to begin the discussion of the American church in the new millennium? There are two reasons—first, church attendance in Marin County offers a glimpse of the future. For counties with at least 60,000 residents, the weekly church attendance percentage in Marin County is the lowest, less than half that of the typical American county.[4] Talk to pastors in Marin and most will tell you that the spiritual soil is hard and rocky toward any expression of Christianity.

Art Greco is a pastor in the heart of Marin County. "The context here is one of spiritual openness and hunger," he says. "The mentality is hedonistic in a 'classy, upscale' sort of way. Every way life has to scar and destroy people can be found here. In fact, those ways don't need to be 'found' at all; they are such a part of this county that they will find *you*!"[5] The majority of people have no memory of Christianity, no meaningful experience of Christian community. While the specific lifestyles and demographics make Marin County a unique locale, church attendance projections make the county a portent for the future of the entire country.

Second, Marin County straddles two "earth-shattering" geographic features. I will never forget watching the third game of the World Series on Tuesday, October 17, 1989, as more than 62,000 hopeful fans jammed into Candlestick Park. Just before the first pitch, a 7.1 magnitude earthquake struck the Bay area. The television showed fires blazing throughout San Francisco. The Loma Prieta earthquake was the strongest earthquake in California since the 1906 San Francisco earthquake, causing 62 deaths and $10 billion in damage. The San Andreas Fault traverses under 800 miles of California real estate, bisecting San Francisco and cutting under the ocean on the west end of San Francisco, then continuing north parallel to the Golden Gate Bridge and the coastline of Marin.

Ten miles to the east, on the bay side of Marin County, runs the parallel Hayward Fault. Contrary to the popular belief that the sins of Californians will cause the state to slide into the ocean soon, the tectonic plate is sliding into California. Earthquakes occur because of subduction, the process whereby the Pacific plate is slowly pushing into and under the North American plate. Eventually, the two plates will become stuck and the accumulated pressure will increase until a portion gives way, causing an earthquake along the fault line.

Just as tectonic forces exert great pressure against each other at a fault line, three cultural-religious forces simultaneously clash in Marin County and throughout America. They are (1) the continuing secularization of our culture, (2) the loosening grip of the historically dominant strains of American Christianity, and (3) the surprisingly vital expressions of Christianity bursting out in new and unexpected ways.

Fig. 3.1. Cultural-religious fault lines.

These three forces exert movement and pressure against each other to create two fault lines. One exists where secularization seeks to subduct American Christianity. These tremors are felt every day in the cultural values, families, and religious institutions of America. At the other fault line, new expressions of American Christianity are subducting the dominant expressions of the faith. These tremors are felt in the changes occurring in the religious picture of America, as growth and decline patterns reshuffle the size and influence of churches and denominations. These cultural and spiritual earthquakes have increased in frequency and magnitude since the beginning of the new millennium.

Church attendance for the American church this millennium peaked during the five Sundays following the 9/11 attacks. That national trauma sent worshipers to church services in record numbers, but the memory of the event and the attraction to church was short-lived. On the sixth Sunday, attendance returned to normal. Since then, American church attendance has declined in an unprecedented fashion. Most of the deterioration is in mainline and Roman Catholic churches, although some evangelical groups are also struggling. What does this tell us about our culture? What does this tell us about the American church?

Degeneration occurs silently at first. Having personally passed the 50-year milestone, I now receive unsolicited mail from the American Association of Retired Persons that I refuse to open. Yet I am beginning to notice that I am not as young as I once was. Maintaining good muscle tone is more difficult, I need more sleep, and I cannot work as long or as hard as before. Not wanting to accept this new reality, I prefer delusion.

In the same way, most Christians have not noticed the silent decay of the American church. Instead, we hear the success stories of Willow Creek, The Potter's House, Saddleback, and Rob Bell's Mars Hill; we discover that more than 30 million people have read *The Purpose-Driven Life*; and we believe the results of opinion polls that show thriving church attendance. Beneath this veneer of success, however, lies a church in decline.

To discover the changes happening in this new millennium, we will examine the three main branches of American Christianity: the Roman Catholic Church, the mainline church, and the evangelical church.

What Is Happening to the Roman Catholic Church?

The Roman Catholic Church has good news for which to be thankful. While attendance is declining, membership in the church is increasing at the same rate as population growth, due to Hispanic immigration. In addition, the death of Pope John Paul II brought forth an outburst of acclaim for the leadership he provided for the Christian church. Yet in the midst of the good news are sobering reports. The number of men entering the priesthood continues to decline. The sexual abuse scandal has profoundly affected the church. The average age of priests keeps rising. Mass attendance continues to decline. This downward attendance trend began after

Vatican II (1963), coinciding with the beginning of decline in mainline denominations. The waning was slow until 2001, then accelerated.

Yet the polling numbers of Roman Catholic attendance by the Center for Applied Research in the Apostolate (CARA) at Georgetown University,[6] the most influential Catholic research organization, have stayed the same from 2000 to 2005. Those stable numbers were trumpeted in this headline throughout the nation's papers: "Study Shows Mass Attendance Steady Despite Sex Abuse Crisis."[7] But actual attendance head counts conducted by Catholic parishes show significant decline in Mass attendance. "The most damaging change in Catholic life is the precipitous decline in Mass attendance. It's the sign of a church collapsing," says Catholic University sociologist William D'Antonio, coauthor of numerous statistical studies of American Catholics.[8]

Here are the facts:

- In 2000, 17.3 million Catholics (27.9 percent of the membership) attended Mass on any given weekend. By 2005 that number had declined to 15.7 million (24.1 percent).
- In 2000, 6.1 percent of the American public attended a Roman Catholic church on any given weekend. By 2005 the percentage was 5.3 percent, a decline of almost 14 percent in the percentage of Americans attending a Catholic church on any given weekend over those five short years.

The Roman Catholic attendance decline is most pronounced in the Northeast and Midwest. The 2000 and 2005 attendance numbers from seven representative Roman Catholic dioceses and archdioceses in these two regions illustrate this decline:

	2000	2005
Philadelphia	387,393	318,978
Boston	397,069	319,559
Milwaukee	230,687	196,629
Rockford, IL	112,900	109,072
Chicago	561,000	500,000
Toledo	113,023	96,919
Madison	79,177	67,584

Fig. 3.2. Roman Catholic attendance decline.

As the chart shows, each of these dioceses has sustained attendance decline over the last five years, in most cases substantial numbers.

In Boston the decline in attendance, coupled with mounting legal costs from the sex abuse scandal, forced the archdiocese to the brink of bankruptcy. On May 25, 2004, 65 parishes received word that they would be closed by the end of the year. Their churches would be sold off, their priest reassigned.[9]

Robert Penta, a member of Sacred Heart Church in nearby Medford, summed up the response of many parishioners. He told the *Boston Globe* that closing parishes was "almost like an attack, to some degree, on the faithful. The archdiocese is asking people to bear the brunt of their ineptitude."[10]

In a few places, the closures did not go as planned, as parishioners refused to leave. At St. Albert the Great in Weymouth, Massachusetts, the faithful held around-the-clock prayer vigils for months. One night a *Boston Globe* reporter visited the church and found more than 30 people there. Among them was Elizabeth Griffin, there with her two daughters who were asleep on the pews with their stuffed animals while their mother talked with other parishioners. "I've never believed in anything as strongly as I believe in this," she told the *Globe*. "The people are so brave here. One night an 83-year-old woman was sleeping behind me."[11] In the end, a reprieve came, at least for St. Albert's, when the archdiocese rescinded its decision to close the church. Nevertheless, no reprieve came for most other parishes, despite vigils and lawsuits.

The decline of the Roman Catholic Church in the Northeast and Midwest contrasts sharply with patterns in the South and West, as seen in the figure 3.3. From 2000 to 2005, churches in the Northeast and Midwest lost more than a million attendees. Attendance in the South and the West remained virtually steady. Some of the Northeast and Midwest decline was produced by Anglos from the Boston to Milwaukee crescent migrating to Southern states, and some of the Southern and Western stability came from the Catholic Hispanic increase in the South, Southwest, and West.

	2000	2005
Northeast and Midwest	9.4 million	8.2 million
South and West	7.7 million	7.6 million

Fig. 3.3. Roman Catholic regional church attendance.

What has caused the Roman Catholic Church to experience accelerated decline in much of the United States during this decade? Here are five observations.

1. *Traditional loyalties to the Roman Catholic Church are diminishing where Catholicism was historically the strongest.* This is occurring primarily in the European ethnic communities of the Northeast and Midwest urban areas. The loyalty of each successive generation to the Roman Catholic Church is diminishing. According to the American Religious Identification Survey (ARIS) of 2001, more than twice as many people switched out of the Roman Catholic Church as switched in.[12] A priest from the East Coast describes the current challenge: "We are suffering from several generations of poor catechetical formation, and Catholics have lost a sense of their faith identity. Certainly preaching in the way that he [their cardinal] exemplifies would help: breaking open the Scriptures, stirring the people to holiness, and showing how the faith has meaning and importance in their lives."[13]

2. *Historically, Catholic churches are located in urban areas more so than Protestant churches, and most urban Catholic churches are old.* Decline in the American church is more pronounced among older churches, particularly in those urban areas, as people move into the suburbs.

3. *The abuse scandal undercut the confidence of many Catholics in the trustworthiness of their leaders.* In the dioceses where sexual abuse occurred and was publicized, attendance immediately dropped. Some leaders have asked whether church attendance will recover once the abuse scandal is in the past. While the decline has slowed, few dioceses have returned to prescandal attendance levels.

4. *The shortage of priests is a critical problem in the American Catholic church.* In 1990 there were 1,111 Catholic parishioners for every priest. In 2000 that number grew to 1,328. By 2005 that ratio had risen to 1,573. The parishioner to priest ratios in many regions are staggering: in the Dallas archdiocese there are 6,552 Catholics per priest; in the El Paso diocese, 5,607 Catholics per priest; and in the Orange County, California, diocese, 4,225 Catholics per priest. Virtually every diocese across the country is projecting that this acute shortage will escalate during the next 20 years, as the largest cohort of the priesthood (now averaging over 55 years old) goes into retirement. In Austin, Texas, the diocese reports that while there is one priest for every 1,914 Catholics today, in 30 years there will be one priest for every 6,866 Catholics![14] The Trenton, New Jersey, diocese projects that by 2020 each priest in the diocese will be serving 8,147 Catholics. While lay workers can assume some of the priests' roles, the diminished contact parishioners have with their priest will lower Mass attendance.

5. *The Roman Catholic Church does not start enough new parishes to keep up with population growth.* Most of a church's attendance growth occurs

in the first generation of its life. As adult children of Catholics move out to new suburbs, they find fewer Catholic churches and often lose connection with the church. The critical stress the abuse scandal has created on the financial reserves of most dioceses and the lack of available priests makes an increase in the number of new parishes unlikely.

What Is Happening to the Mainline Protestant Churches?

Mainline Protestant churches have good news for which to be thankful. While mainline churches have experienced more than 40 consecutive years of membership decline, their attendance loss has not been as pronounced. In the decade of the 1990s, attendance at mainline churches declined by only 1.9 percent.[15] However, the decline from 2000 to 2005 accelerated to seven times the yearly rate of the previous decade.

Here are the facts:

- In 2000, 9.5 million people attended mainline worship services on any given weekend. By 2005 the number had declined to 8.8 million.
- In 2000, 3.4 percent of the American public attended a mainline church on any given weekend. By 2005 that number had declined to 3 percent.
- While some mainline churches are withdrawing from their historic denominations, less than 10 percent of the mainline attendance loss from 2000 to 2005 was from seceding churches.

Figure 3.4 shows what happened in attendance between 1990 and 2005 in six of the largest mainline denominations.

	1990	2000	2005
Episcopal Church	826,661	848,847	787,500
Evangelical Lutheran Church	1,582,589	1,561,776	1,431,811
Presbyterian Church (USA)	1,349,388	1,303,549	1,198,148
United Methodist Church	3,492,246	3,515,650	3,403,080
Christian Church (Disciples of Christ)	349,588	316,291	299,643
United Church of Christ	667,809	569,138	495,284
All Mainline Denominations	**9,687,507**	**9,502,806**	**8,838,793**

Fig. 3.4. Mainline church attendance 1990–2005.

Figure 3.5 shows what their estimated attendance will be in 2010 if the decline continues at the present rate.

	2000	2010
Episcopal Church	848,847	726,095
Evangelical Lutheran Church	1,561,776	1,298,877
Presbyterian Church (USA)	1,303,549	1,092,747
United Methodist Church	3,515,650	3,260,086
Christian Church (Disciples of Christ)	316,291	282,994
United Church of Christ	569,138	421,430

Fig. 3.5. Estimated mainline church attendance in 2010.

As a group, mainline churches are projected to decline by 14 percent in numeric attendance in this decade, a loss of well over a million weekly attendees. When the 2000—2010 population growth is factored in, the percentage of the population attending a mainline church on any given weekend will decline by 24.4 percent in this decade. In addition, from 2004 to 2006 the number of churches leaving mainline denominations dramatically accelerated. Why did this attendance decline happen? Here are five observations.

1. *Mainline denominations are made up primarily of older churches, and those older churches are declining consistently.* The average mainline church started before 1965 declined by 2.7 percent in attendance from 2004 to 2005. Mainline churches also have older members and older clergy than evangelical churches. In a 2001 survey, they had twice as many self-identified members over 65 years old as did evangelical and Roman Catholic churches, half as many 18- to 29-year-olds, and one-third fewer singles.[16] Birthrates are also lower for mainline members.[17] While birth rates are definitely one factor in the growth of evangelical churches and the decline of mainline churches, the subject is much more complex than a 2001 study by Hout, Greeley, and Wilde indicates.[18]

2. *The human sexuality discussion is negatively affecting mainline churches.* More problematic to many traditionalists is the perception that the arguments regarding homosexuality lack a "commonsense" hermeneutic of Scripture. This quote from the Anglican bishops of Africa about the Episcopal Church (USA) reflects this sentiment: "The unscriptural innovations of North American and some western provinces on issues of human sexuality undermine the basic message of redemption and the power of the Cross to transform lives. These departures are a symptom of a deeper problem, which is the diminution of the authority of Scripture."[19]

According to C. Kirk Hadaway, director of research for the Episcopal Church, about one-third of the recent membership loss in the Episcopal Church can be attributed to churches in internal conflict over the homosexuality issue.[20]

3. *Mainline denominations face a severe shortage of new churches.* Only 10 percent of new Protestant churches started in the United States are mainline; the rest are evangelical. The only possible tactic available to recoup the attendance losses occurring in established churches and through closures is to start new congregations. For the Evangelical Lutheran Church in America (ELCA) just to maintain its present size, they would need to plant eight times as many new churches a year as they currently do. Their established churches are declining by 26,500 attendees per year, and their new churches add only 3,100 new attendees each year. The Presbyterian Church (U.S.A.) (that is, PCUSA) needs to plant 10 times as many churches as they currently do. Their established churches are declining by 30,000 attendees per year, and their new churches add fewer than 2,500 each year. Given the lack of church planting in most mainline denominations, church attendance will continue to decrease.

4. *Fifty years ago, mainline denominations were very good at planting new churches.* In every mainline denomination, the 1950s is the decade with the largest number of churches and the highest attendance. Today that has turned into a problem as many of these churches are in their fifties and are facing a severe generational challenge. They are primarily in first-ring suburbs, which have an aging population of original homeowners. Unfortunately, the young families purchasing these homes have no interest in attending the previous owner's 50-year-old church! For example, the greatest yearly numeric attendance decline in the ELCA comes from churches started between 1954 and 1966.

5. *Leaders of mainline denominations, on both the national and regional level, do not seem to be able to understand and articulate the root problems the mainline churches face.* Often they mention the challenge of birthrates and demographics, say their churches are not doing poorly considering their challenges, yet make no structural changes to stop the decline. Robert Coats, a retired Episcopal priest and chaplain, says his denomination ignored serious problems for too long. Looking at his church's official statistics, he could see that in 1965, 880,000 children attended Episcopal Sunday school. By 2001 that figure dropped to 297,000. Confirmands dropped from 128,000 in 1965 to 34,000 in 2001. "In other words," he wrote, "over the years, the Episcopal Church has had fewer and fewer people coming into the church at the entry level." On top of that, he adds, the church made little effort to connect

with new immigrants. The results were disastrous, says Coats. "By paying little or no attention to changing ethnic patterns, the declining birthrate or other demographic shifts, our myopic laziness has cost us dearly."[21]

What Is Happening to the Evangelical Church?

The evangelical church has experienced a more encouraging story this millennium, but even evangelicals are experiencing a slowdown in a variety of key areas. Here are the facts:

- In 2000, 25.3 million people attended evangelical worship services on any given weekend. By 2005 that number had grown to 26.9 million.
- In 2000, 9.2 percent of the American public attended an evangelical church on any given weekend. By 2005 that number had declined to 9.1 percent.
- Between 2000 and 2005, while the combined decline in the number of Protestant mainline and Roman Catholic churches was almost 2,500, the number of evangelical churches increased by 4,500.

There are, however, signs that the evangelical growth rate is beginning to slow down and even decline. From 2001 to 2005, the growth rates of Pentecostal denominations have diminished. Worship attendance in Southern Baptist churches has lagged behind the robust population growth in the South. The largest conservative Lutheran denomination, the Lutheran Church–Missouri Synod (LCMS), declined at nearly the same rate as that of the more liberal Evangelical Lutheran Church in America (ELCA).

Here are five observations regarding the growth trends in the evangelical churches.

1. *Evangelical churches are outperforming the Roman Catholic and mainline churches because they are better at the two fundamentals of growing denominations:* (1) Their established churches are nearly maintaining their current attendance level, which produces a stronger overall base, and (2) they are starting many new churches. Figure 3.6 compares the growth rate of evangelical and mainline churches between 2004 and 2005 based on the age of the church. Evangelical churches outperform mainline churches in every category.

2. *Virtually every evangelical denomination has renewed its focus on church planting since 1990, expanding their systems and processes for starting new churches.* The result is higher survival rates and increased ministry fruitfulness from these new churches.

3. *Evangelical groups have many more large churches than do mainline denominations.* More than 95 percent of Protestant megachurches are

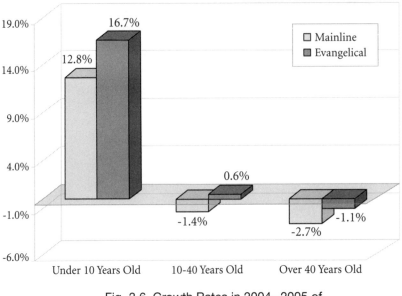

Fig. 3.6. Growth Rates in 2004–2005 of
churches based on age of church.

evangelical. Large churches are the second leading growth factor in the
American church (new churches are the leading growth factor), providing
a significant boost to evangelical growth.[22]

4. *Evangelical churches started before 1965 are seeing more attendance
erosion in this decade than in the 1990s.* Since 2001 these older churches
have declined by 1 percent each year. This small yearly change will translate to an attendance decline of almost 10 percent by 2010.

5. *Evangelical churches have two demographic advantages that cause higher
growth rates.* First, their members have higher birthrates than mainline
members. Second, more people are "switching in" to evangelical churches,
many from mainline or Roman Catholic churches, than are "switching
out."[23] Figure 3.7 shows the switching in and switching out percentages
for evangelicals, mainliners, and Roman Catholics. ("Switching in" means
a person joins a new group from another group. "Switching out" means a
person leaves their group to go to another group.)

The study concludes that "the top three 'gainers' in America's vast
religious marketplace appear to be evangelical Christians, those describing themselves as nondenominational churches and those who profess no
religion."[24]

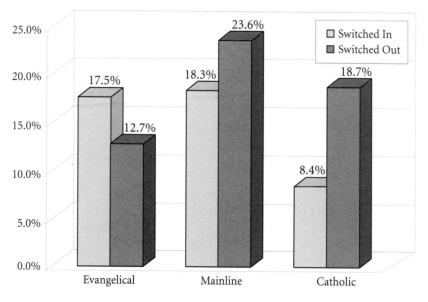

Fig. 3.7. Switching in and out.

Millennial Turmoil

Christian churches are experiencing new and alarming challenges in this new millennium. The Christian church had one other experience of a millennial transition. Richard Landes, director of the Center for Millennial Studies at Boston University, describes what happened when the calendar turned to the year AD 1000:

> Most medievalists still hold that 1000 was a "year like any other," and that it passed largely unnoticed by a chronologically ignorant and confused population. [Other medievalists, including Landes] see various popular and elite behaviors as manifestations of a millennial "spirit": e.g., waves of conversion to Christianity, imperial and ecclesiastical reforms, mass pilgrimages (especially to Jerusalem), popular "heresies" and apostolic movements, the execution of "heretics" and popular violence against the Jews, and, most importantly, the "Peace of God," the first mass peace movement documented in world history. When 1000, for all its excitement, failed to bring the awaited end, contemporaries re-dated to 1033 [1000 years after Christ's death], triggering a second wave of peace councils, pilgrimages, and reforms. The period between 1000 and 1033 mark, then, a particularly apocalyptic "millennial generation." We may see some resemblances with the period 2000–2033.[25]

The first millennium ended without the cataclysmic, earth-shattering changes many predicted, and some spiritually positive events occurred. At the second millennial transition, in spite of Landes's optimism, few signs of renewal occurred, and the American church definitely saw a fundamental shift leading to decline and decay. Why are these changes occurring? Chapter 10 will describe the transformations happening in our culture that affect churches and the adjustments that are needed to thrive in this new world.

The American church varies distinctly and surprisingly across each of the four primary regions of the country. The geographic strength of the American church is based on physical topography, immigration patterns, each region's missional enthusiasm and practices, and the story of the church's connection with the culture of its region. In the next chapter we will board a transcontinental flight to explore America's spiritual geography.

Questions for Reflection and Discussion

1. What was the most surprising information presented in this chapter? What made that surprising?
2. Why do you think the American church is challenged in this new millennium? What has changed?
3. In the group to which you belong, how well do the leaders understand the changes that are occurring? What adjustments are taking place in response?
4. Sometimes the church cyclically oscillates between growth and decline. Do you think a return to growth is on the horizon? Why or why not?

Please go to www.theamericanchurch.org/TACIC/Chapter3.htm for updates and additional information and resources for this chapter.

Chapter 4

THE CHURCH'S REMARKABLE REGIONAL LANDSCAPE

When I was young, my father was a pastor, so we moved to a new church every three to five years, as was the custom in those days. Then he returned to graduate school, so we moved again and again and again. By the time I was thirteen years old, I had lived for seven years in Canada and Scotland. I regret never learning to skate in Canada, although my dentist applauds my choice. I am slightly embarrassed to admit I wore a kilt in Scotland, but the manly men wore them, complete with knives in their stockings. I lost my friends yearly by attending a different school each year in grades four through ten.

My wandering ways continued in college: I spent summers as a door-to-door book salesman in Arkansas, Tennessee, Florida, Rhode Island, New Hampshire, and California. I sold in Arcadia, Florida, a town with a legacy of old Southern white culture, which included starting each day with eggs and grits at the Magnolia Hotel. Only after I returned months later did I discover that I had missed the 30 percent of Arcadia's residents who were African American, their community segregated into a geographically hidden, poverty-stricken part of town I never noticed. I lived in a raucous University of Rhode Island dorm in West Kingston and in the home of an eighty-six-year-old woman in idyllic Keene, New Hampshire. I was sent to Earle, Arkansas, which sadly did not allow door-to-door salesmen. So I hitchhiked to the neighboring town of Parkin, where a white policeman shot a black man to death the day I arrived. On the top of the charts that summer of 1972 were Roberta Flack and Donny Hathaway asking, "Where Is the Love?" I sweltered during my final summer in Bakersfield, California, and vividly remember selling in nearby Taft, a remote town with a legion of oil derricks and stray dogs in the semiarid landscape, where the hot sun so brilliantly reflected on the sand and the white rickety houses that I became temporarily blind.

My early life, which seemed disrupted, eventually became an advantage vocationally. I have spent significant amounts of time living in the four major regions of the United States: the Northeast, the Midwest, the South, and the West. Those experiences have helped me appreciate the unique cultures of each region and have made me aware of nuances in the values and worldviews of each. The expression of the church in each region reflects a diverse culture and unique history. This chapter investigates how Christianity is shaped by these features and will bring to light a composite picture of the strengths and weaknesses of the Christian church in each region.

One way to understand the regional makeup of the American church is to map the three major branches of Christianity, showing which one has the largest weekend church attendance in each of the 3,141 counties of the United States. Figure 4.1 shows that evangelical churches dominate in 2,044 counties, many in the South and West. Mainline churches are prevalent in 421 counties, many in the Midwest, West Virginia, and parts of the rural Northeast. Roman Catholic churches are dominant in 630 counties, most in the Northeast, parts of the Midwest, and the border and coastal counties from Louisiana to the Napa Valley in California. Orthodox churches are dominant in three counties in Alaska.

A Geographic Religious History

A condensed geographic history of the American church can be told in the six short paragraphs that follow. The early churches along the East Coast were predominantly Anglican (Episcopalian) or Congregationalist. So in 1775, when a church sexton named Robert Newman climbed to the steeple of the Old North Church in Boston, with Paul Revere's instructions in mind, he was hanging two lanterns—"One if by land, two if by sea"—from the top of an Anglican church, built in 1723. Boston's Old South Church was founded in 1669 and was Congregational.

As the pioneers began to move west, they encountered a daunting obstacle called the Appalachian Mountains. Most eastern Anglicans and Congregationalists were not built for the "rough and ready" life of the frontier. The newly emerging Methodists and Baptists, on the other hand, moved in with a vengeance. They filled the central and southern sections of middle America with churches on virtually every mile of country road.

Methodist churches were often founded by traveling preachers known as circuit riders. In 1771, when a young English Methodist preacher named Francis Asbury arrived in New York City, less than 2.5 percent of the population in American colonies was Methodist.[1] Soon afterward, Asbury mounted his horse and began traveling from town to town, preaching. By the time he retired, forty-five years later, he had traveled "an estimated 300,000 miles, delivering some 16,500 sermons," according to *Christian History and Biography*.[2] As the leader of American Methodists, he organized the efforts of other circuit riders as well. Sociologist Roger Finke points out that by 1850, Methodists made up more than 34 percent of the U.S. population.[3]

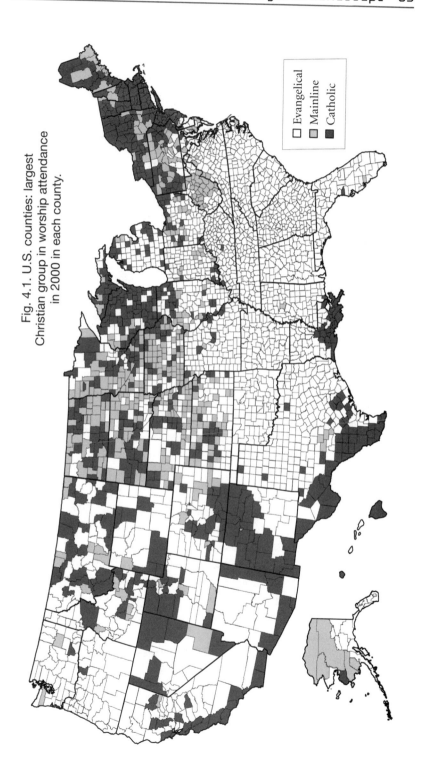

Fig. 4.1. U.S. counties: largest Christian group in worship attendance in 2000 in each county.

Evangelical
Mainline
Catholic

Lutherans, who originally settled in New York, New Jersey. and Pennsylvania, later began to fill the Upper Midwest. Those northern European immigrants seemed to love cold and desolate landscapes. They inspired a young writer named Garrison Keillor in the 1970s to create a fictional town called Lake Wobegon, where "all the women are strong, all the men are good looking, and all the children are above average."[4]

Roman Catholics immigrated in a very different pattern, settling in the large industrial cities of the Northeast and the Midwest. A third wave of migration occurred between World Wars I and II when millions of African Americans came to those same cities in search of jobs.

The Rocky Mountains proved to be a more difficult barrier to the church than were the Appalachians. No group did well at scaling the vast heights of the Rockies. Thus, the West historically is rather unchurched. The mainline presence in the West is very low. The Catholic percentage would be low as well if not for Hispanic immigration. Most church attendance in the West tends to be from "homegrown" American evangelicalism rather than from immigrant European Christianity.

These idiosyncrasies of history and geography cause Christianity to be expressed very differently in the four major regions of the country. In the two least churched regions, the Northeast and the West, about 14 percent of people attend church each week. In the two most churched regions, the Midwest and the South, the attendance percentage increases to 20 percent.

Where the Three Branches are Located

The next maps will illustrate the geographic pattern of the three main branches of American Christianity. Figure 4.2 shows the attendance percentage of evangelical churches for every county in the year 2000. The map shows that evangelicalism is prominent in the South, while much less pronounced in the rest of the country. In fact, more than half of evangelical church attendance is found in the South. Irrespective of where an evangelical lives in the country, the southern dominance of evangelicalism affects the public's view toward them. (Please note that the scales on these three maps are different.)

Mainline Christianity reveals a very different nationwide profile. These churches are weakest in the West, while strongest in the Upper Midwest. Mainline Christianity has moderate influence in much of the rest of the country east of the Rockies, except in the South where its presence is overpowered by the size of the southern evangelical church.

The regional location of Roman Catholic Christianity was created by the immigration patterns of European Catholics. Figure 4.4 shows that Catholics are most dominant from the Upper Midwest to New England, in Louisiana and in the states along the Mexico border. Catholics historically were absent from the South.

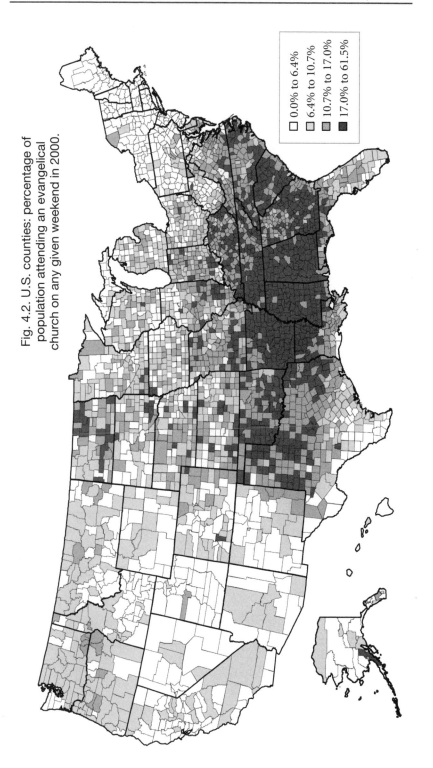

Fig. 4.2. U.S. counties: percentage of population attending an evangelical church on any given weekend in 2000.

☐ 0.0% to 6.4%
☐ 6.4% to 10.7%
▨ 10.7% to 17.0%
■ 17.0% to 61.5%

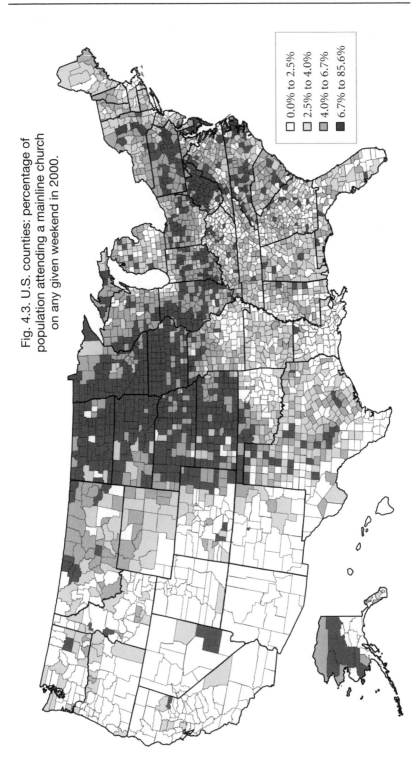

Fig. 4.3. U.S. counties: percentage of population attending a mainline church on any given weekend in 2000.

0.0% to 2.5%
2.5% to 4.0%
4.0% to 6.7%
6.7% to 85.6%

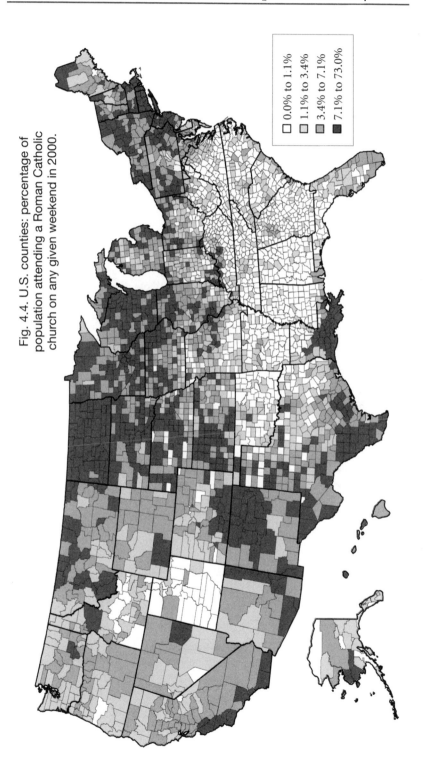

Fig. 4.4. U.S. counties: percentage of population attending a Roman Catholic church on any given weekend in 2000.

☐ 0.0% to 1.1%
☐ 1.1% to 3.4%
☐ 3.4% to 7.1%
■ 7.1% to 73.0%

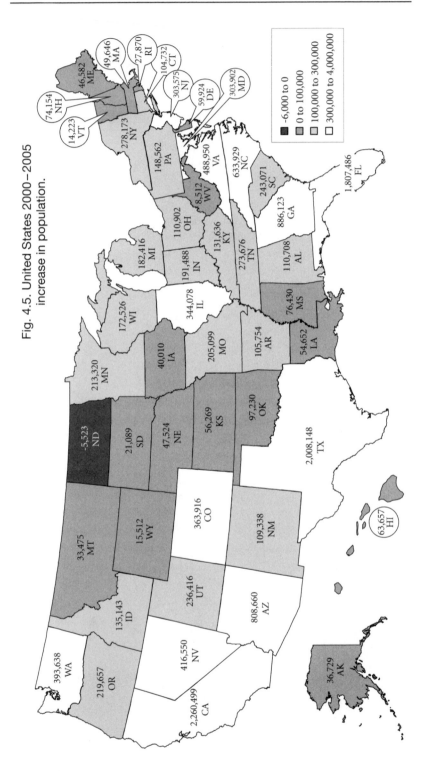

Fig. 4.5. United States 2000–2005 increase in population.

Demographic Change

Population shifts in a community or state will influence the growth or decline potential of its churches. Figure 4.5 shows population changes from 2000 to 2005 in state population. Most growth is in the South and West, led by California, Texas, Florida, Georgia, Arizona, and North Carolina.

Appreciating population growth or decline by ethnicity is also critical in understanding the changes in the American church. Figure 4.6 shows how the four regions grew in population from 2000 to 2005 among the four primary ethnic divisions. Anglos are moving south and west. African Americans are headed back to the South. Surprisingly, Hispanic population growth is stronger in the South than the West, primarily because of growth in Texas and Florida.

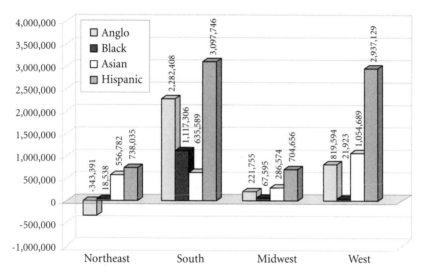

Fig. 4.6. Population growth from 2000 to 2005 by region.

Four factors shape the population growth of a state: births, deaths, internal migration from another state, and immigration from outside the United States. Figure 4.7 shows the internal migration between states from 2000–2005. Internal migration is a state's net gain or loss in residents, and shows where American citizens are moving. The figure graphically shows three migrations: the migration to the South from the Midwest and the Northeast; the migration from Louisiana in the aftermath of Hurricane Katrina, especially to Texas; and the migration from California to Arizona, Nevada, Oregon, and Washington. More than 1.2 million residents left New York from 2000 to 2005. California was next in decline, losing almost one million residents, followed by Illinois, Louisiana, Massachusetts and New

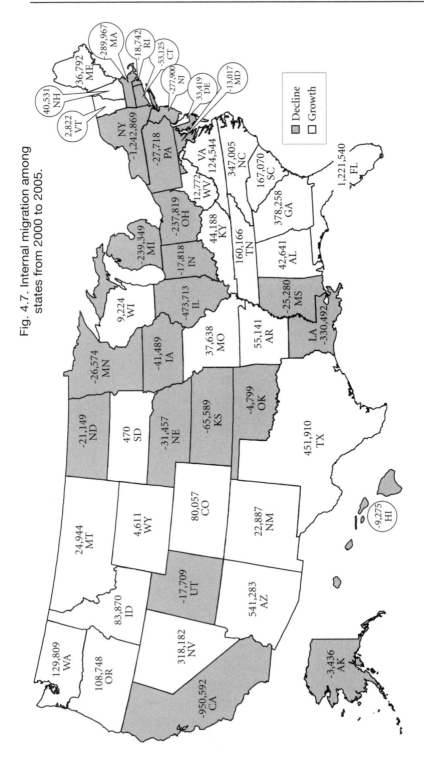

Fig. 4.7. Internal migration among states from 2000 to 2005.

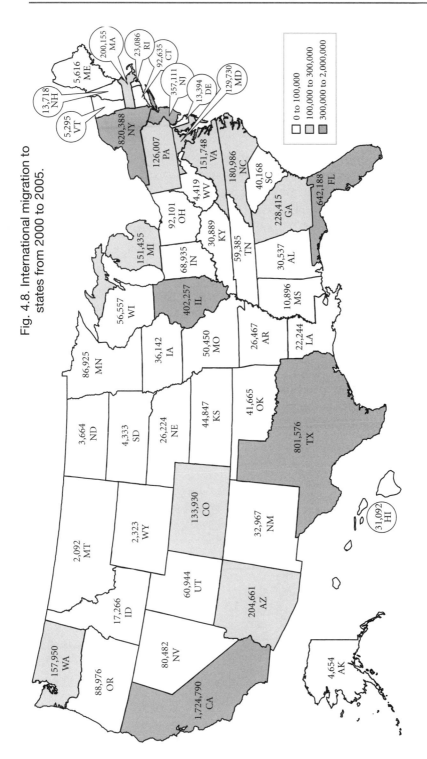

Fig. 4.8. International migration to states from 2000 to 2005.

0 to 100,000
100,000 to 300,000
300,000 to 2,000,000

200,155 MA
23,086 RI
92,635 CT
5,616 ME
357,111 NJ
129,730 MD
13,718 NH
13,394 DE
5,295 VT
820,388 NY
126,007 PA
151,748 VA
180,986 NC
40,168 SC
642,188 FL
4,419 WV
228,415 GA
92,101 OH
151,435 MI
30,889 KY
59,385 TN
30,537 AL
68,935 IN
402,257 IL
10,896 MS
56,557 WI
36,142 IA
50,450 MO
26,467 AR
22,244 LA
86,925 MN
3,664 ND
4,333 SD
26,224 NE
44,847 KS
41,665 OK
801,576 TX
133,930 CO
32,967 NM
31,092 HI
2,092 MT
2,323 WY
60,944 UT
204,661 AZ
157,950 WA
88,976 OR
17,266 ID
80,482 NV
1,724,790 CA
4,654 AK

Jersey. Internal migration influences the growth or decline of church attendance, as members leave their church and move to another state, with many
moving to the South.

International migration is also unequally influencing the growth of states.
Figure 4.8 shows the net international immigration to each state from 2000
to 2005. Six states led the way in this immigration: California, Texas, New
York, Florida, Illinois, and New Jersey. These states comprise 62 percent of
all immigration. Notice that most of the states with the largest immigration
also had the highest level of losses from internal migration. This dynamic is
changing the cultural identity and religious makeup of those states.

These demographic changes produce both challenges and opportunities
for the American church. To understand what this means, the next section
will focus on the religious composition of the four regions of the country.

The Northeast

Profound changes are happening to church attendance in the Northeast. Most
significant is the decline in Roman Catholic Mass attendance. The downward trend in the 1990s accelerated rapidly this decade. Mainline churches
also have declined sharply, while evangelical churches are growing faster in
the Northeast than in any other region of the nation. Figure 4.9 tracks the
change in the percentage of the population attending church from 1990 to
2005, in which the percentage share of mainline church attendance declined
by 20.3 percent. Catholic church attendance declined by 30.5 percent.

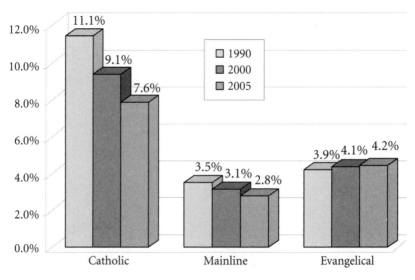

Fig. 4.9. Percentage attending a Christian church in the
Northeast region each weekend.

While much of this decline is caused by internal issues, some of the mainline and Roman Catholic decline is from Anglo migration to Southern states; some of the evangelical growth is from the sharp increase in Asian, Hispanic, and other immigrant populations. In the Northeast, most Roman Catholic and mainline church attendees are predominantly Anglo, while many evangelical churches in urban areas are non-Anglo.

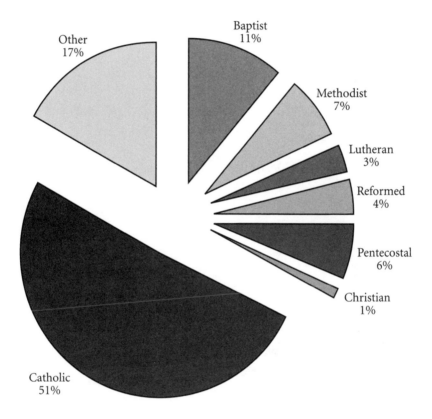

Fig. 4.10. Northeast region church
attendance share 2005.

Figure 4.10 shows the division of attendance among the eight primary denominational families.[5] The Roman Catholic Church is still the dominant force in religion in the Northeast, but the Catholic share of church attendance declined from 59 percent in 1990 to 51 percent in 2005. Only Pentecostals and "Other Evangelicals" grew faster than population growth.[6]

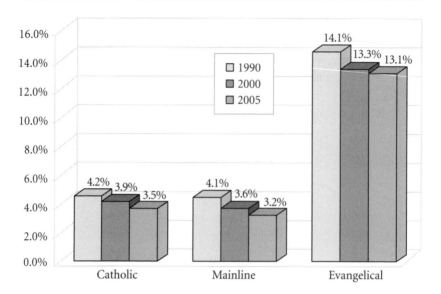

Fig. 4.11. Percentage attending a Christian church in the South region each weekend.

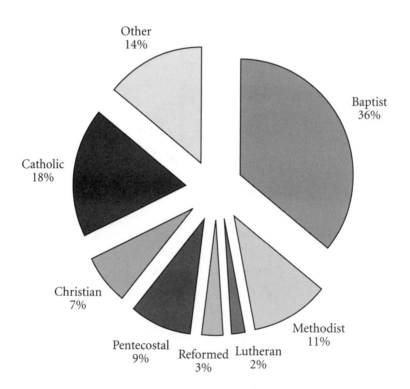

Fig. 4.12. South region church attendance share 2005.

The South

The South is seeing significant immigration, particularly from the North-east states. Population numbers for Anglos, African Americans, Asians, and Hispanics are all growing. Church attendance is also growing. Unfortunately, for each of the three major Christian branches, the population grew faster than attendance growth, as shown in Figure 4.11. This chart also reflects how dominant evangelicalism is in the South.

The Southern Baptist Convention (SBC) illustrates the challenge churches face in keeping up with the population growth. Nationally, Southern Baptists are growing faster than population growth. That is not the case in the South, however, because of the region's rapid population growth. From 2000 to 2005, the Southern Baptists grew by 5.6 percent in attendance in the Southern states. Unfortunately, the population growth rate was 7.1 percent in those states, causing the SBC to decline in its attendance percentage. Figure 4.12 shows the percentage of total church attendance for the eight denominational families in the South region. There are twice as many Baptists in church each week as in any other family group.

The Midwest

Figure 4.13 illustrates that Roman Catholic and mainline churches saw rapid decline in their attendance percentage in the Midwest, while evangelical churches kept up with population growth and actually grew slightly faster than population growth from 2000 to 2005. The evangelical growth occurred primarily in suburban areas.

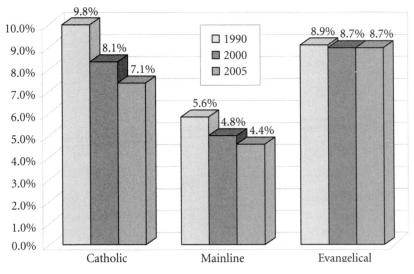

Fig. 4.13. Percentage attending a Christian church in the Midwest region each weekend.

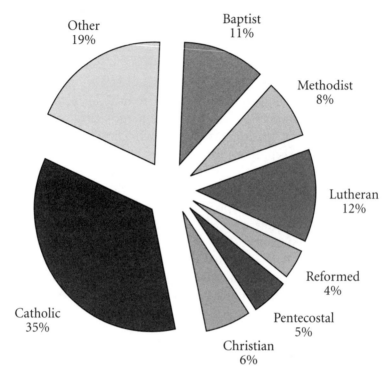

Fig. 4.14. Midwest region church attendance share 2005.

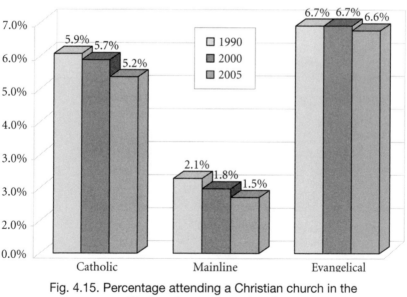

Fig. 4.15. Percentage attending a Christian church in the
West region each weekend.

Figure 4.14 shows the attendance share for each of the eight major denominational families. Roman Catholics have the largest attendance in the Midwest. The Lutheran share in the Midwest is three times higher than the Lutheran share in any other region.

The West

The religious makeup of the West is unique. Figure 4.15 shows that mainline churches have experienced rapid decline in their attendance percentage. Roman Catholic churches have experienced modest decline, while evangelicals have almost kept up with population growth. Mainline churches declined by almost 30 percent from 1990 to 2005 in attendance percentage. Of all four regions, mainline churches are declining the fastest here.

Common sense would suggest that since mainline churches are the most "liberal" churches in Protestantism, they would do best in states that are more "liberal." In fact, the opposite is true. Mainline churches do best in conservative states, and decline the most in liberal states. This is because many mainline churches in conservative states are theologically conservative, and liberal mainline churches are declining more rapidly than conservative mainline churches.

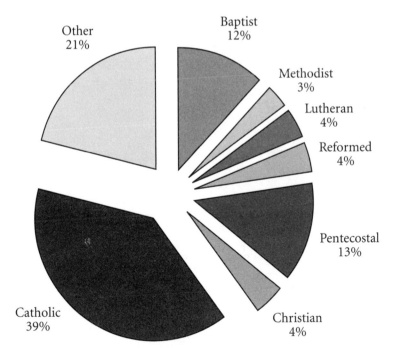

Fig. 4.16. West region church attendance share 2005.

Figure 4.16 shows the attendance share of the eight major denominational families in the West. While Catholic attendance is the largest, the "Other" and the Pentecostal families have the next highest share in this region. This feature, combined with the small size of mainline denominations, shows how Protestant churches in the West are primarily indigenous American forms of Christianity.

Millennial Decline

Figure 4.17 shows the yearly numeric attendance growth for each region from 1990 to 2000 and from 2000 to 2005. The yearly rate in every region from 2000 to 2005 was lower than the 1990s rate. The yearly growth rate from 2000 to 2005 in the South and West was half as much as the 1990s. The yearly decline rate in the Northeast and Midwest was twice as high as in the previous decade. This reflects the more challenging environment facing Christian churches in every region in this new millennium.

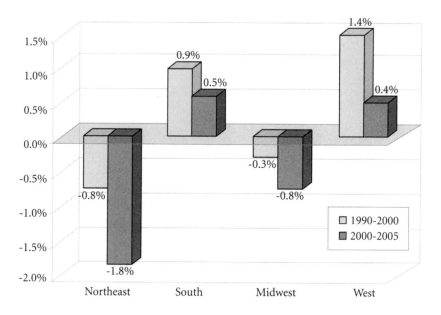

Fig. 4.17. Yearly numeric attendance growth or decline
by region.

Figure 4.18 factors in population growth by showing the regional decline in church attendance percentage from 1990 to 2005. While the South and West experienced significant numeric church attendance growth in these 15 years, each region's population grew by 25 and 29 percent respectively. Church attendance growth did not come close to keeping up with population growth. The Northeast and the Midwest had slower population growth, but declined in attendance percentage even more.

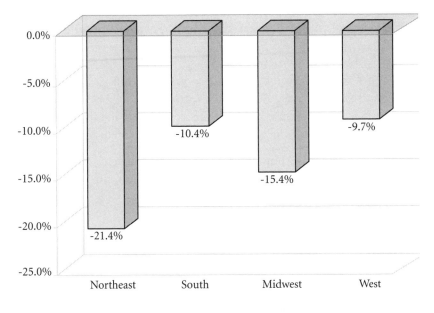

Fig. 4.18. Decline in attendance percentage by region
from 1990 to 2005.

What Does the Church's Regional Geography Mean for the Future?

Historical immigration trends set the original pattern of American Christianity, but the energy and enthusiasm with which each group expands is now reshaping the American religious picture. This regional look highlighted how the ecclesiastical players are being reshuffled. Many historic denominations appear to be losing energy and focus, while newer denominations and independent churches are gaining ground.

This reshuffle can be seen in the 2007 sale of the Cathedral of Christ the King in Portage, Michigan. In 1965 members of the Episcopal Diocese of Western Michigan voted to build a new cathedral on 30 acres of land near Kalamazoo. Designed by an award-winning architect and housing a massive 49-rank Aeolian/Skinner organ, the building cost $1,653,729.81, according to the cathedral's official website. "The Cathedral ... stands as a constant reminder to Christians of each generation that it is the mission of the Church of the Living God to minister to all of God's people and to all forces in society."[7]

According to the *Kalamazoo Gazette*, "tight finances and a dwindling church maintenance fund" caused the diocese to sell the cathedral.[8] The Kalamazoo Valley Family Church, an independent, charismatic congregation of 2,300 people, purchased the building in 2007, and the Episcopalians began holding their worship services at a nearby athletic club.

While this chapter focuses on changing demographics and church attendance trends in each region, many factors within your community and congregation also affect the church's growth or decline and have major implications for the future. In particular, six external and internal demographic features are having a significant effect on your church:

1. *Affluence* of the community in which your church is located
2. *Educational attainment* of your church's community
3. *Age* of your church and its constituency
4. *Size* of your church
5. *Gender* makeup of your church
6. *Location* of your church

We now turn in the next chapter to these six dimensions of your church, to discover how they are shaping your church's future.

Questions for Reflection and Discussion

1. Are you surprised at the regions where evangelical, mainline, and Roman Catholic churches are strongest?
2. Given that historic immigration patterns laid the foundation of Christianity in your region, how do you think missional enthusiasm will now influence the expression of Christianity in your region in the next decade?
3. Looking at the region in which you live, what trends are most significant to your church?
4. What have you learned in this chapter about the branches of Christianity that are not your own tradition?

Please go to www.theamericanchurch.org/TACIC/Chapter4.htm for updates and additional information and resources for this chapter.

Chapter 5

"POOR, UNEDUCATED, AND EASY TO COMMAND"

On February 1, 1993, the *Washington Post* became embroiled in a religious firestorm. In a front-page story, reacting to a volatile political battle over gays in the military, writer Michael Weisskopf described followers of television evangelists Jerry Falwell and Pat Robertson as largely "poor, uneducated, and easy to command." Facing immediate protests, the *Post* issued a correction the next day, stating, "There is no factual basis for that statement." *Post* writer Howard Kurtz, on February 6, quoted Robert Kaiser, *Post* managing editor at the time, as saying, "We really screwed up." In spite of the correction, Weisskopf's line has lived on in infamy.[1]

The firestorm erupted because there was a collision between certain unspoken presuppositions our society possesses about certain Christian groups and the direct, provocative statement of those assumptions. That stereotype of the American church is deeply rooted in the psyche of much of the non-churchgoing public.

H. L. Mencken was a famous journalist and one of the most influential American writers in the early part of the twentieth century. According to Jon Meacham, managing editor of *Newsweek*, "Mencken famously called evangelical Christianity 'a childish theology' 'rounded upon hate' for 'half-wits,' 'morons,' 'rustic ignoramuses,' and 'yokels from the hills.' "[2] The prevailing theory invoked by both Weisskopf and Mencken was that religion attracts poor, uneducated, and easily manipulated people who are hoping for a better life in this world and in the "sweet by and by." According to this theory, Christians believe an illusionary myth and follow religious leaders who prey on the weak and gullible.

Does this cultural stereotype describe the church of today? What is the true profile of the people who attend and of the communities in which churches minister? To find out, the American Church Research Project studied six demographic qualities of the American church.

Affluence and Education

The U.S. Census Bureau publishes data on the household income and educational attainment for every zip code in America. When combined with church attendance data sorted by zip code, a picture emerges of how churches in different economic and educational environments are progressing.

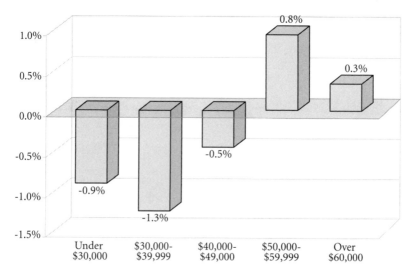

Fig. 5.1. 2004–2005 United States church attendance growth rate based on 1999 median family income of church's zip code.

The American church is growing the fastest in zip codes that are more affluent. Figure 5.1 is based on 2004 to 2005 attendance numbers of 70,000 Protestant churches, sorted by the median income of their zip code. Church attendance in poorer communities declined, while churches in wealthier neighborhoods grew. A similar study on educational attainment produced a virtually identical graph.

Evangelical churches, in particular, are growing in suburbs that are home to affluent, educated residents. The median income in Lake Forest, California, home of Saddleback Community Church, is $78,681,[3] more than $25,000 higher than the national median. In South Barrington, Illinois, home of Willow Creek Community Church, the median income is more than $200,000 a year.[4]

Writing in the June 2000 issue of *Christianity Today*, Seattle Pacific University professor Michael S. Hamilton worried about the effect wealth was having on the church. "At the beginning of the 20th century, evangelicalism gave up much of its wealth and social status so that it could be more faithful to the gospel," he wrote. "A century later, North American evangelicalism has recouped its lost wealth, and then some."[5]

Age

My first ministry position was as youth pastor at the 120-year-old South Isanti Baptist Church in rural Minnesota. We loved it. My new bride and I lived in the minuscule "janitor's house" behind the church building. We filled the 400-square-foot, two-story house with raucous teenagers as our newborn daughter tried to sleep in the tiny landing at the top of the stairs.

Thirty-seven percent of American churches join South Isanti Baptist Church in surpassing the century mark in age. As a church grows older, identifiable patterns, similar to that of the human body, become apparent. The Merck website describes the aging process:

> Aging is a process of gradual and spontaneous change, resulting in maturation through childhood, puberty, and young adulthood and then decline of many bodily functions through middle and late age. It involves both the positive component of development and the negative component of decline. *Normal aging* refers to the common complex of diseases and impairments that affect many older people. It encompasses a wide spectrum, because people age very differently, including how they develop diseases and impairments.[6]

Churches follow a similar pattern. The growth rate of churches is highest in their early years. Once churches reach 40 years of age, on average they enter a period of long and sustained decline. Figure 5.2 displays the yearly growth rate of churches in their first to tenth year and then every decade thereafter.[7]

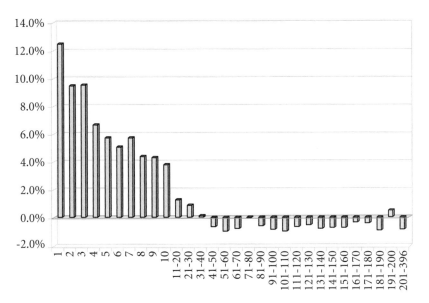

Fig. 5.2. Yearly growth rate by age of church.

Churches, it turns out, are not like André the Giant, the well-known professional wrestler and actor in the movie *Princess Bride*. Born on May 19, 1946, André René Roussimoff of Grenoble, France, suffered from acromegaly—"an overabundance of growth hormones," according to his official biography. At 17 he was six feet seven inches tall, and he eventually grew to seven feet four inches and weighed more than 500 pounds.[8] His body would not stop growing! Mercifully, for most humans, our bodies reach an age where growth stops. Unfortunately, for most churches, the growth and decline cycle replicates the typical human life cycle rather than Andre's amazing growth.

On average, churches begin to decline in size when they reach 40 years of age. From 2004 to 2005, 57 percent of churches over age 40 declined. For mainline churches, the statistics are more dire: 66 percent of these older mainline churches declined.

An important parallel between the body and the church exists. It is noteworthy when a world-class athlete can still perform at a professional level after age 40. Like aging athletes, many churches over 40 are less flexible, move more slowly, and no longer respond well to change. Denominations differ greatly in the percentage of decline among their churches over 40 years of age. The following chart evaluates 10 denominations and tracks the percentage of the churches over 40 years of age that declined over the last 10 years.

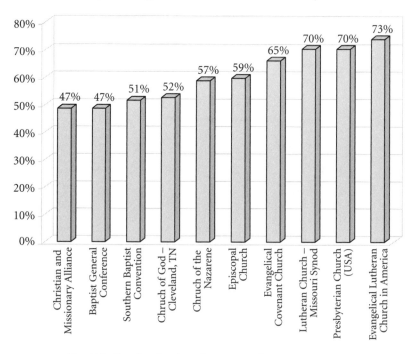

Fig. 5.3. Decline in churches more than 40 years old.

One reason mainline churches are declining faster than evangelical churches is that they are significantly older. In a study of more than 100,000 churches from a variety of denominations, the average mainline church was 105 years old while the average evangelical church was only 64 years old.

Age of Members and Clergy

The age of church members and the age of a congregation's pastor also influence a church's growth pattern. The average age of members in established churches is older than the average in younger churches, and the average age in mainline churches is older than in evangelical churches. In the Presbyterian Church (U.S.A.), the average age of church members is 58. For United Methodists, 61 is the average age. Sixty percent of Episcopalians are over age 50; 38 percent are over age 60. The older the members of a church are, the slower the church grows. Why? Older members do not have children, so they do not help the church grow through reproduction. Older members also tend to adjust slowly to cultural changes.

The average age of senior pastors is increasing as well. This is especially true among Roman Catholic priests and mainline clergy. As an example, before 1960, 85 percent of Presbyterian ordinands (seminarians ordained to the ministry) were under the age of 30. Today only 20 percent of ordinands are that young. In mainline churches, the percentage of priests and ministers under the age of 35 stands at around 7 percent.[9] Only 4 percent of Episcopal priests are under 35.[10] The Assemblies of God ministerial age is increasing as well, while Catholic priests average 59 years of age. Only 5 percent of priests are under age 35.[11]

Older members often attend older churches pastored by older clergy, and these three combine to create a "triple elder factor." This means that when all three are present together, the growth potential becomes very limited. The age factor is a critical issue for the American church to address. The Merck study cited above includes a final paragraph that provides hope for the church: "Successful (healthy) aging refers to a process by which aging is not accompanied by debilitating disease and disability. People who age successfully may maintain an active healthy life until death."[12]

My wife, Shelly, works part-time as an activities director at a retirement center. As part of her job, she leads a program called "Exercise with Shelly." One of her regulars is Signe Broberg, who is a young 108 years old. As well as exercising, she reads, creates handmade Christmas cards and valentines, enjoys a supportive family, lives out her faith, and still has purpose in life. She visits elementary schools and tells first graders what school was like a hundred years ago!

Churches can live a healthy life, even as they age. Chapter 8 will explore in depth how established churches, their members, and their clergy can maintain a life of activity, health, and even growth.

Size

The size of a church's worship attendance affects its growth pattern. Most casual observers would guess that large churches are growing, while mid-sized and small churches seem to be declining. What does the research show? Figure 5.4 displays the results of a study of more than 100,000 Protestant churches, tracking their attendance growth or decline from 1999 to 2005.[13] These churches were divided into 10 categories according to their 1999 worship attendance.

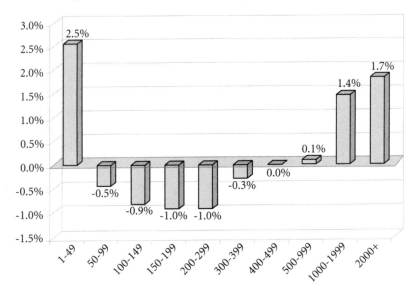

Fig. 5.4. Yearly rate of growth or decline in attendance
by size of church.

While the larger churches grew according to expectation, the smallest churches actually grew at a faster yearly rate. The churches that declined most were those with a weekly attendance between 100 and 299.

There are several reasons why small churches are growing. In a small church, everyone knows everyone else by name, creating intimate bonds. Small churches also have a much larger growth upside than downside. A church with fewer than 50 people has very little room to shrink. On the other hand, they have a large potential upside, since a church of 25 could grow to 75, 125, or even 200.

While most large churches are not intimate, they usually offer a wide range of high-quality ministries. Many features of American culture, such as sports stadiums, shopping malls, and superstores have made Americans more comfortable in large group settings. Bigger is synonymous with better. In one sense, Christians who leave smaller churches to attend larger churches are "upgrading to first class."

This double trend of upgrading to the large and specializing in the small is seen in how retail markets are changing. In my hometown, five mega-dealers have absorbed almost every independent auto dealer and now control the market through multiple locations. Yet there is a thriving business at the opposite end of the car market. Former auto salespeople are advertising on the radio, offering to find the right car for you at the right price. Craig's List, Carmax, and eBay have also become popular places to search for the right car. Midsize dealers, however, have all but disappeared. Unfortunately, midsize churches seem to face a similar problem. They are too large to be intimate yet too small to offer the range of services that large churches provide. They are being squeezed out by either side of the continuum.

What are midsize churches to do? One half of Protestant church attendance comes from midsize churches, so this is a critical question to address. The answer is that midsize churches need to embrace both intimacy and ministry excellence if they hope to grow. In midsize churches, intimacy is best fostered in a variety of small group settings—often gatherings that meet in a home for a meal together, a Bible study, or a monthly service project. Midsize churches can improve their ministry excellence by (1) developing the gifts of the pastor and staff; (2) motivating, training, and deploying lay leaders; and (3) focusing on a manageable number of ministries that reflect quality and spiritual depth. Midsize churches will continue to decline if these challenges are not addressed.

Gender

A gender gap exists in the church: many more women than men attend church. Reporting on David Murrow's book *Why Men Hate Going to Church*, Biola University's *Connections* magazine noted the following:

> Worldwide, the church is 66 percent women. In America, among evangelical churches, 57 percent of members are women and, among mainline Protestant churches, 66 percent are women, according to a 1998 book *American Evangelicalism* (University of Chicago Press). The imbalance is greatest in rural churches, small churches, older churches, traditionally black denominations, and in liberal churches, Murrow said, citing research from the 1998 National Congregations Study. It's smallest in nondenominational and Baptist churches, he said.[14]

Research studies agree that 61 percent of those who attend religious congregations are women.[15] In Roman Catholic churches two-thirds of Mass participants are female.[16] African American churches have an especially high percentage of female attendees, with most research estimates finding that women comprise 70 to 85 percent of their worship attendance. The predominance of women in American churches is not a new phenomenon but has been true throughout much of U.S. religious history.

Research has also found that younger churches and growing churches have more balanced male-female ratios. In older churches and declining churches there are more female attendees. Figure 5.5 shows the result of a TACRP study of Presbyterian Church (U.S.A.) churches. The higher the percentage of females in the membership of a church, the faster the church is likely to decline in attendance.

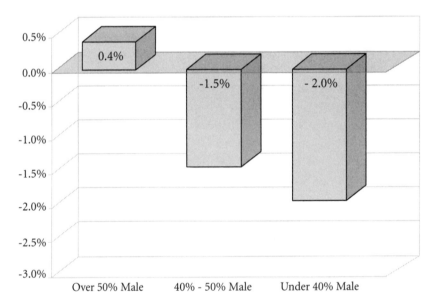

Fig. 5.5. Presbyterian Church (U.S.A.) 2005–2006 attendance growth based on the gender of the membership.

While studying megachurches, James Twitchell, a marketing professor from the University of Florida, discovered that megachurches like Willow Creek have found ways to attract men to church. Doing that, he argues, is crucial to their success. In his book *Branded Nation*, he describes how Bill Hybels and a group of volunteers went door-to-door, asking people about their churchgoing habits. They discovered that in most cases "the impediment to family faith was, in a word, men." "If there is one marketing secret Hybels learned, it is this: Men are the crucial adopters in religion," Twitchell writes. "If they go over the tipping point, women follow, children in tow."[17] A study in 2000 from Switzerland provides insight on the importance of male attendance on the religious development of children in that country. "In summary, if a father does not go to church, no matter how regular the mother is in her religious practice, only one child in 50 becomes a regular church attendee. But if a father attends regularly, then regardless of the practice of the mother, at least one child in three will become a regular church attendee."[18]

The research seems to indicate that a balanced male-female ratio in a church correlates positively with growth.

Location

Historically, most Protestant churches were originally located in counties classified as rural, small town, and large town. In 2000, 17 percent of the population in these counties attended a Protestant church on any given week, while the attendance rate for suburban and urban counties was 11.5 percent. However, these percentages have changed since 1990. Figure 5.6 shows that numeric church attendance is declining in nonmetropolitan counties while remaining the same in metropolitan counties.

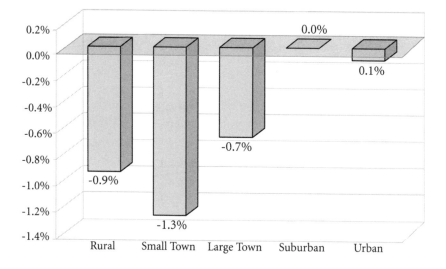

Fig. 5.6. United States church attendance growth rate 2004–2005 based on location of church's zip code.

Reflection

While research does not show that Christians are "largely poor, uneducated, and easy to command," there are some disconcerting trends in the American church. The gospel is for all people. Whenever the focus of the church bends toward the wealthy, the well educated, and the properly scrubbed, I feel concern. This pattern is a potent indicator of the captivity of American Christianity to our culture. Christianity has an amazing ability to connect with a great variety of cultures, whether rich or poor, educated or uneducated, liberal or conservative. Yet Christianity is also profoundly countercultural.

If there is a bias in Scripture, Jesus' inaugural sermon in Luke 4:18–19 reveals the predisposition. His heart was drawn toward the poor, the captive, the brokenhearted, and the oppressed. The stereotype about Christians mentioned in this chapter's introduction shows a repugnant elitism, implying that the poor, the uneducated, and the easy to command somehow deserve the scorn of the ruling elite. That very same elitism can be true of much of the American church today—the sting becomes much more personal when we are the guilty ones. If the church is indeed becoming the home of affluent, educated, and suburban Americans, we had better let the countercultural power of the message of Jesus reshape our lives. That gospel is for all classes and types of people. That was part of the appeal of the church from the beginning:

> It was in the way of love revealed, in the witness of community (*koinonia*), in a fellowship which took in Jew and Gentile, slave and free, men and women, and whose solid practicality in their care for the needy won the admiration even of Lucian. "How these Christians love one another!" was a respectful affirmation.[19]

Chapters 13 and 14 suggest a model to bring us back to the original message and mission of the original messenger and missionary, Jesus himself.

One final portrait needs to be painted before moving from observation to evaluation. American religion is dominated by eight families of Christianity that have all left their unique mark on our country's religious landscape and history. Chapter 6 will explore the variety and vitality these ecclesiastical breeds bring to American Christianity.

Questions for Reflection and Discussion

1. This chapter refers to a "triple elder factor," when the age of the church, its members, and its clergy all reinforce the fact that the institutional profile is not becoming younger. Do you think this is a major challenge? Why?

2. If your church is more than 40 years old, what strategies of successful aging apply to your church?

3. Were you aware that growth patterns are influenced by the size of a church? What difference might that make in how your church looks at intimacy and excellence?

4. Are you concerned that the American church is becoming more educated, affluent, and suburban? Why or why not?

Please go to www.theamericanchurch.org/TACIC/Chapter5.htm for updates and additional information and resources for this chapter.

Chapter 6

DENOMINATIONAL WINNERS AND LOSERS

The array of dogs at the Westminster Kennel Club Show is astounding. Large and small, slow and fast, lively and sleepy all abound. The unusual names seem endless. In the giant dog class alone, there is the Akita, Anatolian shepherd, Caucasian mountain dog, Dogue de Bordeaux, Great Dane, Great Pyrenees, Greater Swiss mountain dog, Irish wolfhound, Kuvasz, mastiff, Neapolitan mastiff, Newfoundland, Saint Bernard, Scottish deerhound, and Tibetan mastiff.

From the opening moments when the 2,500-plus champions begin to compete in 162 different breed and variety rings at Madison Square Garden in New York, to the final crowning of the "Best in Show" dog, the Westminster is the greatest spectacular of dog adoration in North America.

The American church is also comprised of a variety of "breeds." Like their canine counterparts, denominations each have characteristics formed by their genetic history. Some are large and slow. Others are small and fast.

Some live in packs, while others are very independent. Some were born to live in an earlier world and are struggling with the present environment. Some are becoming increasingly barren, while others are multiplying rapidly.

These American church "breeds" can be grouped into seven major denominational families: Baptist, Methodist, Lutheran, Reformed, Pentecostal, Christian, and Roman Catholic families. Churches that do not easily fit into one of these seven are referred to as "Other" in this chapter's research. Figure 6.1 shows the 2005 weekly church attendance share by denominational family.

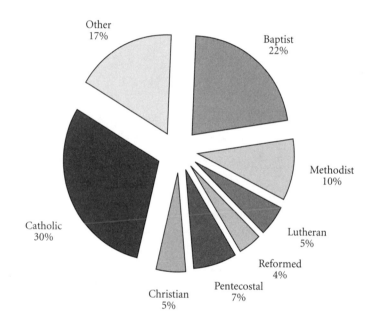

Fig. 6.1. 2005 Church attendance by denominational family.

In this chapter we look at these eight families to see where they are clustered in America and whether they are growing or declining in attendance percentage.

How Is the Baptist Family of Churches Doing?

Baptists are the largest group in Protestant weekend attendance. They have more than twice as many attendees as any other identified Protestant family. As seen in figure 6.2, Baptist church attendance is very strong in the South, particularly in the Bible-belt crescent from Oklahoma to North Carolina. The percentage declines sharply outside the South. The Great Lakes region is the next leading Baptist area, with much of the Baptist population being African American Baptists in urban cities. Baptists are numerous because of their historic emphasis on conversion and growth. Because each congregation is self-governing and ordains its own pastor, Baptist churches are easy to start. Today there are more than 90,000 Baptist churches in the United States.

Figure 6.3 shows that Baptist attendance is growing faster than population growth in states where Baptists were not historically strong, such as in the middle of the Midwest and in the Ohio-Virginia-Vermont triangle. None of the Southern states is seeing Baptist attendance keep up with population growth, even though Baptist churches in those areas are growing numerically. The strong Baptist growth in Minnesota is due to the growth of a denomination called the Baptist General Conference (BGC). Twenty-five percent of BGC attendance is concentrated in that state.

How Is the Methodist Family of Churches Doing?

Methodists are the second largest family of American Protestants. They have their roots in the movement started by John Wesley in late eighteenth-century England. The three largest American Methodist denominations are the United Methodist Church, the African Methodist Episcopal Church, and the African Methodist Episcopal Zion Church. Methodists are most numerous in Alabama, followed by South Carolina, North Carolina, Mississippi, West Virginia, Kansas, and Indiana.

Methodists are declining in attendance percentage in every state except Mississippi. The decline is particularly strong west of the Rockies. Because Methodist denominations start few new churches, this family struggles to keep up in states with rapid population growth.

How Is the Lutheran Family of Churches Doing?

Lutherans originally came to America as immigrants in the 1800s and the early 1900s from Scandinavia and Germany. Their denominations are strongest in the Upper Midwest. The farther the state is from the Minnesota-Dakota border, the lower the percentage of Lutherans.

Lutheran churches declined in attendance percentage in 43 states from 2000 to 2005. The states that showed an increase have very small Lutheran populations.

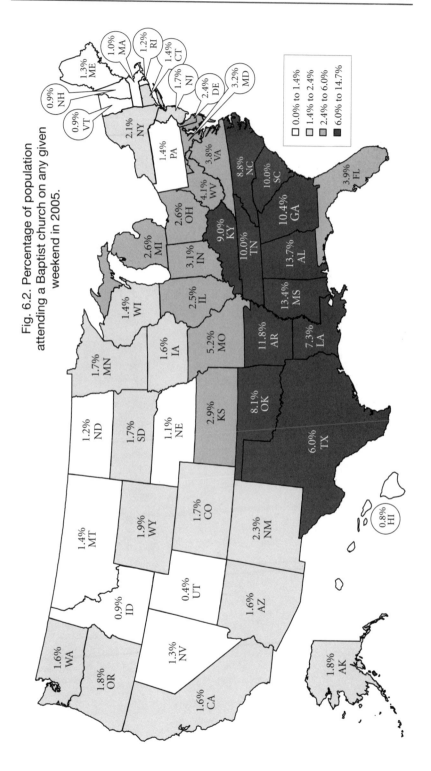

Fig. 6.2. Percentage of population attending a Baptist church on any given weekend in 2005.

Legend:
- 0.0% to 1.4%
- 1.4% to 2.4%
- 2.4% to 6.0%
- 6.0% to 14.7%

0.9% NH
0.9% VT
1.3% ME
1.0% MA
1.2% RI
1.4% CT
1.7% NJ
2.4% DE
3.2% MD
2.1% NY
1.4% PA
3.8% VA
8.8% NC
10.0% SC
3.9% FL
4.1% WV
2.6% OH
2.6% MI
3.1% IN
9.0% KY
10.0% TN
13.7% AL
10.4% GA
1.4% WI
2.5% IL
13.4% MS
1.6% IA
5.2% MO
11.8% AR
7.3% LA
1.7% MN
2.9% KS
8.1% OK
1.2% ND
1.7% SD
1.1% NE
6.0% TX
1.4% MT
1.9% WY
1.7% CO
2.3% NM
0.9% ID
0.4% UT
1.6% AZ
1.6% WA
1.8% OR
1.3% NV
1.6% CA
1.8% AK
0.8% HI

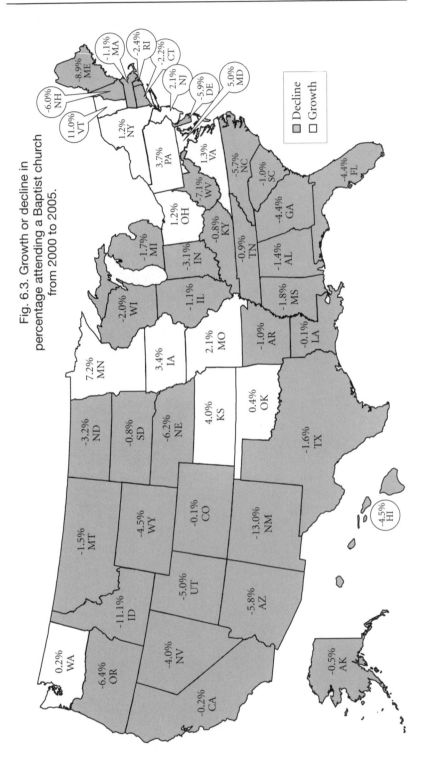

Fig. 6.3. Growth or decline in percentage attending a Baptist church from 2000 to 2005.

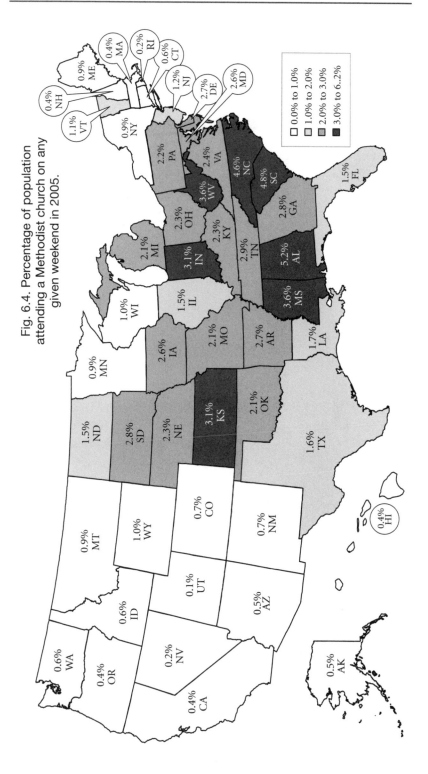

Fig. 6.4. Percentage of population attending a Methodist church on any given weekend in 2005.

Legend:
- 0.0% to 1.0%
- 1.0% to 2.0%
- 2.0% to 3.0%
- 3.0% to 6.2%

0.4% NH
1.1% VT
0.9% ME
0.4% MA
0.2% RI
0.6% CT
1.2% NJ
2.7% DE
2.6% MD
0.9% NY
2.2% PA
2.4% VA
4.6% NC
4.8% SC
1.5% FL
3.6% WV
2.8% GA
2.3% OH
2.3% KY
5.2% AL
2.1% MI
3.1% IN
2.9% TN
3.6% MS
1.0% WI
1.5% IL
2.1% MO
2.7% AR
1.7% LA
0.9% MN
2.6% IA
2.1% OK
1.5% ND
2.8% SD
2.3% NE
3.1% KS
1.6% TX
0.9% MT
1.0% WY
0.7% CO
0.7% NM
0.4% HI
0.6% ID
0.1% UT
0.5% AZ
0.6% WA
0.4% OR
0.2% NV
0.4% CA
0.5% AK

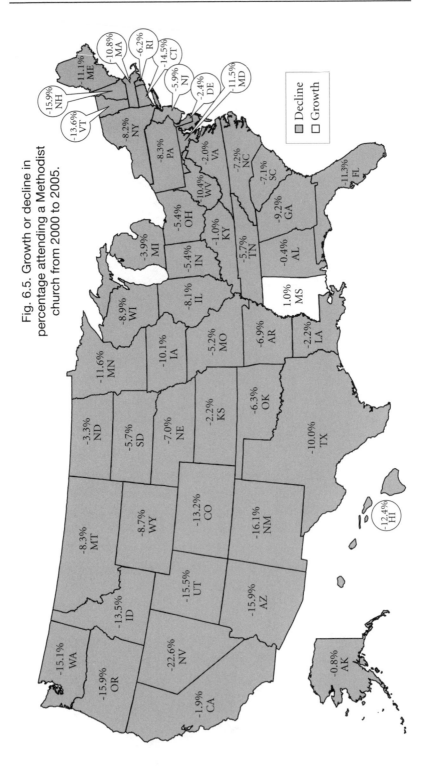

Fig. 6.5. Growth or decline in percentage attending a Methodist church from 2000 to 2005.

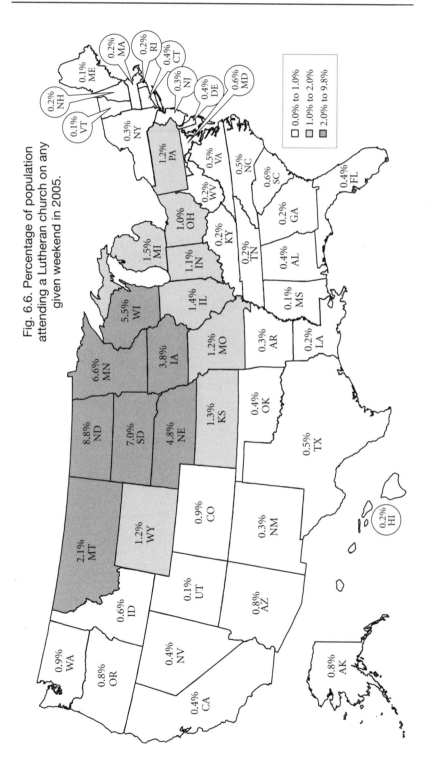

Fig. 6.6. Percentage of population attending a Lutheran church on any given weekend in 2005.

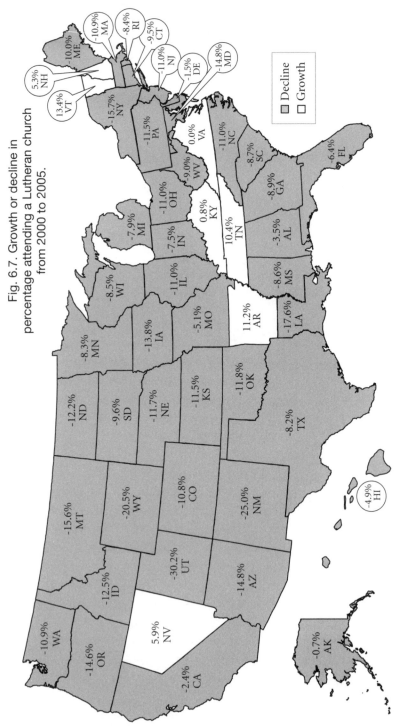

Fig. 6.7. Growth or decline in percentage attending a Lutheran church from 2000 to 2005.

How Is the Reformed Family of Churches Doing?

The Reformed family is rooted in the Calvinist expression of Christianity. These churches are called either Presbyterian or Reformed. The largest Reformed denomination is the Presbyterian Church (U.S.A.). They are followed by the Presbyterian Church in America, the Christian Reformed Church, the Reformed Church in America, and the Korean Presbyterian Church. The three states with the highest percentage of attendance are Iowa, Michigan, and South Dakota, states with many residents of Dutch ancestry. Churches that are called Presbyterian (rather than Reformed) are strongest in the mid-Atlantic region.

The Reformed family declined in 48 states, growing only in Hawaii and New Hampshire, states with a small Reformed population. Nineteen states saw a percentage decline of more than 10 percent from 2000 to 2005, including Arkansas, Minnesota, Nevada, Arizona, and South Dakota.

How Is the Pentecostal Family of Churches Doing?

Pentecostal churches are an outgrowth of the Asuza Street Revival in Los Angeles in 1906. They emphasize the work of the Holy Spirit in their members' lives and their churches, and they are strongest in the South and the West regions. Their two strongest states are Oklahoma and Mississippi. The largest Pentecostal group is the Church of God in Christ, followed by the Assemblies of God.

Pentecostals are growing faster than population growth in 40 states. The states that are in decline are in the far north or the far south. The fastest growth has occurred in Massachusetts, Rhode Island, Iowa, South Dakota, Hawaii, and Virginia.

How Is the Family of "Christian" Churches Doing?

"Christian" churches come from the Restorationist branch of American Christianity. This began in the mid-1800s as an attempt to restore New Testament Christianity. The three largest groups are Christian Churches, Churches of Christ, and the Disciples of Christ (Christian Church).[1] Technically, these groups do not consider themselves denominations. As can be seen in the map, Christian Churches are strongest in the midsection of the country, with Oregon also having a higher percentage.

How Is the Catholic Family of Churches Doing?

The Roman Catholic Church is strong historically in the urban centers of the Northeast and the Midwest as well as Louisiana and the states that border Mexico. Rhode Island has the highest percentage of Catholic attendance of any state.

The Catholic Church is declining in the areas of its greatest historic strength, but growing faster than population growth in much of the South, where the church is least populous. Much of the growth in the South is from the migration of Catholics moving south from the Northeast and Midwest, as well as from Hispanic immigration.

How Are Non-Baptist, Non-Pentecostal Evangelical Churches Doing?

The eighth family, the "Other" family, includes those denominations and churches that do not easily fit into one of the other seven families. There is a bewildering variety in this family, ranging from very liberal to very conservative. One important subset of the "Other" category is a collection of evangelical denominations that are neither Baptist nor Pentecostal, but have affinities in culture, theology, and mission with each other. This subset is the fastest-growing segment of the American church. All of these denominations are midrange in size with a weekly attendance of 50,000 to 500,000. These 12 denominations are

Church of God—Anderson, Indiana
Church of the Nazarene
Christian and Missionary Alliance
Christian Reformed Church
Evangelical Covenant Church
Evangelical Free Church
Evangelical Presbyterian Church
Free Methodist Church
Missionary Church
North American Baptist Conference
Presbyterian Church of America
Wesleyan Church

Since 1990 these "other" evangelicals have experienced the strongest attendance growth of any of the eight families. There are many reasons for this: they have relatively healthy established churches and extensive church planting systems, and their colleges and seminaries are seeing robust growth in enrollment. They are strongest in the northern half of the country, particularly the Upper Midwest.

These twelve denominations are seeing very strong growth throughout the country. They increased in attendance percentage in 37 states and declined in 13 states.

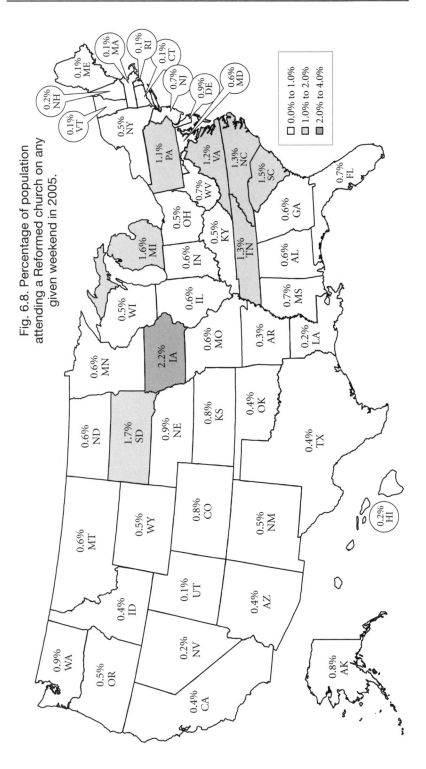

Fig. 6.8. Percentage of population attending a Reformed church on any given weekend in 2005.

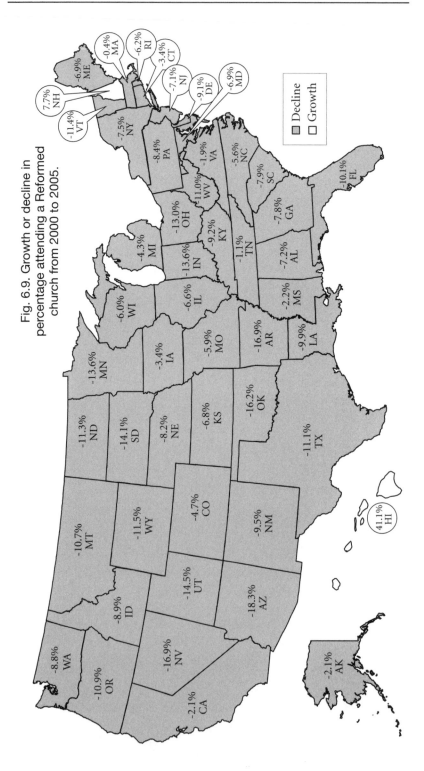

Fig. 6.9. Growth or decline in percentage attending a Reformed church from 2000 to 2005.

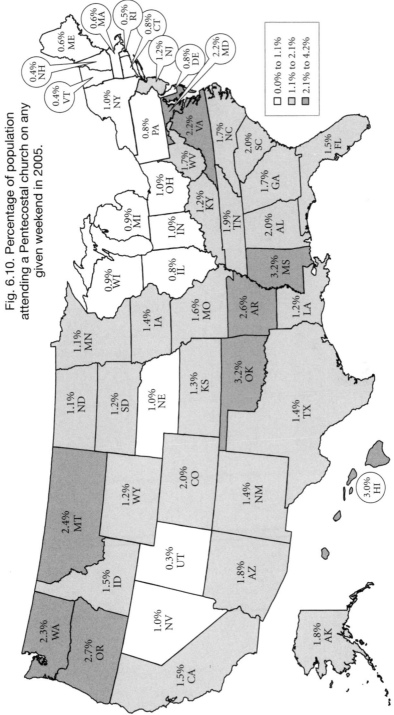

Fig. 6.10. Percentage of population attending a Pentecostal church on any given weekend in 2005.

Legend:
☐ 0.0% to 1.1%
▨ 1.1% to 2.1%
▨ 2.1% to 4.2%

0.4% NH
0.4% VT
0.6% ME
0.6% MA
0.5% RI
0.8% CT
1.2% NJ
0.8% DE
2.2% MD
1.0% NY
0.8% PA
2.2% VA
1.7% NC
2.0% SC
1.5% FL
1.7% WV
1.7% GA
1.0% OH
1.2% KY
1.9% TN
2.0% AL
0.9% MI
1.0% IN
3.2% MS
0.9% WI
0.8% IL
1.2% LA
1.4% IA
1.6% MO
2.6% AR
1.1% MN
3.2% OK
1.1% ND
1.2% SD
1.0% NE
1.3% KS
1.4% TX
2.0% CO
1.4% NM
2.4% MT
1.2% WY
3.0% HI
1.5% ID
0.3% UT
1.8% AZ
1.8% AK
2.3% WA
2.7% OR
1.0% NV
1.5% CA

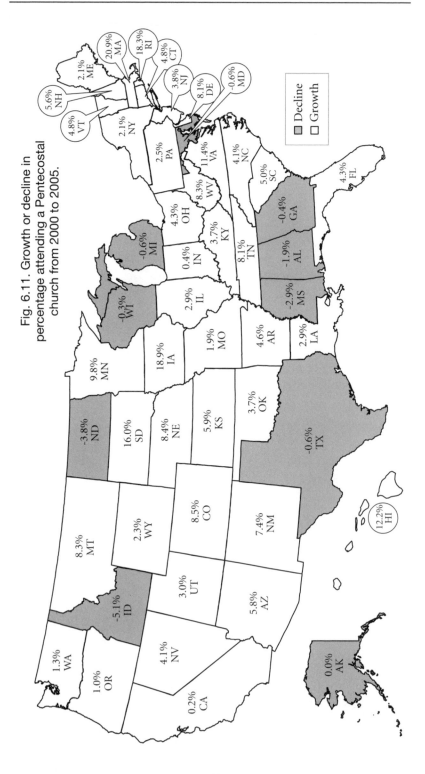

Fig. 6.11. Growth or decline in percentage attending a Pentecostal church from 2000 to 2005.

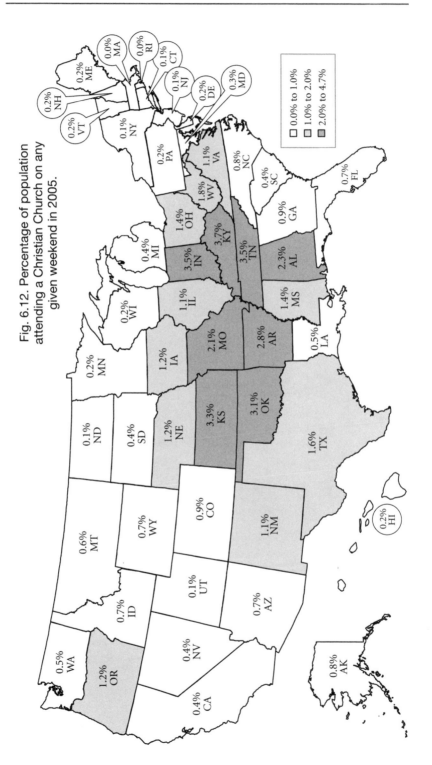

Fig. 6.12. Percentage of population attending a Christian Church on any given weekend in 2005.

Legend:
- 0.0% to 1.0%
- 1.0% to 2.0%
- 2.0% to 4.7%

0.2% NH
0.0% MA
0.0% RI
0.1% CT
0.1% NJ
0.2% DE
0.3% MD
0.2% ME
0.2% VT
0.1% NY
0.2% PA
1.1% VA
0.8% NC
0.4% SC
0.7% FL
1.8% WV
1.4% OH
3.7% KY
3.5% TN
2.3% AL
0.9% GA
0.4% MI
3.5% IN
1.1% IL
1.4% MS
0.2% WI
2.1% MO
2.8% AR
0.5% LA
0.2% MN
1.2% IA
0.1% ND
0.4% SD
1.2% NE
3.3% KS
3.1% OK
1.6% TX
0.6% MT
0.7% WY
0.9% CO
1.1% NM
0.2% HI
0.7% ID
0.1% UT
0.7% AZ
0.5% WA
1.2% OR
0.4% NV
0.4% CA
0.8% AK

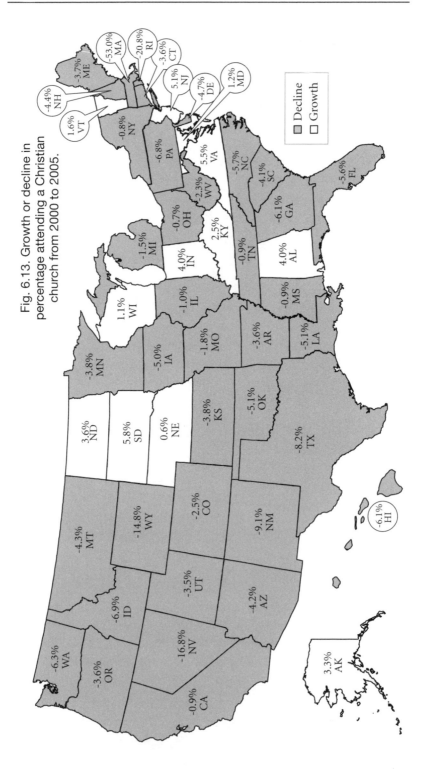

Fig. 6.13. Growth or decline in percentage attending a Christian church from 2000 to 2005.

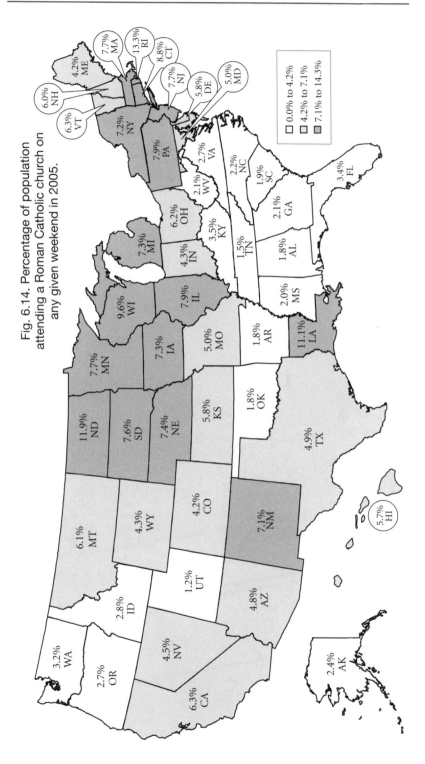

Fig. 6.14. Percentage of population attending a Roman Catholic church on any given weekend in 2005.

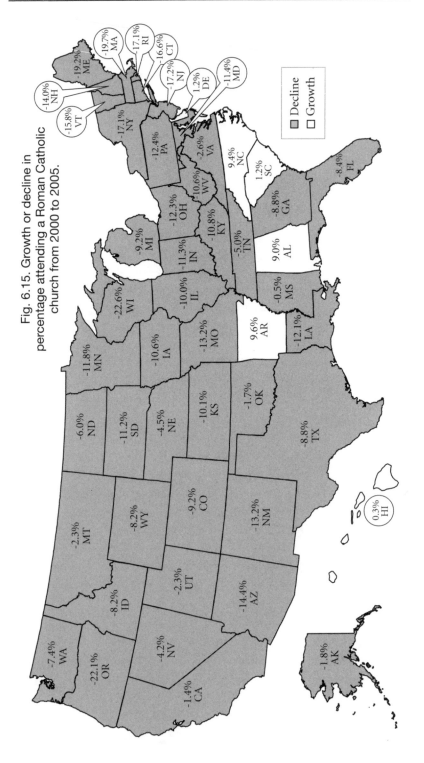

Fig. 6.15. Growth or decline in percentage attending a Roman Catholic church from 2000 to 2005.

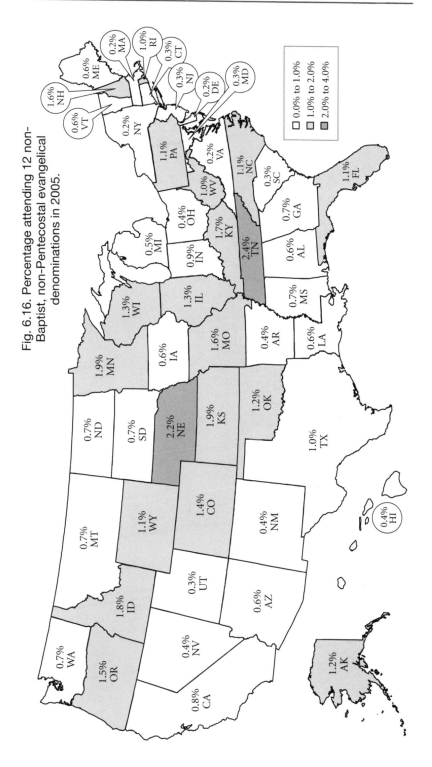

Fig. 6.16. Percentage attending 12 non-Baptist, non-Pentecostal evangelical denominations in 2005.

Legend:
- 0.0% to 1.0%
- 1.0% to 2.0%
- 2.0% to 4.0%

1.6% NH
0.6% VT
0.2% MA
1.0% RI
0.3% CT
0.3% NJ
0.2% DE
0.3% MD
0.6% ME
0.2% NY
1.1% PA
0.2% VA
1.1% NC
0.3% SC
1.1% FL
1.0% WV
0.4% OH
1.7% KY
2.4% TN
0.7% GA
0.6% AL
0.5% MI
0.9% IN
0.7% MS
1.3% WI
1.3% IL
1.6% MO
0.4% AR
0.6% LA
1.9% MN
0.6% IA
1.2% OK
0.7% ND
0.7% SD
2.2% NE
1.9% KS
1.0% TX
0.7% MT
1.1% WY
1.4% CO
0.4% NM
0.4% HI
0.7% WA
1.8% ID
0.3% UT
0.6% AZ
1.5% OR
0.4% NV
0.8% CA
1.2% AK

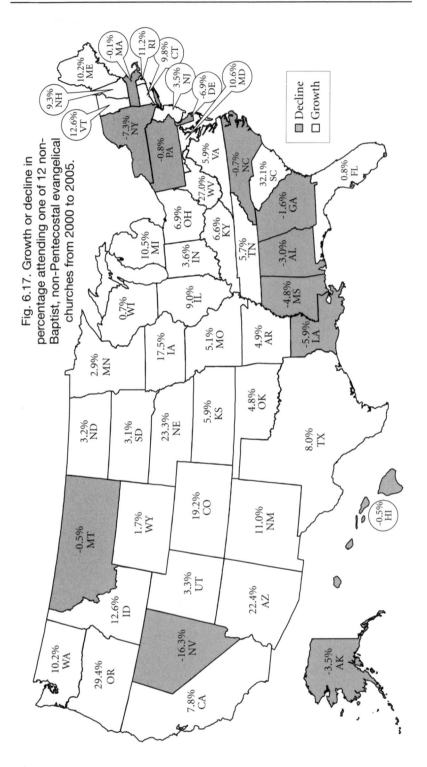

Fig. 6.17. Growth or decline in percentage attending one of 12 non-Baptist, non-Pentecostal evangelical churches from 2000 to 2005.

Decline

Growth

9.3% NH

10.2% ME

-0.1% MA

11.2% RI

9.8% CT

3.5% NJ

-6.9% DE

10.6% MD

12.6% VT

-7.3% NY

-0.8% PA

5.9% VA

-0.7% NC

32.1% SC

0.8% FL

27.0% WV

6.9% OH

6.6% KY

-1.6% GA

3.6% IN

5.7% TN

-3.0% AL

10.5% MI

9.0% IL

-4.8% MS

-5.9% LA

0.7% WI

17.5% IA

5.1% MO

4.9% AR

2.9% MN

5.9% KS

4.8% OK

3.2% ND

3.1% SD

23.3% NE

8.0% TX

-0.5% MT

1.7% WY

19.2% CO

11.0% NM

-0.5% HI

12.6% ID

3.3% UT

22.4% AZ

10.2% WA

29.4% OR

-16.3% NV

7.8% CA

-3.5% AK

How Have These Eight Families Fared in This New Millennium?

Figure 6.18 compares the yearly growth rates of these eight families from 1990 to 2000 with the growth rates from 2000 to 2005. While three families stayed virtually the same (Pentecostals, Christian, and "Non-Baptist, Non-Pentecostal Evangelicals"), the other five declined rather significantly from the 1990s rate. This figure reflects the continuing challenge that churches are facing in this new millennium.

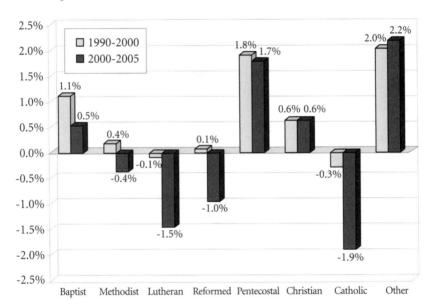

Fig. 6.18. Yearly growth rates by denominational family
1900–2000 and 2000–2005.

Independent Churches

Totally independent churches are fewer than might be expected. Most independent churches have some connection to a voluntary association of churches or a loosely affiliated denomination.[7] In that way, they are similar to the independent polity of Baptist and Christian churches. *Independent churches have been increasing in number and size over the last 15 years.* This is an important trend for the American church. Much of that growth comes from independent megachurches, which comprise about a third of all megachurches.

However, most independent churches tend to have relatively short life spans. They grow quickly in their early years but are prone to rapid decline. The personality of the founding pastor strongly influences its growth, and decline occurs when crisis or retirement comes. Their limited connection with other churches and the lack of a larger external stabilizing structure make independent churches vulnerable over time.

A Historic Reshuffling

The many different breeds of the American church are finding that the competitive environment of its culture is causing a historic reshuffling. The denominations that are declining today are slow and cautious, concerned about preservation and safety, often alienated from many of their own churches and its members. The denominations that are thriving today are nimble, fast, and multiplying strategically through grassroots ownership of the denomination's missional vision. The subject matter of the second part of this book illustrates both the growing and the declining segments of the church.

The challenges facing the American church can best be quantified in the answer to these three questions:

1. How many churches close each year?
2. How well are established churches doing?
3. How many new churches are started each year, and how well are they growing?

The answers to these three questions may surprise you.

This chapter marks the end of the section on observation; the next three chapters are devoted to evaluation. We will look at why the detailed data and observations of the first six chapters are occurring. Chapter 7 looks at the survival of the species, in this case the church species. Every species' survival depends on its health and its birthrate. Survival becomes especially difficult when living in a stressed environment, an apt description of the present religious milieu of America.

Questions for Reflection and Discussion

1. How did this chapter help you gain a more comprehensive picture of the American church? Why is that important?
2. How is your own denominational family doing? Are you encouraged or discouraged?
3. Often churches located in the geographical region of their denomination's historic strength are finding growth most difficult. Why is this, and how could these churches resist that trend?
4. How do you think the denominational families will fare in the next 40 years? Do they have a future?

Please go to www.theamericanchurch.org/TACIC/Chapter6.htm
for updates and additional information and resources for this chapter.

Part 2

EVALUATION

When nesting consistently fails to replace the numbers lost over the course of a year, extinction becomes inevitable.

Jack L. Griggs[1]

Christian leaders tend to react to challenges in the American church with one of three responses. First is the Chicken Little response: "The sky is falling. The future looks bleak. Is there any hope?" Surprisingly, the worse things are and the more alarming the statistics, the happier they often become, because their prophecies of doom are vindicated.

A second reaction is that of the ostrich: "We're not doing that poorly. In fact, we are doing quite well, all things considered. If it were not for changing demographics and low birthrates, we would be doing fine. I rather like my head in the sand." These Christians leaders expect the church to decline and consider a modest decline acceptable considering the challenges their churches face.

The third response is that of the eagle: "We are the church of Jesus Christ. The gates of hell will not prevail against us. We soar above the fray and do not pay attention to mundane matters such as attendance." Those with an eagle mind-set often lose sight of what is happening on the ground. This response discourages public discussion of attendance or its significance as an indicator of church health.

The four-stage model outlined at the beginning of part 1 requires the abandonment of the Chicken Little, ostrich, and eagle approaches. Having observed the terrain of the American church, the second stage of the model, *evaluation*, examines the data and asks, "Why is this happening?" and "What do these observations mean?" This stage attempts to foster understanding. What values and habits of the larger culture affect the church? What values and habits of Christian culture affect the church? Evaluation focuses on *objective analysis.*

In the book of Numbers, the twelve spies returned from their scouting expedition of the land of Canaan with this report: "We went into the land to which you sent us, and it does flow with milk and honey! Here is its fruit. But the people who live there are powerful, and the cities are fortified and very large" (Num. 13:27–28). Their objective evaluation? It is a good land, but there are significant challenges.

The next three chapters will use evaluation to provide a sober objective analysis of the observations collected. The best way to understand the dynamics behind the growth and decline of churches is to evaluate the data through the lens of closed churches, established churches, and new churches.

Chapter 7

THE SURVIVAL
OF THE SPECIES

Extinction. The word creates deep sadness, a feeling of tragic loss. The dodo bird, *raphus cucullatus*, was a large, comical, flightless bird that weighed up to 30 pounds.[1] The island of Mauritius in the Indian Ocean was its only home. Having developed in isolation, with no known predators, the dodo was perfectly suited for its environment. When its environment changed quickly, the dodo was unable to adapt.

Dodo birds were first discovered by Dutch sailors in 1508. Unused to predators, the dodos had no fear of human beings and walked up to their visitors, who promptly shot them. Sailors later introduced pigs, goats, cats, rats, and monkeys to the island. These animals became competitors and predators for the dodo bird. By 1681 the dodo was extinct.

Stories of other extinctions abound. Great auks were a 30-inch tall, flightless bird that lived in the islands of the North Atlantic. On June 3, 1844, at Eldey Rock near Iceland, the last known pair in the world was seen and then shot. John Audubon, who died in 1851, reported that in Ohio he once saw a flock of more than one billion passenger pigeons. Sadly, only 63 years after Audubon died, the last remaining passenger pigeon died in the Cincinnati Zoo. Audubon called the ivory-billed woodpeckers the  "king of the woodpeckers." The bird was so striking that people referred to it as the "Lord God" or "Good God" bird—as they were so struck by its beauty that all they could say was "Lord God."[2] As Audubon wrote,

> It could vigorously rip bark from a tree in large chunks, and could shred a
> dead tree into a splintered trunk barely taller than the mound of chips and

bark left around its base. The ringing echoes of the powerful blows from
its beak were mixed with its loud, excited calls—yam, yam, and yam.[3]

Eventually, the only remaining ivory-bills were in a 120-square-mile section of old forest along the Tensas River in Louisiana. The forest was cleared
for agriculture in 1948. There was not sufficient national will to save either
the forest or the birds, and the ivory-billed woodpecker disappeared, seemingly forever.

Why Do Species Become Extinct?

Why does extinction occur? It is a complex question. Extinction occurs
most often when a species faces a crisis or change in its environment and
is unable to adapt. Predators, often human, invade and take over a niche,
bringing disease and destruction. As a species begins to be threatened,
these changes combine to produce a low fertility rate. Survival comes down
to simple math: the number of births must outnumber the deaths for a species to survive. When deaths outnumber births, the species goes extinct.

A sequence of indicators denotes the health of a species. First is the
birthrate, followed by the infant mortality rate. Later, the group's ability to
help adolescents survive until they become adults and reproduce becomes
critical. Environmental changes, genetic adaptations, competition, and
predators affect the health of the adult members of the species. Yet the
ultimate end result hinges on whether more members of a species die than
are born. If so, that species faces extinction.

The American church lives in an ecosystem and in its own right can be
called a species. The long-term survival of the church can be evaluated by
the number of new churches born each year that survive and prosper, by
the health and reproductive rate of established or "adult" churches and by
the number of churches that close each year. This chapter looks specifically
at how many churches close each year and how that affects the survival of
the species. Chapter 8 will examine the health and growth of established
churches, while chapter 9 will investigate the birth of new churches. The
next three chapters will seek to objectively evaluate the data by asking three
"why?" questions: Why do churches close? Why is the future of so many
established churches at risk? Why start additional churches when there are
so many half-empty churches already?

How Many Churches Close Each Decade?

A popular prediction made fifteen years ago was that 100,000 churches
would close within the decade.[4] Did that many churches actually close?
Today many observers assume that large numbers of mainline churches

close every year. Is that true? How many Christian churches close each decade and why? To begin our investigation we will look at two case studies that illustrate church closures from opposite poles of the ecclesiastical spectrum.

The United Methodist Church is by far the largest mainline denomination in America. It has a proud and distinguished history, dating back to the early part of the nineteenth century. It also has many old churches and many small churches: more than 21,000 of its 35,000 local congregations have a weekly attendance under 75. From 1990 to 2000, out of a total of 37,129 churches, 2,212 closed. That resulted in a closure rate of 0.6 percent per year. During that same period, 706 new churches were started that remained in existence in 2000. The small number of new churches resulted in a very low reproduction rate—new churches replaced only one-third of the closed churches.

The International Pentecostal Holiness Church (IPHC) is a growing, midsize Pentecostal denomination located predominantly in the South. From 1996 to 2005 the IPHC closed 777 churches out of an average base of 1,839 churches. Their annual closure rate was 4.2 percent—every year four out of every 100 IPHC churches close, seven times the rate of the United Methodists. During that same period, however, the IPHC started 1,088 new churches, which is one of the highest church-planting rates of any denomination. The IPHC closure rate is high because slightly more than half of their new church plants close within ten years—75 percent of their closures are failed new churches. Because the IPHC starts so many new churches, the number of surviving new congregations is more than enough to replace the number of closed churches, causing the denomination to grow.

Because this chapter has focused on the death of churches, one might expect that closures are quite common. Actually, they are not! Most churches are amazingly resilient. Very few older churches close over the course of a decade. Ask any denominational official who has encouraged a church to close, and you will hear a report of how feisty churches can be. At the United Methodist closure rate, only 18,038 of America's 300,000-plus Christian churches would close each decade. At the IPHC closure rate, 127,924 Christian churches would close each decade. Fortunately, the closure rate for all churches in the United States in the 1990s was much closer to the UMC closure rate—it was only 1.1 percent per year. That means that over the course of that decade, 32,000 churches closed their doors.

The frequency of restaurants closings can provide a comparison with church closures. Have you had the experience of going to dine at a favorite restaurant and discovered that it was gone? Restaurant ownership seems to be a high-risk enterprise. Two separate studies conducted by Ohio State University and by Cornell and the University of Michigan show that the closure rate for restaurants is 57 percent during the first three years of operation and 70 percent after 10 years.[5]

In this decade, both the number of closures and the number of new churches have increased. Unfortunately, the increased net gain in churches has slowed down as the closures have increased more than the new churches. Figure 7.1 shows the number of churches that closed in the United States each year in the 1990s and in the decade of the 2000s, followed by the number of new churches started each year for both categories.[6] The third column shows the yearly net gain in churches across the United States, which is 303 per year. The final column shows that there needs to be a yearly net gain of 3,205 churches to keep up with American population growth.[7] This number is ten times higher than the actual net gain. For the American church to keep up with population growth, 2,900 additional new churches need to be started each year.

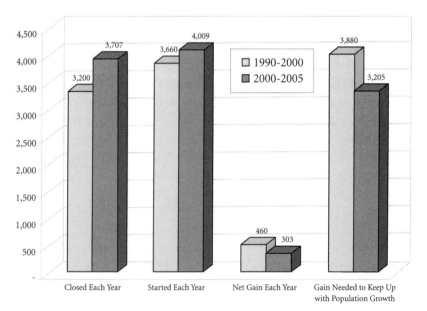

Fig. 7.1. Churches closed and churches started per year.

Why Do Churches Close?

In most cases, a process of decline leads to closure. Churches lose members, income, energy, vision, and the ability to minister in a changing world. Unless they are able to reverse those dynamics, death will inevitably occur.

Stated differently, individual churches of the "American church" species die through old age, environmental changes, fierce competition, predators, or low birth weight.

Ely Cathedral is a magnificent Norman church in Cambridgeshire, England, whose original monastery was founded in 673. Our family visited in August of 1994, when our children were still young. I remember how our then eight-year-old daughter, Andrea, collected a number of cushions she found, stacked five of them onto a chair, and sat atop them like the princess in *The Princess and the Pea*. We did not understand at first why people stared at her with such a surprised expression, until we realized the cushions were actually kneeling pads meant for prayer. The nave of the cathedral is 80 feet wide by 250 feet long, and could potentially seat close to 2,000 worshipers. We were there on a Sunday morning for the primary worship service, with only 50 other worshipers in attendance. Two-thirds seemed to be visitors, while only 20 seemed to be attendees from the community.

Ely Cathedral functions primarily as a museum that attracts a quarter million visitors each year. The admission fee to view the cathedral helps to cover its operating costs of more than 1 million British pounds. The glory of this unique church architecture makes this tourist attraction economically feasible. In reality, the cathedral has become a museum and has essentially ceased to function as a living church. Could our churches someday become museums rather than vital churches?

Researching why churches close can help us understand how to prevent closures. How are churches that close different from those that survive? To find out, TACRP researched the Evangelical Lutheran Church in America (ELCA) churches that closed from 1993 to 2005. In summary, the research revealed the following:

- Churches that closed declined eight times faster than did those that remained open.
- Closed churches were less likely to be in rural, small town or large town communities. Instead, they were much more likely to be urban.

- Closed churches were in communities that had lower median incomes, educational attainment, and age but a higher percentage of households with children and a higher poverty rate than those that stayed open.
- ELCA churches were three times more likely to close when they were in communities where less than 75 percent of the population was white.

Two observations from the study are noteworthy. First, rapid demographic changes within urban centers can make survival much more challenging than in other locations. Second, churches close after a period of rapid decline, which ends all hope for its future. While closure can be related to poor pastoral leadership, the church has often had a limited ministry impact for years. Eventually the financial pressures of remaining open become overwhelming.

By far, the highest closure rates come from new churches. Depending on how a denomination starts its new churches, the closure rates can vary from between 10 and 50 percent of new churches started. Just as low birth weight is a risk factor in the birth of a human, beginning with too few people and resources is a risk factor in the birth of a church. Many of these churches are never able to overcome their anemic beginning. Over time, the unusual pressures of small new churches wear down the energy of the committed core, and with one final gasp, they expire.

Figure 7.2 shows the yearly closure rates of 12 denominations from 1990 to 2000.

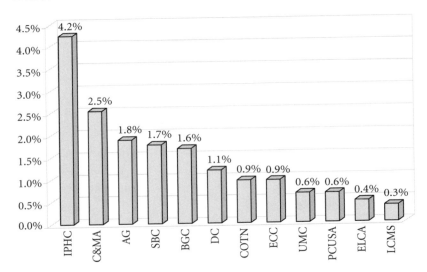

Fig. 7.2. Yearly closure percentages of 12 denominations.

Evangelical denominations, predominantly displayed on the left of the chart, have the highest closure rates. The lowest closure rates are in mainline denominations, which are primarily on the right of the chart. The perception that many mainline churches are closing is inaccurate. The two case studies and the graph can help explain two very counterintuitive facts about closures. *First, mainline churches have the lowest closure rates, and evangelical churches have the highest closure rates, the exact opposite of what most observers would assume.*

There are many reasons for this surprising result. For example, the United Methodists create "circuits" among two, three, or four small churches, with one pastor assigned to the circuit. This allows very small churches to keep their doors open. In addition, many mainline churches are in their fourth or fifth generation of life and have had hundreds of years to practice and hone their survival skills. Mainline churches are also more stable than evangelical churches. Evangelical churches fluctuate more in yearly attendance, with individual congregations seeing higher peaks and lower valleys in their attendance graph than do mainline churches. Finally, because evangelical churches plant nine times as many new churches as mainline denominations, new churches that only survive for a short time cause a much higher closure rate in evangelicalism.

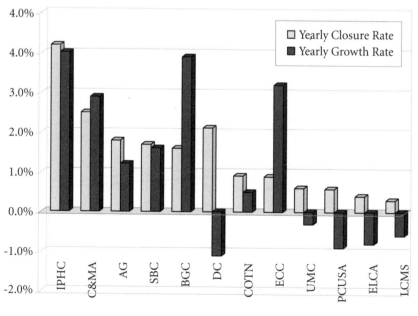

Fig. 7.3. Yearly closure rate and yearly
attendance growth.

The two case studies also highlight the second counterintuitive fact about closures. *There is an inverse relationship between the closure rate and the growth of a denomination. The lower the closure rate, the more likely the denomination is declining. The higher the closure rate, the more likely the denomination is growing.* Figure 7.3 shows that the denominations with high closure rates are growing rapidly and those with low closure rates are declining. The mainline instinct never to let a church die actually discourages energy from being directed toward the development of new churches. Growing denominations create an atmosphere that encourages and provides for health and growth in all their churches while allowing unhealthy or marginal churches to die with dignity. Growing denominations also reinvest the assets of closed churches into new church-planting projects, usually producing multiple new churches to replace each closed church.

The surprising conclusion from these two facts is that closed churches are not a significant factor in the survival of the American church species. Closures occur at a rather consistent rate year after year, and the rate likely will not change much — in the same way that the mortality rate of Americans is very stable. The variable that is critical in the survival of any species is the birthrate of new offspring. For the church species to survive, three types of births are necessary. Is your church (or denomination) attracting and connecting with young adults and families so that there is a significant natural birthrate? Is your church (or denomination) seeing substantial numbers of people become new followers of Jesus? Is your church (or denomination) planting sizeable numbers of strong new churches? New churches naturally produce the first two types of birth. New churches have a much younger age profile than do older churches, and new churches have two to four times the conversion rate of new Christians than do older churches. New babies, new Christians, and new churches are required to keep the church species healthy and strong.

Understanding the Healthy Denominational "Species"

Many years ago, Martin Marty, professor emeritus of history at the Divinity School of the University of Chicago, wrote a fictional account of the demise of the Presbyterian Church (U.S.A.) in *Christian Century* magazine. In it, he predicted the denomination's future demise. Lewis Wilkins of the Plains Institute recalled that story in a 2006 Presbyterian Church (U.S.A.) research page commentary:

> When the General Assembly published its statistics for that year, Marty turned them over for analysis to his statistically talented son. The younger

Marty projected demographic and fiscal trend lines, and Marty Sr. interpreted the patterns in a fictional obituary of "The Last Presbyterian." As I recall, the last spiritual heiress of Calvin, Knox and Witherspoon described by Marty died in Charlotte, North Carolina, in 2038. Ever since Marty's tongue-in-cheek interpretation of Presbyterian statistics, the trends he played with have held.[8]

Unfortunately, in Marty's fictional account, she was a rich woman who willed billions of dollars in the last year of her life to perpetuate the future of her beloved but now peopleless denomination.

As with every species, the number of babies born that survive and prosper, the health of the adult stock of the species, and the number of church closures determine the future of any denomination. In Marty's fictional piece, 2038 became the date that the Presbyterian Church (U.S.A.) would become an extinct species.

How does a denomination evaluate the health of its population, its reproductive potential, and the possibility of extinction? Just as the American Heart Association creates benchmarks for healthy cholesterol levels and blood pressure, the American Church Research Project has developed benchmarks for the "healthy denominational" species. In this profile, 16 percent of the denomination's attendance come from churches under 11 years of age, 36 percent of its attendance are from churches 11 to 40 years old, and 48 percent are from churches over 40 years old.[9] The critical factor for the health of any denomination is the successful birthing of new churches. Without new birth, the species has no other option but to decline and eventually become extinct.

Figure 7.4 shows the attendance percentages for the three segments of the "healthy denominational" species compared to a representative evangelical denomination and mainline denomination.[10]

	Healthy Species	SBC Species	ELCA Species
New Churches	16%	8%	2%
11–40 Years Old	36%	23%	17%
Over 40 Years Old	48%	69%	81%

Fig. 7.4. A denomination's percentage for each segment.

The Southern Baptists plant many new churches, but most are quite small. They should maintain their high planting rate while increasing the quality and size of their new churches. The Evangelical Lutheran Church in

America plants very few churches and will need to change some foundational values and behaviors to begin recovery from 40 years of inattention to church planting. A denomination lays the foundation for its future by (1) each year planting quality new churches equal to at least 2 percent of the number of congregations in the denomination, (2) creating synergistic systems of health and growth between both new and established churches, and (3) reinvesting the assets of closed churches into the planting of multiple new churches.

No Longer an Endangered Species

Our friend Ruth knocked on our door a few days ago and exclaimed, "Do you see what is across the street?" Shelly and I dashed outside and scanned the trees in the nature preserve across the road. There, not more than 100 yards away, was a bald eagle sitting on the top branch of a tree. I have seen eagles in Alaska and Canada, but never have I seen one in my neighborhood. The eagle was huge, with broad shoulders and regal bearing. It peered down at us and seemed to say, "I am the most magnificent bird in all of America."

Before the first European settlers arrived, bald eagles may have numbered half a million in the United States. Essentially, eagles and humans competed for the same food, and humans, with weapons at their disposal, had the advantage. As the human population expanded westward, they destroyed the natural habitat of the eagles, leaving them few places to nest and hunt. This caused the population of bald eagles to decline sharply. In 1940 the United States Congress passed the Bald Eagle Act, reducing harassment by humans. Eagle populations began to recover. However, just a few years later, DDT and other pesticides began to be widely used. Those pesticides made their way up the food chain, eventually affecting eagles. Not long afterward, the eagles began laying eggs with very thin shells. Many of those eggs failed to hatch, and the numbers of eagles plummeted.

On July 4, 1976, the U.S. Fish and Wildlife Service officially listed the bald eagle as a national endangered species. Because of the banning of DDT and the restoration of habitat, by the year 2005 the birthrates were increasing and the eagle population was recovering. Experts estimated that there were more than 8,000 nesting pairs in the contiguous United States and 17,500 pairs in Alaska. On June 28, 2007, the American bald eagle was officially removed from the endangered species list. Bald eagles are thriving again in North America.

And the "Lord God" bird? On February 11, 2004, Gene Sparling of Hot Springs, Arkansas, was kayaking in the Cache River National Wildlife Refuge of Arkansas when he caught sight of an unusual woodpecker with an ivory bill. Since then researchers from Cornell University and the Nature Conservancy have been searching for more evidence that the ivory-billed woodpecker still exists. During their search, a team of researchers shot video of what appears to be the "Lord God" bird.[11]

According to a news story by the Big Woods Partnership,[12] which is funding the search, researchers believe they found the bird once thought extinct. "The bird captured on video is clearly an ivory-billed woodpecker," said John Fitzpatrick, director of the Cornell Lab of Ornithology and leader of the project's research team. "Amazingly, America may have another chance to protect the future of the ivory-billed woodpecker and the awesome forests where it lives."[13]

The Shakers

One summer evening while on vacation in New England, our family happened upon a historic tourist attraction, a Shaker village in Canterbury, New Hampshire. The village had closed for the day, but we walked its grounds and were able to view some of the buildings that remained open. We visited the carpenter's shop where the Shakers' simple furniture was fashioned. We peeked into the windows of the creamery and the schoolhouse. We admired the large and well-kept flower and vegetable gardens.

This religious group, also known as "shaking Quakers," was founded in England in 1772 by Ann Lee. She and eight followers emigrated to America two years later, forming a communal, utopian religious group known for its unusual, unorthodox beliefs and worship practices. Shaker culture has left behind the lasting legacy of a strong work ethic, simple timeless crafts, and lovely spirituals and ballads. At their height, there were over 6,000 Shakers living in 19 communities.

Unfortunately, the group adopted two strategies that guaranteed their eventual demise. The first was their practice of a celibate lifestyle. Conversion and the adoption of children became the Shakers' only means of growth. They officially adopted their second lethal strategy in 1965, deciding to allow no new members into their group. As a result, there are only three Shakers left in the United States—two brothers and a sister—living their remaining years in the Sabbathday Shaker Community in Maine. With their death, the more than 200-year-old Shaker movement will become extinct.

Reflection

What about your church or denomination? Will it become extinct or will it flourish? Will declining churches and denominations learn new habits of health and growth? These are vital questions to ponder. Churches and denominations can make dramatic and unexpected comebacks, as did the bald eagle and the ivory-billed woodpecker. Two factors will determine the future of the American church species. The first is the health and growth of its established churches: whether they thrive and reproduce or diminish and close. The second is the fertility rate of the American church: whether new offspring survive and flourish, replacing closed churches as well as providing new churches for the new Americans. Within each factor is a complex combination of cause and effect, which we will investigate in the next two chapters.

Chapter 8 will examine why so many established churches are struggling and will look particularly at the differences between declining churches and growing churches. Ministry for established churches has become more challenging since 2001, and many churches are desperate to understand how they can thrive again. The solution is in learning to age successfully and focusing on the three keys to growth: spirituality, chemistry, and strategy.

Questions for Reflection and Discussion

1. Are you surprised at the low number of churches that close? Why or why not?
2. Why do you think the lowest closure rates are in declining denominations?
3. Of the five factors that negatively influence a species (low birth weight, environmental changes, competition, disease, and predators), which is the most challenging for your church?
4. Many churches never remember the small group of visionary people that started their church many years in the past. In your church, what was the vision of those people? Is it still being lived out today? Telling the stories of your pioneers is an important part of a church's revitalization.

Please go to www.theamericanchurch.org/TACIC/Chapter7.htm for updates and additional information and resources for this chapter.

Chapter 8

WHY ESTABLISHED CHURCHES THRIVE OR DECLINE

Two apple trees grow in the side yard of our home. One tree appears to be barely alive, yielding few leaves and bearing little fruit. The other has incredible foliage every year yet is mostly barren one year then produces hundreds of apples the next. The mystery of the oscillating harvest was solved by some horticultural research. Apple trees set more fruit than they are capable of carrying to maturity. The good arborist will remove the excess fruit from the trees so that the remaining fruit can develop. When the excess fruit is not removed, the tree adapts and forms fewer flowers the next year. This causes the cycle that produces a crop of apples every other year.

The Scriptures use the tree as a metaphor for a fruitful, productive life. At times the Bible portrays barren trees that produce neither leaves nor fruit. Other references portray leafy trees yet without fruit. The third and most honored trees are both leafy and fruitful, such as the tree portrayed in Psalm 1:3: "They are like a tree planted by streams of water, which yields its fruit in season and whose leaf does not wither—whatever they do prospers." These three trees illustrate three types of churches. The barren tree is a picture of the church that is neither healthy nor growing. The leafy tree is a healthy church that mysteriously does not bear fruit. The leafy and fruitful tree is a church that is both healthy and growing.[1]

Health and Growth

Growth is a controversial word in the American church. The phenomenal success of megachurches has created a backlash in many small congregations. Weekly attendance counts can be seen as badges of honor—those with smaller counts are seen as somehow inferior. This leads to questions such as, "Is it necessary for a church to grow?" "Isn't a fixation on growth just an example of the American success syndrome?" "Isn't health enough?"

Some churches exist in environments where growth is very difficult. Yet in every county in America, Christian churches have the potential for growth, because in almost every county the majority of people do not have a consistent connection with a Christian church. The gospel is not to be only inwardly focused, but outwardly directed as well. The early church understood that the message of Jesus was to spread to every country, people group, family, and individual in the world. God's heart for each person in the world is that they joyfully confess Jesus as Savior and Lord.

Both health and growth should be the normal and natural result of the gospel working in peoples' lives. Churches should bear fruit, both by inward change in the lives of believers and in outward change through conversion, community transformation, and global impact.

What is the level of health and growth in established churches?[2] The first word, *health*, is difficult to study empirically. The second word, *growth*, is easier to quantify. This chapter will look at both health and growth, presenting three preventative actions that facilitate health and four proactive activities that produce growth.

Two questions help us assess the true condition of established churches. First, "Why do the majority of established churches decline in attendance?" This question points to the habits a church needs to practice to counter the debilitating effects of age, producing "healthy aging." Second, "What causes a healthy, established church to produce fruit?" The answer will create understanding of how this kind of church grows through increased fruitfulness.

How are established churches faring in recent years? To find out, a study of attendance data from 1999 to 2005 evaluated 85,000 established Protestant churches founded before 1965. Figure 8.1 shows the yearly rate of attendance growth from 1999 to 2006.

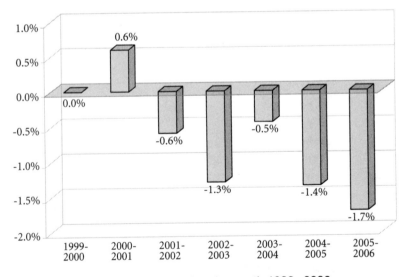

Fig. 8.1. Established church growth 1999–2006.

In 2000, established churches stayed the same as in the previous year. In 2001, established churches saw slight growth based on an anomaly—church attendance spiked by 25 percent for the five Sundays after 9/11, artificially raising the yearly average. Since 2001, established churches have declined in attendance every year, with the rate of that decline escalating. Why are established churches declining, and why is that decline increasing?

Do External Demographics Cause Established Churches to Decline?

One way to answer that question is to find out whether growth or decline in established churches occurs primarily because of external demographic changes in the community or because of internal dynamics within the church. To answer this question, TACRP evaluated the 10 external factors listed in figure 8.2.

1. The median income of the zip code of the church.
2. The median age of the zip code of the church.
3. The average household size of the zip code of the church.
4. The average educational attainment of the zip code of the church.
5. The location of the church—rural, small town, large town, suburban, or urban.
6. The average percentage of households with children under 18 in the zip code of the church.
7. The average percentage of poor households in the zip code of the church.
8. The average percentage of residents who were "white alone" in the zip code of the church.
9. The year the church was founded.
10. The population growth from 1990 to 2000 of the zip code of the church.

Fig. 8.2. Ten external demographic factors that might influence growth and decline.

More than 70,000 Protestant churches were sorted by their attendance growth or decline rate from 1999 to 2005. The "Decline" category is comprised of churches that declined by more than 10 percent in attendance over the six-year period and includes 52 percent of the sample. "Stable" churches grew or declined by less than 10 percent and comprised 17 percent of the churches. The remaining 31 percent of churches were in the "Growth" category, growing by more than 10 percent over the time period.

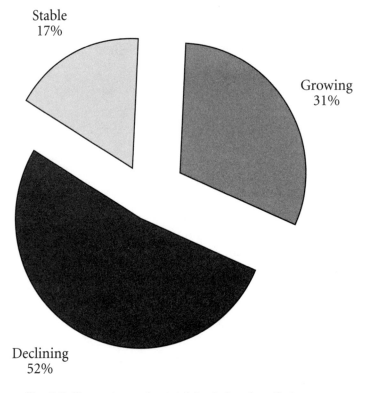

Fig. 8.3. Percentage of established churches that were growing, stable, or declining.

Surprisingly, there was no statistical difference between the declining and the growing churches in nine of the external demographic factors evaluated. The median age of the community, the average household size, the percentage of households with children under 18, the poverty rate, and the level of racial diversity did not correlate with either growth or decline. The research did show one slight variance worth noting. Growing churches were more likely to be rural and less likely to be small town, suburban, or urban. While the common assumption is that rural churches are under the most stress, the research supports the opposite.

Only one external factor was significant in the growth or decline of the church—the change in the population of its zip code. Fast-growing churches—those that increased by more than 20 percent in attendance—were more likely located in zip codes where the population growth was *higher* than the national average. If a church declined or was stable, it was more likely located in a low-growth zip code where population growth was *lower* than the national average. In figure 8.4 the left seven categories were predominately in slower growth communities, and the right five were in faster growth neighborhoods.

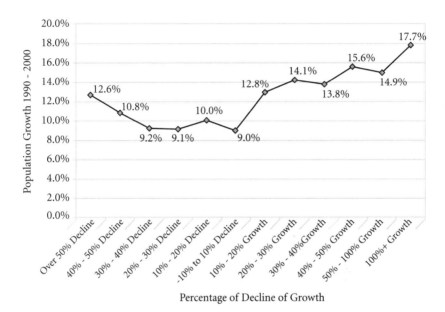

Fig. 8.4. Population growth in zip codes of declining, stable, and growing churches.

What does this research mean for established churches? *Population growth in your community is a positive factor* in the growth of established churches. One example is the recent growth in downtown Orlando, Florida. At least 12,000 new people moved into the area since 2001, according to the *Orlando Sentinel*. Some of those newcomers have begun to filter into older churches, like Broadway Methodist Church, where the congregation grew from 50 to 75 people in about a year. Half of the congregation are newcomers, Pastor Clare Watson Chance told the *Sentinel*, adding that newcomers are "absolutely a godsend."[3] A nearby Roman Catholic church planned to increase its sanctuary by 150 seats to allow for growth. Other churches were sending brochures and postcards to new residents or starting Bible studies in new condominium complexes. The churches have responded proactively to the new influx in their community, which may lead to more growth.

The fact that population growth can enhance church attendance growth is not surprising. The surprising finding of this study is that none of the nine remaining external demographic factors correlated with the growth or the decline of established congregations. *This suggests that most of the reasons for growth or decline are internal factors.*

How Can a Church Counter the Debilitating Effects of Age?

As described in chapter 5, a primary reason for decline in established churches relates to aging. This quote from that chapter describes the process of successful aging that correlates closely with successful aging strategies for established churches: "Successful (healthy) aging refers to a process by which aging is not accompanied by debilitating disease and disability. People who age successfully may maintain an active healthy life until death."[4]

What are the diseases and disabilities that produce the negative effects of aging in established churches, and how can they be avoided? Three primary sources negatively affect the internal health of a church.

1. Inability to Adapt to Cultural Change

Environmental change in the natural world is parallel to cultural change in human societies. Just as dodo birds found it difficult to adjust to changes in the environment, churches will struggle if they cannot adjust to changes in the culture. This does not mean that a church should change the content of the gospel. Although the gospel message should not change, a church needs to find new methods and styles of communication—in art, music, dialogue, and preaching—that truly engage people in the community. In the early 1990s a former Pentecostal evangelist named Pat McKinstry became pastor of Upton United Methodist Church in West Dayton, Ohio, a church that had been in decline for years. As she told the *Toledo Blade* newspaper, the denomination sent in Reverend McKinstry "to prepare the West Toledo church for its last rites."[5]

McKinstry had different plans. She wanted to find a way to revitalize the church. "They just wanted me to follow their programs," she told the *Blade*. "But why should I follow a program that was not giving life?" Instead, as the *Blade* recounted, she "decided to hold two Sunday services, one for the longtime members biding their time until the church closed, and a second with lively music and a solid Gospel message."

Today that formerly dying congregation draws 500 people on Sunday mornings, and they recently built a new, $2 million sanctuary on eight acres of land. Despite the changes in style, the church's core theology remains the same. The church has what McKinstry calls "a lively worship service that involves everybody"—so lively that neighbors once called the police to complain about the volume.

Many churches mistake culturally bound ministry styles for core theology. For many churches, their music, stories, programs, and means of community outreach no longer resonate with those outside of their church. A generation can become "culture-bound" and not notice they are increasingly out of touch with the changes. It is always easy for a generation to see the flaws in the previous generation, yet miss their own shortcomings. For example, boomer Christians believe they clearly saw the flaws of the builder generation's church as well as the shortcomings of the emerging generation, but they have difficulty seeing the limitations of their own expression of Christianity.[6]

2. Inability to Fight Off Disease

Churches often develop Immune Deficiency Syndrome—they do not fight back against the diseases that afflict them. Many declining churches suffer from "family system dysfunction." The two primary signs of a dysfunctional family system in a church are destructive communication patterns and the improper use of power.

Destructive communication patterns occur when church members find it impossible to communicate clearly and directly with each other in a context of genuine love. Paul described healthy communication succinctly in Ephesians 4:15 as "speaking the truth in love." Dysfunctional churches often have buried stories that never surface and members who keep longstanding grudges against other members.

Misuse of power occurs when powerful leaders or families dominate a church, disenfranchising most of the other members. Their intentions may be good, but the results rarely are. Most power struggles are over who should lead and who should leave. Jesus stressed that his followers should not lead by coercion but instead "serve one another in love" (Gal. 5:13).

3. Inability to Delay Decay and Diminishment

Reduced energy and progressive deterioration are two natural results of aging. In humans, five habits ward off decline and debilitation as a person advances in age. These healthy habits are proper diet, exercise, relational connections, mental stimulation, and spiritual vitality. When practiced daily, these habits promote health while slowing decline and debilitation.

These five factors have a direct analogy to the habits of healthy churches. In the same way that they revitalize a person, they are also necessary for a church. Proper diet is the spiritual food that a church ingests, typically through preaching, teaching, and Bible study. Exercise means active ministry involvement. Healthy relational connections form deep and authentic interpersonal interactions with others both inside and outside the church. Mental stimulation occurs when the church grows in the knowledge of Jesus, the gospel, our world, and our culture. Spiritual vitality occurs when we set apart Christ as Lord in one's heart (1 Peter 3:15).

Chapter 5 revealed a remarkable fact: churches from 190 to 200 years old are actually growing. While humans cannot reach the age of 190, established churches can thrive no matter how old they are. A church can be renewed regularly through cultural relevance, nourishing relationships, and life-giving behaviors. Those qualities attract vigorous young members who revitalize and remake the body. This can produce health, but it does not necessarily produce growth. How then does a healthy church grow?

Becoming a Thriving Church

Figure 8.5 visualizes a simple model that can help a healthy church grow. The visual of a three-legged stool represents the four critical foci of a thriving church. Three observations about the design of a stool are necessary to note. First, all three legs are critical—one or two will not do. Second, without the strength and stability of the seat, the three legs by themselves will collapse. Third, it is most helpful if the legs are of similar length. Each leg and the seat correspond to a dynamic quality necessary for growth to occur:

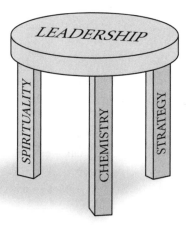

Fig. 8.5. Components of a thriving church.

The first leg of the stool represents *spirituality*, which is a commitment to deep spiritual transformation that brings about the live-changing work of God in people. The second leg represents *chemistry*, which creates an inviting relational atmosphere within the church. The third leg of the stool is *strategy*, a process of sequential actions that produce fruitful ministry in line with God-directed goals. Finally, the seat represents *leadership*, which rests on the three supporting legs and ensures that spirituality, chemistry, and strategy are internalized within the church and lived out in the community by the church's leaders and members.

Spirituality

Fruitful growth begins with spirituality, which is a commitment to deep spiritual transformation that brings about God's work in people's hearts. Four elements comprise the core of Christian spirituality.

The first element is clarity on the question "*what is the gospel?*" Because this question is vital to the health and growth of your church, chapters 12 to 14 are devoted to this foundational topic. The American church will not thrive in its current culture until it intentionally refocuses on the message and mission of Jesus.

The second element is the *necessity of transformation.* One result of the message and mission of Jesus is to deconstruct the damaging worldview formed within each person and reconstruct a new, life-giving worldview. The most effective way to do this is to allow the powerful words and actions of Jesus to reshape our lives. Anything less than this produces "cultural Christianity," which gives lip service to change but does not produce deep transformation.

Third is *spiritual formation* (or *discipleship*), what Jesus called "turning hearts of stone into hearts of flesh." Spiritual formation builds on transformation to create the type of heart that Jesus seeks to produce. Dr. John Perkins, a pioneer in the Christian Community Development Association and a powerful African American voice in the United States for racial reconciliation for more than 30 years, recently told me, "We have overevangelized the world too lightly." When I asked the 76-year-old Dr. Perkins what the phrase meant, he said that evangelism actually becomes counterproductive to God's purpose for the church when it is not partnered with discipleship. Evangelism and discipleship should be an inseparable pair!

The fourth component is *reliance on the Holy Spirit.* First Corinthians 3:6 describes the necessity of divine intervention: "I planted the seed, Apollos watered it, but God has been making it grow." Fruitful ministry is a remarkable combination of God-directed human effort converging with the work of the Holy Spirit to manifest the touch of God himself. In their own power, Christians can never produce spiritual transformation in themselves or in other people. Rather, transformation is solely the work of the Holy Spirit.

Chemistry

Chemistry focuses on the church's personality as it lives out the fruits of the Spirit relationally. Two crucial components create good chemistry in a church.

A healthy family system. When a pastor, the staff, lay leaders, and the members are set free to be whom God created them to be, the church can live an authentic, joy-filled life together. As mentioned earlier, healthy family systems prosper in atmospheres of truth and love, without the exercise of abusive power.

An attractive group personality. When people visit your church, they usually decide within the first 10 minutes whether to return. Visitors sense the group's personality and intuitively know whether they wish to connect with you. While some believe a church should be filled with dour Christians, true followers of Jesus should be marked by joy. The book of Psalms describes a group of joyful, attractive believers: "Our mouths were filled with laughter, our tongues with songs of joy.... Then it was said among the nations, 'The Lord has done great things for them'" (Psalm 126:2).

Strategy

Strategy creates a process of sequential actions that produce fruitful ministry in harmony with God-directed goals. Five components make up a church's strategy.

Vision. Vision is the conceptualization of God's future for each church. What should this church look like? What is the specific niche that God wants our church to fill? How can our church expand the kingdom of God? Clarity of vision is critical for growth.

Division of ministry. Each church needs to determine how to delegate ministry responsibilities. This is established by the church's structure, which is often managed by the pastoral staff and/or lay leaders, and is spelled out in the church's constitution. For many churches the five essential divisions are

1. The weekend experience (preaching, worship, fellowship)
2. Spiritual formation (discipleship)
3. Outreach (evangelism, missions, and compassion/justice)
4. Ministry to children and youth
5. Facilities and finance

Ministry development. In each division there is a four-step process to build and strengthen ministries. The prerequisite to this process is to clarify reality by telling the truth about the present ministry fruitfulness of that division. Then develop the pathways of ministry fruitfulness by implementing the following sequence:

1. Set God-directed, attainable goals.
2. Develop a strategy to reach the goals—plan relational activities, processes, and events.

3. Implement the strategy—work out the logistics of leaders, workers, and funding.
4. Regularly evaluate the progress. Tweak, refocus, reinvent, improve, and advance.

Connection with new people. While health is the prerequisite to growth, growth is the more difficult of the two to produce. *The lack of growth in a church usually stems from the inability to make personal connections with new people.* This is why the healthiest growing churches are committed to conversion growth. Conversion growth happens when a person experiences the love of God in Christ combined with the love of Christians and responds with repentance and faith to wholeheartedly follow Jesus. Walter Hooper described the role that J. R. R. Tolkien played in C. S. Lewis's conversion this way: "Not only was Tolkien a Christian, but one of the human carriers of the Faith to him."[7] If the pastor and people are not committed to being "human carriers of the Faith," the chances of healthy growth are slim.

Patience. The goal is to build strong ministries, which produce fruit that will last, fruit that is ever increasing. Take the time to build a strong foundation, because that underpinning will determine the future ministry scope of your church. Prayer and leadership development are typically the two major omissions when creating a foundation for long-term ministry growth.

Leadership for Growth

"Leadership for growth" is the seat that provides stability and strength for the three legs. The purpose of leadership for growth is to focus the energy of the whole church on spirituality, chemistry, and strategy.

Churches do not grow without godly and gifted pastoral and lay leaders. Pastors are severely limited in their leadership effectiveness unless they know how to lead authentically in all three categories. I have observed that most pastors of rapidly growing churches have gifts in all three. If a pastor is naturally gifted at one, average at a second, and challenged at the third, that church has little chance for growth. For a church to grow, at a minimum the pastor needs to be strong in two of the areas and be motivated to develop competence in the third. With good coaching and a teachable attitude, most pastors can dramatically improve in all three areas. While lay leaders can augment the gifts of the senior pastor, seldom can they compensate for a lack of leadership in more than one category. Authentic spiritual pastoral leadership is one of the great challenges in the church today.

Spirituality, chemistry, and strategy are listed in the order of development. If a pastor leads with strategy first, the congregation will miss the spiritual dynamic. Feeling that human effort rather than divine initiative is driving the church forward, the members will often react negatively. When the first priority is chemistry, with little attention given to spirituality and strategy, the members may like each other, but little will be accomplished for God's kingdom. When spirituality and chemistry are in place, then add strategy, and the three will produce fruitful growth.

Pastoral and lay leaders lead with integrity only when they authentically live out spirituality and relational chemistry in their own lives. The pastoral and lay leadership of a church needs to model these qualities personally and communally, so the team is spiritually unified and relationally connected to each other before they lead with strategy.

Reflection

In the fall of 2006, 24 new members joined St. Mark Evangelical Lutheran Church in Yorktown, Virginia. For several years the church was part of a nationwide study of "thriving mainline churches," led by historian Diana Butler Bass. Many of these churches had struggled for years before making remarkable turnarounds.

At St. Mark's this meant growing from 500 members with 200 in weekly attendance in 1997 to a membership of more than 1,200 with a weekly attendance of 500 in 2006. The church's service is traditional, with chanting and hymn singing accompanied by the church's pipe organ. On Wednesday nights, the church offers dinner to families attending weekday programs.

During the study, the church's pastor, Gary Erdos, told Butler Bass that revitalizing the church "was not rocket science." He said, "You preach the gospel, offer hospitality, and pay attention to worship and people's spiritual lives."[8] Erdos says that getting the small things right has helped the church grow. "We pay attention to the small things that show respect," he told *USA Today.* "Our worship doesn't sound or look like a third-rate high school play. There are no typos in the newsletter or halfhearted sermons."[9]

As St. Mark's illustrates, I believe there is great hope for established churches. However, there is no "silver bullet" that provides an easy solution. God's solution is healthy churches led by healthy leaders. These churches then experience internal and external growth by living out their vital relationship with Christ through spirituality, loving each other through attention to chemistry, and serving each other and the world through strategic life-giving ministries.

Ever since Alexis de Tocqueville wrote *Democracy in America*, chronicling his exploration of the United States and its institutions in the early 1800s, commentators have marveled at how religious Americans are. They have wondered where all of the churches dotting the landscape of America came from. With so many established churches, should we even consider starting new ones? Chapter 9 will complete the evaluation section by investigating whether there is still a role for new churches.

Questions for Reflection and Discussion

1. Is your church declining, stable, or growing in size? What are the internal factors that are affecting your church?
2. Proper diet, exercise, relational connections, mental stimulation, and spiritual vigor are the five key activities for successful aging. How will your church live out each one?
3. If you are the pastor, are you strongest in spirituality, chemistry, or strategy? Which is the weakest? What specific action plans can you make to improve in each of the three areas?
4. Who could your church use to conduct a yearly physical of the health and growth of your church?

Please go to www.theamericanchurch.org/TACIC/Chapter8.htm
for updates and additional information and resources for this chapter.

Chapter 9

IN THE BIRTHING ROOM
OF THE AMERICAN CHURCH

My ministry passion is planting new churches. Last month I took part in an assessment center for potential church planters held at First Covenant Church of Seattle in their glorious in-the-round hundred-year-old sanctuary.[1] The assessment center chose this historic church as host because of its long history of vision and expansion. Located downtown on Pike Street, just east of Seattle's famous Pike Street Market, the church was founded by Swedish immigrants in 1889. The Reverend E. August Skogsbergh became pastor in 1909 and began holding revival meetings.

> The intent was to proclaim the gospel of Jesus Christ to Swedish immigrants in fast-growing Seattle. Large numbers of young Swedes attended these revivals and the little congregation grew very large, very fast. In response, it changed itself and built a new, larger sanctuary. By 1911, over 2,000 immigrants regularly attended services at the new Swedish Tabernacle.[2]

This church became a megachurch before anyone knew what a megachurch was! By the 1930s, Otelia Hendrickson became their "city missionary," and First Covenant was sending missionaries to China and Alaska. In the 1950s First Covenant started six new churches around the edge of metro Seattle, which are still thriving today. Those six churches have themselves planted yet another generation of churches. Today First Covenant is again seeking to reinvent itself in the midst of a complex, regentrified city-center neighborhood.

> Located in the heart of scenic Seattle's downtown, we are an historic old First church, which after decades of birthing new churches, is being reborn

itself through the power of God's Spirit. Already a century old and nearing 100 years on this plot of land, our church is driven by the quest for spiritual renewal and call to the urban community. It is a home for many: the rich, poor, well-educated, homeless, old and young, and those searching for a vital faith and spiritual home.[3]

How was your church started? What vision, passion, and need caused a small group of people to begin the adventure of faith that became your church? What are the stories of your church's pioneers? Why did they plant your church? I have asked these questions to hundreds of established churches. Every time their answer is wrapped up in a fascinating story of the founders' love for God, concern for their neighbors, and willingness to venture outside of their safety zone. Usually they were ordinary, faith-filled people driven by an extraordinary dream from God.

While almost every established church can recite its proud history, few of the present members ever consider that their congregation was itself once a new church. The thought of church planting is usually foreign to them, even though their own place of worship exists because it was planted.

To help them further appreciate what God has done in their midst and to comprehend the critical role of church planting, I ask them another set of questions:

- How many people have become Christians through the ministry of your church?
- How many children and teenagers has your church ministered to since you began?
- How many baptisms, marriages, and funerals have been performed?
- How many broken hearts, shattered lives, and divided families have been mended through your church's ministries?

They have never considered the scope of those questions. They are not sure how to proceed. I ask the group to make a guess at how many people became Christians each year throughout their history. After hearing a number of suggestions, we settle on a yearly estimate. Then on the whiteboard, we multiply that number times the age of the church. It always produces an impressively large number. We multiply the cumulative numbers for children, teenagers, baptisms, marriages, and funerals by the age of the church and add them to the whiteboard. By this time, the light in their eyes begins to flicker on as if to say, "Our church *has had* an incredible influence for Christ over the years!" Then I go back to the first question: "How was your church started, and why?" Then they begin to make the connection. All of this ministry fruit was produced because a group of visionary people stepped out in faith and founded their church. Without their church, the loss to the kingdom of God would be enormous. One final question remains for me to ask: "Have you ever considered that your church could replicate your own incredible story by planting a new church?"

The ability to convey our faith to the next generation should play a critical role in the life of every church. The Old Testament has a particular interest in how we transmit the story of God to the next generation.

> Even when I am old and gray,
> do not forsake me, my God,
> till I declare your power to the next generation,
> your mighty acts to all who are to come. (Psalm 71:18)
>
> We will not hide them from their descendants;
> we will tell the next generation
> the praiseworthy deeds of the LORD,
> his power, and the wonders he has done. (Psalm 78:4)

While many established churches have a vital ministry to multiple generations, new churches play an equally important role in passing the faith from generation to generation. New churches are critical to the health and vitality of the American church in general and denominations in particular. Strong, healthy new churches produce enormous benefit to their denomination and to the whole American church.

To understand the influence new churches have on the religious landscape today, the answers to the following five questions will create a portrait of church planting in America.

1. How Many New Churches Are Started Every Year?

Graphing the start dates of churches throughout the history of the United States produces a fascinating picture. Figure 9.1 displays the number of churches in existence today for every 1 million citizens at the year of its founding, while also graphically revealing the traumas and trials of American history.

Notice the dramatic drops during the War of 1812, the Civil War, World War I, and the Great Depression. From 1945 until the peak in 1957, the number of new churches planted every year more than doubled. Then the rate gradually declined to the lowest planting level in American history by 1970. Since then, the rate has only marginally increased.

Fig. 9.1. Churches started per 1 million residents. Based
on start dates of 92,677 churches in the United States.

Counting the number of new churches can be surprisingly difficult.
Some new churches begin and end within a matter of months, leaving little evidence of their existence. Other new churches start as a small group
meeting in a house — and plan to stay that size indefinitely. The number of
these "house churches" has increased over the last five years.[4] This chapter
looks at new churches that stay in existence at least one year.

Each year from 2000 to 2005, an estimated 4,000 new churches were
started in America. That is an increase from the 1990s, when an average of
3,600 new churches started each year.

You can find out the percentage of new churches your denomination is
starting by dividing the number planted each year into the total number
of churches in your denomination. Figure 9.2 shows this percentage for 12
denominations. The chart reveals that denominations vary greatly in the
number of new churches they start. For example, mainline churches plant
few churches — in most cases, not even one new church for every 200 established churches. The United Methodist Church and the Episcopal churches
start one new church each year for every 500 established congregations.
The Southern Baptists, on the other hand, start one new congregation for
every 50 churches. The International Pentecostal Holiness Church (IPHC)
starts one new church for every 15 established churches. All told, nine new
evangelical churches are started for every new mainline church.

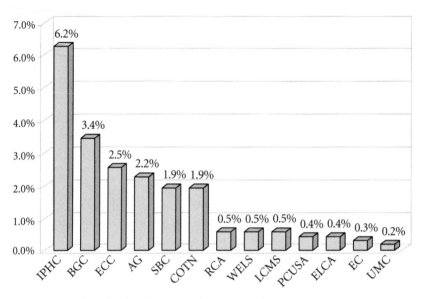

Fig. 9.2. Yearly planting rate of new churches by denomination.

Every group with less than a 1 percent planting rate — less than one new church for every 100 established churches — is declining numerically in attendance. For a denomination to keep up with population growth, it needs a planting rate of more than 2 percent each year — or 1 new church started for every 50 established churches. Many evangelical groups plant three or four new churches a year for every 100 established churches, which is why their attendance growth exceeds population growth.[5]

Unfortunately, the 3,700 churches that close per year reduce the impact of the 4,000 new churches that start, leaving a net yearly gain of 300 churches in the United States. A net gain of 3,205 churches is needed each year for the American church to keep up with population growth; this is far less than the actual yearly gain of 300 churches. This means that an additional 2,900 new churches need to be started each year in the United States to match population growth. Since the closure rate is quite consistent year after year, the only solution to this challenge is to plant more churches.

In a 2005 address at Princeton Divinity School, pastor-author Brian McLaren urged mainline church leaders and seminary professors to do just that. He began by acknowledging that the mainline churches are in crisis. In recent years fierce debate over the decline of mainline churches has occurred. In 1960 mainline churches had more than 29 million members — by 2000, that figure had dropped to 22 million. As Michael Hamilton and Jennifer McKinney pointed out in a *Christianity Today* article called "Turning the Mainline Around," this decline represented "a 21 percent drop in mainline membership—during the same period that overall church membership in the United States *increased* by 33 percent."[6]

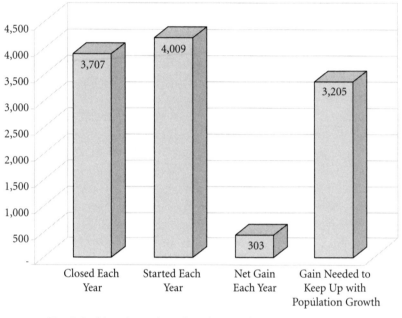

Fig. 9.3. Churches closed and started and net gain each
year from 2000 to 2005

Some factions blame mainline leadership for this decline, pointing to a "liberal shift" in church theology. Others point to declining birthrates among mainliners as the primary culprit. McLaren, however, was not concerned why the mainline churches had declined. He asked the pastors, bishops, and seminarians gathered at Princeton to do something about the decline. The first step, he said, was admitting that the mainline church was in a state of crisis. Rather than waiting for things to worsen or trying to conserve the remaining resources of the church, he said, "Let's have our emergency now." In an emergency, people act decisively rather than place blame.

Pointing to the example of Jesus, who said,[7] "Whoever wants to save their life will lose it, but whoever loses their life for me will save it," McLaren advocated pouring "disproportional, absurd, extravagant amounts of money" into new churches. "I believe that the best way to reinvigorate the existing church is by planting new churches," he said, adding that he believed new churches can be laboratories where new approaches to "doing church" can be tried, where old practices can be reinvented, and where pastors and leaders can try creative approaches without fear of anyone saying, "We never did this before."

Those new churches can discover ways to save the mainline church, McLaren argued. Those discoveries can then be passed on to established congregations. "New churches innovate," he said, "and old churches imitate."[8]

2. How Many New Churches Survive the First Ten Years?

The survival rate of new churches depends on many factors. They include whether a supportive parent church starts the church, whether a rigorous assessment of the church planter is required, whether there is a quality launch process and extensive training in church planting, and whether coaching and support systems are available to help the new church continue to grow.

The survival rate varies greatly among denominations. My colleague Gary Walter insightfully labels the two basic systems of church planting *reptilian* and *mammalian*. Reptilian systems reproduce churches in the same way reptiles reproduce offspring: they procreate as many as possible—and hope that enough survive to keep the denomination growing. In essence, the church planter is told, "Good luck, God bless, we hope you make it." The denomination offers little help. This method does perpetuate the species, but in its wake it frequently leaves the carnage of failed church plants and disillusioned pastors. In addition, the more challenging the culture is toward Christianity, the less fruitful will be this type of planting. Baptist and Pentecostal denominations are most likely to employ reptilian systems.

In mammalian church-planting systems, starting new churches echoes the way mammals give birth to and raise offspring. They produce fewer new churches but provide advantageous support systems to ensure that as many as possible survive. The goal is for all to become healthy and growing adult churches, quickly achieving self-support without creating dependence. While this means fewer church plants than reptilian systems, the new churches have a higher survival rate and grow more quickly. Mammalian systems can have potential downsides. Sometimes the new church receives too much money, creating financial dependency. In other cases, a denomination is satisfied with too few new churches, focusing on quality while forgetting to balance it with quantity. The best solution for denominations is to develop "turbocharged" mammalian church planting—planting as many as possible while maintaining high standards.

Many denominations have attempted to improve the quality of their church-planting systems over the past fifteen years, often with dramatic results. There are many parachurch organizations that specialize in helping a church or denomination plant new churches, providing the assessment, training and coaching for church planters and their launch teams. Both of these quality systems have contributed to the increased number of new churches started from 2000 to 2005. Figure 9.4 shows the survival rates of church plants for 10 denominations in the last ten years.

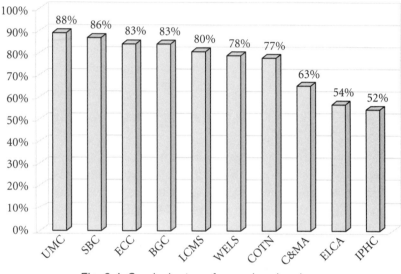

Fig. 9.4. Survival rates of new churches by denomination.

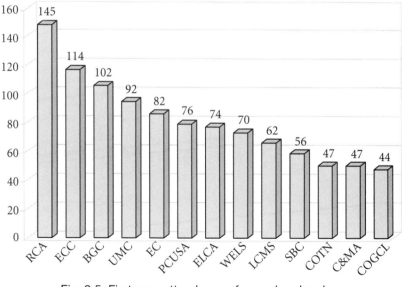

Fig. 9.5. First-year attendance of new churches by denomination.

3. What Is the Average Size of a New Church after Its First Year?

Reaching a critical mass of more than 70 in attendance has proven crucial for new churches. Once they reach their benchmark, new churches find that growth comes more easily.

When a majority of a denomination's new churches average under 70 in attendance at the end of the first year, those churches will experience a higher closure rate and a slower future growth rate. *Strong attendance in a church's initial year is often a product of support by a parent church and a solid launch process.* Figure 9.5 shows the average attendance during the first year for new churches in 13 denominations.

4. What Is the Growth Rate for New Churches in Years Two to Seven?

The fourth question investigates how quickly new churches grow from their second through seventh year. The strength and habits of the new church by the end of its first year provides the platform for its future growth. These six years usually provide the highest growth potential throughout the entire church's life. *Growth in the second to seventh year reflects the quality of the church planter and its launch team, and the strength of the training and coaching they receive.* Figure 9.6 shows the average yearly growth rate during these years for 14 denominations.

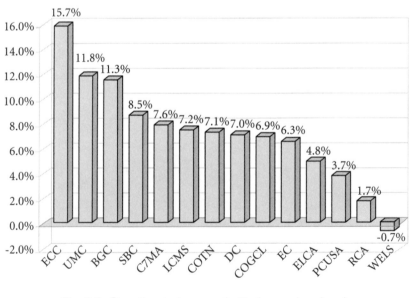

Fig. 9.6. Growth rate in years 2–7 of new churches by denomination.

5. What Are the Building Blocks of a Strong Church-Planting System?

Four building blocks are necessary to create a strong church-planting system. The first is *parenting*. This means an established church takes a major role in helping start a new congregation, known as a daughter church. They provide funds (usually one-third of the external funding comes from the parent church) and pledge a tithe of their attendees. Parenting is most effective when the parent church plants within 5 to 10 miles of its own facility. Territorialism, defined as the fear that other churches will intrude on a church's God-given geographic birthright, is the primary inhibitor to parenting. When a church plants a daughter church, both the new church and the parent church benefit. In growing perennials, the more you divide them, the quicker they will grow. "To keep plants healthy and strong, it is necessary to divide them periodically."[9] Congregations that parent new churches grow faster than those congregations that do not parent. The traits that cause a church to plant a new church are the same traits that will cause the parent church itself to grow. Research also shows that parented new churches grow twice as fast as those started as pioneer plants.[10]

The second building block is identifying *a high-quality pastor, one who knows how to gather and lead people.* An extensive screening process helps identify these pastors and allows them to process their call to church planting. Many denominations use assessment centers, which are multiday intensive events for church-planting candidates and their spouses. Trained assessors observe candidates in a series of ministry settings, simulations, small groups, and interviews. The Covenant Assessment Center looks for 20 specific traits in six major categories: spiritual foundations, leadership gifts, gathering gifts, organizing gifts, ongoing pastoral gifts, and movement connection.

The third building block is an *effective launch process and training program.* The most common launch process used in recent years is the Four Stage Launch Process pioneered at Bayside Covenant Church in Sacramento, California. It allows new churches to grow and develop in a sequential manner, gradually expanding their foundation of strength. The goal is that when the new church begins weekly worship services, they will have at least 75 to 100 worshipers each Sunday and then continue to grow upon that solid foundation. Thousands of new churches from multiple denominations have used this process as a model during the first 12 to 16 months of starting a new church.

The final building block is *coaching and support systems.* Research shows that a new church with a trained and gifted coach will grow at twice the rate of a new church that does not have a coach. Three types of support systems encourage the health and growth of a new church. *Emotional support systems* include retreats, spousal support, think tanks, and spiritual accountability, providing leaders with the necessary spiritual and emotional encouragement. *Financial support* varies greatly by denomination. It is a key factor in the viability of a new church. For a well-conceived project, three years of declining external support seems to be most helpful. This is similar to venture capital in the business world, with a typical three-year total amount of $100,000 to $150,000. The third support system is *availability to resources*, where knowledgeable experts guide the new church in its growth and development and in the task of buying land and building a facility. This usually occurs after at least five to seven years from its founding.

Two Growth Edges in Church Planting

Church planting has changed considerably since 2001. As the first of the baby boomer generation approaches retirement, the emerging generation and the growing non-Anglo populations require new and creative church-planting models. Multiethnicity is the most important and challenging growth edge in church planting. Over the last 15 years, many denominations have been actively engaged in planting new churches in a variety of ethnic communities. Because the future will bring increased diversity in America, planting more first- and second-generation ethnic congregations will be crucial. Planting intentional multiethnic congregations (made up of two or more ethnicities) will also be important for both theological and practical reasons.[11]

The cultural shift toward postmodernism is the other challenging growth edge in church planting. This change is creating transitions in Anglo church planting. The traditional church-planting models of the boomer generation seem dissonant with the emerging generation's values. Their new churches are usually smaller than were the churches planted in the 1990s, because of their emphasis on community. Because of the smaller size, additional new churches need to be planted in the next decade, which then raises the question of whether there will be a sufficient number of leaders. Chapter 10 discusses the influence of both multiethnicity and postmodernism.

Both of these emerging growth edges are already affecting church planting. Figure 9.7 shows the average size of new churches under 10 years old for 1990 and each year from 1999 to 2005. The effects of the boomer church plants of the 1980s and 1990s show up in the spike in size between

1990 and 1999. Since then the average size of new churches has declined, reflecting the smaller size of ethnic and postmodern church plants.

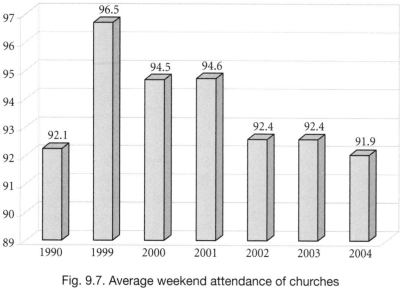

Fig. 9.7. Average weekend attendance of churches
under 10 years old.

Will Your Church Multiply Itself to Impact Future Generations?

At age 116, Elizabeth "Lizzie" Bolden was the oldest person in the world when she died in Memphis on December 11, 2006.[12] The longtime mem-

ber of New Wright's Chapel Baptist Church had lived to be the eighth-oldest person of modern times, according to Guinness World Records. Lizzie and husband, Lewis, had their first child, Ezell, when she was 29 years old, followed by six more offspring. Attending her 116th birthday party were many of her 40 grandchildren, 75 great-grandchildren, 150 great-great-grandchildren, 220 great-great-great grandchildren, and 75 great-great-great-great grandchildren. What a generational legacy!

As evidenced by First Covenant Church in Seattle and thousands more like it, a church that produces a legacy of daughter churches produces a harvest of fruitfulness and righteousness that extends through literal centuries. The best way for pastors to leave a spiritual legacy that will last for generations is for their present church to plant new churches. First Covenant may some day die (we earnestly pray that it will not), but more than 10 times as many people already attend the dozens of daughter and granddaughter churches it has started, ensuring a strong spiritual legacy for generations to come.

I recently attended an overnight retreat with six church planters in Southern California. In our closing session, retreat organizer Jack Hawkins looked at me and said, "Dave, look at what God has done." Those six pastors had each started a new church. The cumulative weekly attendance at all six was more than 2,000 people. Half of the people in attendance at those churches had never consistently attended a church before. Every year more than 200 people became new Christ-followers through the ministry of those six churches. Their stories are not all sunshine and roses—all are struggling to find permanent facilities, and they deal daily with challenging situations and people. Yet a haunting question remained for me: How many people's lives (as well as their children's and grandchildren's lives) would have been left untouched by the gospel if those new churches had not been started?

It Will Take All Churches

Last Easter Sunday our family was on vacation in San Diego. We attended two separate churches as we celebrated the resurrection of our Lord. The first church was a new church of the denomination for which I work. Because it was Easter, they met in a cinema multiplex instead of the elementary school where they normally meet. We attended the second of three services and settled in the top row of the theater, with 500 people filling almost every seat. The theme of the service was "Jesus Showed Up." Interspersed throughout the service were twelve video narratives of new members who had recently

encountered Jesus. Their stories were touching and heartwarming. Person after person testified to experiencing God's presence and grace, often in difficult circumstances. A worship band led the music, and the pastor gave a moving sermon about Jesus and his resurrection.

We attended our second Easter service at the first church founded in California, the historic Mission San Diego. Once again we sat in the very last row, this time in the crowded balcony of the much-loved church building. The organ music, the congregational hymn singing, the sermon by the 85-year-old Irish priest, and a very multiethnic congregation combined to create a memorable experience for our family.

On the surface, the two churches seemed so different. The first is one of California's most recent church plants, the second is the state's oldest. One is Roman Catholic, the other evangelical Protestant. One has a young pastor, the other an elderly priest. Yet both congregations are attempting to embody the mandate of Christ's church to be a living body of believers centered in Jesus and his cross, grave, resurrection, and ascension. Both pray that the Holy Spirit would come in their midst as on the day of Pentecost, that the foundations of the world might be shaken. This is the hope of the world.

The Top 10 Reasons to Plant Churches

10. New churches lower the age profile of the American church, increase its multiethnicity, and better position the whole church for future changes.

9. New churches provide synergistic benefits to established churches. Research shows that denominations that plant many strong churches have more healthy, growing, established churches than those who plant few churches.

8. The continued growth of new churches will extend up to 40 years after their start. The growth that occurs in years 10 to 40 is critical for creating a strong base of churches for the future. The mainline denominations have lost the influence of a complete generation of new churches.

7. New churches provide a channel to express the energy and ideas of passionate, innovative young pastors. Church planting encourages the development of the expansionist gifts of ministry

and leadership. Denominations that plant few churches unintentionally focus on training pastors in stabilizing gifts. A denomination needs both stabilizing and expansionist gifts to be both healthy and growing.

6. New churches are the research and development unit of God's kingdom. New churches create most of the current models and visions for healthy church life. Healthy cultural adaptations and theological vitality occur more often in a denomination that excels at church planting, because the ferment of new ideas and ministry solutions is more robust.

5. New churches are the test laboratory for lay leadership development. Because top lay leadership positions are usually already filled in the parent church, new churches provide a new group of emerging lay leaders the opportunity to grow and develop as primary leaders. In new church plants that do well, most lay members report that being part of the beginning of the new church was one of the defining spiritual events in their life.

4. New churches are historically the best method for reaching each emerging new generation. While many established churches have the ability to connect with the younger cohort, each generation also seems to need their own new type of churches that speak the gospel with their own cultural values and communication style.

3. New churches are the only truly effective means to reach the growing ethnic populations coming to America. Every people group needs to hear the gospel in a way that makes sense to their culture. It is difficult for established churches to become diverse. Church planting can effectively create both ethnic-specific and multiethnic congregations.

2. New churches are more effective than established churches at conversion growth. Studies show that new churches have three to four times the conversion rate per attendee than established churches.

1. Because the large majority of Americans do not attend a local church, many more new churches are needed. In 2005, 17.5 percent of Americans attended a local church on any given Sunday. Seventy-seven percent of Americans do not have a consistent connection with an orthodox Christian church. The best and most effective way for the Christian church to keep up with population growth is to start new churches.

Questions for Reflection and Discussion

1. How was your church started? Spend some time with other members and leaders adding up the ministry impact of your church throughout the years.
2. What are the stories of the pioneers of your church? Why did they start your church? How was their passion for God lived out? What type of people were they?
3. How effective is your denomination or region at starting new churches? What are some of the roadblocks?
4. Could your church plant a new church in the future? Would you parent it yourself or partner with other churches? How would you make sure that it had a long and fruitful ministry?

Please go to www.theamericanchurch.org/TACIC/Chapter9.htm for updates and additional information and resources for this chapter.

Part 3

INTROSPECTION

The Sea of Faith
Was once, too, at the full, and round earth's shore
Lay like the folds of a bright girdle furled.
But now I only hear
Its melancholy, long, withdrawing roar.
                    Matthew Arnold[1]

The third stage of the four-stage process of assessing America's spiritual terrain is *introspection*, which means looking inward before moving ahead. Self-assessment appraises the circumstances, forcing churches to count the cost of change. Introspection requires subjective analysis, asking questions such as, "Are we willing to change the habits and priorities of our church or denomination to reach more people in our community?" Introspection heeds the warning Jesus gave his followers, "You say you want to be my disciples; do you realize the cost of that statement? Will you let the message go so deep in you that you have no choice but to change your thoughts and actions?" (Luke 14:28–33, my paraphrase).

Faith—confidence in God's power—is a crucial element at this stage. The Israelite scouts returned from exploring the land and recognized both the opportunities and difficulties it represented. Ten men looked at themselves and found they were inadequate to face the challenge. Sizing up their circumstances, they found themselves wanting. By contrast, Joshua and Caleb were confident that they would succeed with God's help. Sadly, the Israelites followed the leading of the ten and quickly found themselves stranded in the wilderness because of their Chicken Little mind-set. Because of that response, the people of Israel spent 40 years wandering before Moses' successor, Joshua, led them into the Promised Land.

Wise introspection, like that shown by Joshua and Caleb, prudently adds realism to faith. Introspection becomes fruitful based on the answers to these two questions: (1) Are we willing to pay the price of change? and (2) Are we willing to create new pathways that will allow the work of God to advance?

Many Christian groups show great faith in their goal setting but fail to create the pathways for growth to occur. Consider the following examples:

- A major goal of the Episcopal Church's 20/20 project is to double Sunday attendance in the years between 2000 and 2020. Instead, Episcopalian attendance has declined by more than 7 percent in the first five years of this decade.
- In 2000 the Southern Baptist Convention set a goal of growing to 100,000 churches by the year 2020. In 2000 there were 41,514 SBC churches. By 2005 the number had increased to 43,699 churches. At that rate, the SBC will have 50,254 churches in 2020, far short of their goal.
- The Presbyterian Church (U.S.A.) desires to become multiethnic in composition and has set aggressive goals to turn that desire into reality. Unfortunately, the 2005 "Presbyterian Panel Survey" found that their membership remained unchanged at 97 percent white.

In each case, the group did not create the pathways necessary for the accomplishment of the goal. Pathways are proven activities and initiatives that God uses to accomplish the needed changes. The Episcopal Church needs realistic pathways for attendance growth. The SBC needs to improve in the recruitment of parent churches to plant new churches and in creating greater church-planting quality. The PCUSA needs to improve its understanding of how multiethnic populations develop and grow within a denomination.

The next three chapters will challenge you to engage in introspection. Take the time to be honest and reflective. Are you, your church, and your denomination willing to make the changes necessary to see renewal and restoration in the American church? Are you willing to develop and build the pathways for God's work to go forward? As with the children of Israel, those decisions will determine whether the American church remains in the wilderness or crosses to the place of promise.

Chapter 10

CULTURAL CHANGE IN AMERICA

The world is changed;
I feel it in the water;
I feel it in the earth;
I smell it in the air;
Much that once was, is lost,
For none now live who remember it.[1]

These are the words of Galadriel at the beginning of *The Fellowship of the Ring*, the first movie in the Lord of the Rings trilogy. Middle Earth is changing, and the Elven queen Galadriel's voice is filled with a sense of immense loss and melancholy. Life for Tolkien's Elves, dwarves, men, and Hobbits is undergoing an extraordinary transition. At the opening of the story, their very survival is in doubt. The world is changing, and their future is bleak.

In America our world is also changing. The ongoing downturn in church attendance this millennium is partially related to external cultural changes. Christian ministry faces more challenges today than it did 20 years ago. Many of the people in the emerging culture do not share the philosophical assumptions of 50-year-old churches or even of churches that are just 20 years old. Largely unaware of these changes, many churches continue to operate in modes and mentalities that no longer resonate with our culture.

For many Christians these changes bring up feelings of fear and can lead to a reactive Christianity. When a cultural transition occurs, the world in which we grew up always seems to be the better and safer culture than the new world that is coming.

At its best, Christianity has the adaptive ability to connect with an enormous diversity of cultures around the world. At its worst, Christianity has the lamentable propensity to become completely intertwined with its host culture. When this happens, it is difficult to distinguish where the culture stops and the church begins. While it is imperative that Christians communicate and live out the gospel so people within the culture will connect with the message, at the same time the church is to be, by its nature, countercultural. The message of Jesus challenges all social, religious, and political powers. The church must dance between these two polarities. If the church's message is too aggressively countercultural, few people will hear its words. If the church overidentifies with the culture, the gospel becomes tame and loses its power to transform lives.

This chapter will examine how American culture is changing and why that change must influence how Christians communicate the gospel. My hope is that by the end of this chapter, we will begin to view cultural change in America from a new perspective—that our response to the shifting culture will be "This new world could prove to be an exciting place in which to share the message of Jesus." With such an attitude, we will move from a feeling of loss to a sense of anticipation and hope for what God is doing and will continue to do.

The Church Needs to Discover Which Century It Is Living In

Many churches in America are living in the wrong century. Some of them might have had spectacular ministries if they were operating in the 1910s or 1950s. Other churches act as if they are still living in the 1980s or 1990s. All these churches are trapped in the last century. Unfortunately, the twenty-first century has arrived. A tipping point occurred at the millennial shift, which altered the relationship between American culture and the church, forever changing how the two will relate to each other. This change was in the making for decades. After the turn of the century, America passed the middle point or fulcrum of the transition, forcing us into the new world.

The American church must engage with these three critical transitions:

Our world used to be Christian, but it is now becoming
   post-Christian.
Our world used to be modern, but it is now becoming postmodern.
Our world used to be monoethnic, but it is now becoming
   multiethnic.

In many states and metropolitan areas, these transitions are occurring rapidly. This is especially true in the northern half of the East Coast, the West Coast, in major cities, and in virtually all university towns. In other places, this transition is occurring more slowly and may even take one or two more generations before it arrives at the tipping point, but the transition will eventually happen.

Christian to Post-Christian

What does it mean for the United States to transition from a Christian world to a post-Christian world? In the Christian world, pastors, churches, and individual believers operated as the majority. This close relationship between church and culture was called Christendom. In the early years of the faith, Christians were outsiders in the Roman Empire. They were a small countercultural movement, with little political power or social influence. Because Christians refused to honor Roman gods or to acknowledge the emperor as divine, it was illegal to be a Christian. Nevertheless, by AD 300, the subversive Christian movement numbered in the tens of millions. They had become a force to be reckoned with in Roman culture. So when the Roman emperor Constantine converted to the faith in AD 312, Christianity was legitimized in the eyes of the state. Not long afterward Christianity became the official religion of the empire. The church retained that privileged place in Western culture until recently.

In a largely Christian world, the focus was on building and maintaining Christian institutions. The needs of insiders were most important. Ministry focused on church membership, doctrine, and institutional maintenance. The pastoral role was to attend to the members and keep the ecclesiastical ship sailing smoothly. Preaching the Word, administering the sacraments, and providing pastoral care were the primary tasks of a minister. In the Christian world, people came to church with their needs.

In the post-Christian world, pastors, churches, and Christians need to operate more as the early church did. In the post-Christian world, the needs of outsiders become most important. Ministry is more like missionary work, with a renewed emphasis on the message and mission of Jesus. The role of pastors is to lead the church in its mission and equip members to understand and live out the message and mission of Jesus outside of the church. In the post-Christian world, only the healthy, missional church will prosper. This is not an issue of a traditional or contemporary style of ministry. That perspective is a dated dichotomy from the 1980s and 1990s that no longer is meaningful. Instead, churches must develop a mission mind-set, going out into the world to meet people's needs.

For most American Christians, this is a difficult transition. Many of us grew up in the church. It was a world and a subculture in which we were comfortable. The disappearance of Christendom produces a sense of grief and loss. It is important to acknowledge that grief. However, the world has changed, and the church must move on. The audience for the Christian message has changed. A post-Christian world means we can no longer assume that people know anything substantive about Jesus, his message, his mission, the Scriptures, or the church. The church in the post-Christian world must operate in a way that recognizes the spiritual and cultural situation of those to whom it wishes to minister.

Modern to Postmodern

The second transition is from the modern world to the postmodern world. Various influences formed the modern world, but the defining force in Western culture was the Enlightenment. Observation, logic, and reason determined everything that was important, necessary, and real. The Enlightenment forced people to move from the world of mythology into the world of physical reality. The scientific method facilitated the understanding of how physical processes worked, which led to modern technology and advances in modern health, making life better for most of the world's people. The Enlightenment required the church to leave the premodern world and to engage modernity. That modern world is now passing away.

How does the transition from a modern world to a postmodern world affect the church? In the modern world, pastors, churches, and Christians adapted to the rules of the Enlightenment or were viewed as reactionary. The modern world required rational, scientific proof of everything. Everything was discoverable. Only the objective mattered. Everything was possible. The world was to be used. There was no need for a god. Science was king. Darwin, Freud, and Marx were its prophets. In the modern world, the self was all-powerful.

One of the best ways to understand modernism is through its architecture. Most college campuses have a set of buildings constructed during the 1960s and 1970s. While the buildings looked avant-garde at the time of construction, they now appear hopelessly out of place. They deify the rectangle. They are characterized by severe surfaces, shiny panels, and rectangular footprints, walls, and windows, with little curvature or ornamentation in the architecture. Unfortunately, they were built with donated money, so they are there to stay. New Mexico State University architect Martin Hoffmeister says, "Today we are following Southwest designs and moving away from brutal modernistic styles."[2]

Uncertainty characterizes the postmodern world. Chaos theory and quarks are two scientific paradigms of postmodern uncertainty. Subjective experience replaces objective certainty. There is skepticism and cynicism about overcertainty. Communal life replaces individualism. History and tradition rise in value. We are to care for the world. Story is king. Spiritual curiosity is present yet not necessarily Christian in orientation.

Postmodernism also can be understood through its architecture. It beckons toward a more aesthetic traditional form and makes artistic use of curves, alcoves, and dormers. It uses softer and more natural materials, appearing to be a more integrated part of its environment. The new architectural developments at the campus of Purchase College in New York illustrates the architectural difference between the worlds of modernity and postmodernity.

> To soften the harshness of the school's modernistic architecture, officials at the SUNY College at Purchase have broken ground on a multicolored, U-shaped dormitory that will form a courtyard on campus and also have storefronts, to give it a small-town feeling. The $21 million four-story building is part of a $75 million capital improvement program that will, among other things, reduce the institutional appearance of the stark-looking modernistic campus.
>
> The campus features a dark brown brick plaza lined with similarly brown brick buildings. While the inherent serviceability of the buildings has endured, the aesthetic of unrelenting dark brick has proved increasingly difficult to live with over time. In addition to relieving the austerity of the architecture … the goal now is to erect new buildings that contribute more of a feeling of community.[3]

These architectural changes in aesthetic sensibilities reflect the underlying shift in worldviews. In which world are you most comfortable? I grew up in the modern world, but I am gradually becoming more comfortable in the postmodern world. Much of my transition has occurred because my occupation requires me to live in that new world. Most American Christians find comfort in the familiar modern world. The postmodern world seems dangerous and uncharted. It can seem to have lost the mooring of absolute truth. Yet this new world may be a more fruitful place for Christianity than was the modern world. This is reflected in postmodern interest in spiritual experiences, community life, care for others, care for the earth, the appreciation of aesthetics, and the renewed attraction to narrative form.

To understand the ministry impact of these two transitions, a brief tour will illustrate the differing methods of church ministry as the culture moved from premodernity through modernity to postmodernity.[4] The next four illustrations use the metaphor of a tree to illustrate the function of the church within each culture. The first phase is best described as *Christendom in a religious culture*. This phase was the medieval and Reformation world of Europe before 1800, and the United States from 1800 to 1920, during the period of the Second and Third Great Awakenings.[5]

A fruit basket placed beneath a tree is our first illustration. When the church harvested spiritual fruit in that era, they did not even have to pick the fruit from the tree. The tree was already so laden with fruit that it fell into the basket at the base of the tree, seemingly of its own accord. In this world Christendom was at its apex, the culture was religious, and each reinforced the other. In that synergistic world of church and culture, ministry was done passively. The people came to the church. Missional initiative was not necessary. The conflation of Christianity and culture gave the church enormous power, which allowed the passive approach to ministry.

The second phase was *Christendom in a religious culture that was becoming increasingly secular.* This occurred in Europe from 1800 to 1920. The transition in the United States occurred later, taking place from 1920 to 1965. The influence of Marx, Darwin, and Freud began to challenge the American Christian culture in the 1920s, creating the fundamentalist-modernist controversies. The continuing effect of the Enlightenment and the carnage created by World War I hastened the transition on both sides of the Atlantic.

The second illustration shows how ministry occurred in that phase. The tree was still fruitful, especially on its low-hanging branches. Christian ministry was more challenging than in the previous period, yet there was much fruit still to be picked. The Christian church boomed in America, especially in the 1950s, as the religious and the secular reached a holy truce, allowing each to be considered true within its own arena. That decade gave religious expression to the theme of the movie *Field of*

Dreams: "If you build it, they will come." Tens of thousands of new church buildings were built in this period. Nevertheless, the seeds of decay were sown, for the uneasy truce would not last forever, and the church was harvesting that which it had not sown (see John 4:38).[6]

The third phase was *Christendom in a secular culture that had some religious memory*. This phase happened in Europe from 1920 to 1965 and in the United States from 1965 to 2000. In America it started with the cultural revolution of the mid- to late 1960s. As our nation became progressively more secular, much of the church continued to act as it had for decades, continuing in the Christendom mind-set.[7] Among Christians and those with a religious memory from childhood, the traditional ministry of the church still worked. Unfortunately, for people without religious memory, this style of ministry did not connect well.

A slow change began to happen. As our third photo illustrates, much of the tree was barren, but one branch retained leaves and fruit, and the church spent all of its energy trying to pick fruit from that one leafy branch. In the United States that branch was middle- to upper-middle-class suburban culture. As a result, a slight renaissance occurred, particularly in the evangelical church from the late 1980s to the late 1990s, as the bubble of the boomer generation exerted its leadership influence. However, the bloom was off the rose — or at least off the tree.

The fourth phase is *mission churches engaging a secular yet spiritually curious culture*. In the United States this final phase began with the new millennium.[8] Churches that continue to live in the world of Christendom will see ongoing decline. Churches of influence will be missional churches, reaching an increasingly postmodern culture that is secular yet spiritually curious.

The next photo illustrates the fourth phase. The tree appears to be leafless and fruitless. This is not to imply that many churches are not doing worthwhile ministry, but picking fruit from this tree will yield a minimal harvest. The percentage of the population that will respond to the Christendom model of ministry is declining every year. This is why chapter 6

revealed that Lutheran, Catholic, and Reformed churches are seeing the highest levels of decline, as those churches have the most difficulty transitioning out of the world of Christendom.

A fundamental change in strategy needs to occur for the church to experience fruitfulness in this present age. Picking fruit off a tree can no longer be the primary model for ministry. Instead, the words of Jesus in Luke 13:6–9 give a hint of the new direction needed for a post-Christian and postmodern world.

> Then he told this parable: "A man had a fig tree growing in his vineyard, and he went to look for fruit on it but did not find any. So he said to the man who took care of the vineyard, 'For three years now I've been coming to look for fruit on this fig tree and haven't found any. Cut it down! Why should it use up the soil?'
>
> "'Sir,' the man replied, 'leave it alone for one more year, and I'll dig around it and fertilize it. If it bears fruit next year, fine! If not, then cut it down.'"

When a fig tree is no longer naturally bearing fruit, it needs immediate attention. The tree's owner must dig around the roots and fertilize the tree. If the tree responds to this treatment, it will again bear fruit. Instead of waiting for fruit to grow again on the low-hanging branches, the church needs to relearn how to dig around and fertilize the roots of the tree so that the whole tree begins to bear fruit again. Most American ministry models are based on the fruit-gathering and fruit-picking methods of Christendom. The church needs to rediscover the model of the early Christians, who knew how to dig and fertilize, rather than just collect and pick. What does it mean to dig and fertilize around the tree? For a church this means engaging its community, showing love and servant leadership. It means presenting the Christian message in a manner that connects with true spiritual needs. For Christians it means practicing hospitality, building redemptive bridges to their neighbors. It means living out the full message and mission of Jesus. Chapters 13 through 15 will suggest how to cultivate and fertilize, centered upon a return to the message and mission of Jesus and in relearning the missional strategy and practices of the early church's mission to the Gentiles.

Chapter 3 highlighted California's Marin County as a portent of the future. Marin pastor Art Greco describes for us the greatest challenge of ministry in a post-Christian and postmodern world:

> Ministering in Marin County has helped me to see that *every* place is difficult if the ministry we are doing is truly Christian. But it isn't the culture of Marin County that I find most difficult. In fact, I rather enjoy the context here, as it is one of spiritual openness and hunger. However, the post-Christians of Marin County are not the greatest challenge to the gospel here. In fact, they make for a rather exciting evangelistic opportunity since they are consistently and predictably post-Christian — they are sometimes even *drawn* to an honest, humble, measured approach to doing the gospel.
>
> That introduces what *has* been the greatest surprise and biggest challenge in pastoring here, at least for me. Though I'm privileged to serve an incredibly generous and welcoming congregation, and am acquainted with others like it in the county, it has been the church — the *Christians* of Marin — that have been the most challenging obstacle for ministry here. It's almost as though the anti-Christian attitudes of the county have affected the church more than the church has affected their attitudes. Often the church has responded to the culture's attacks, not by rethinking and reconnecting, but by retreating and redefining mission.
>
> When faithful Christianity is defined primarily as, "protecting the truth, insulating our children, and surviving the onslaught of competing thoughts," the battle is lost. In fact, I sometimes wonder if Satan even has to do much of anything to slow the advance of true Christianity here in Marin; the church seems to be doing most of his work for him by competing for members and dollars, hiding behind the skirts of a few carefully selected Scripture verses about purity, while burying her talents in the sand for fear of making a mistake with them.
>
> Yes, doing ministry in Marin is challenging. But that is not what makes ministry here so difficult. That privilege is reserved for the majority of the Christian community of Marin — one that has too often chosen the way of the ostrich, burying her head in the sands of isolationism and protectionism — as though neither the truth of Scripture nor the well-executed Spirit-filled life could withstand the swirling winds of spiritual deception and confusion.[9]

Monoethnic to Multiethnic

The transition from a monoethnic world to a multiethnic world is the third transition occurring in our country. In the monoethnic world, Christians, pastors, and churches only had to understand their own culture. Ministering in a homogenous culture is easier, but monoethnic Christianity can gradually become culture-bound. The worldview and values of a particular culture can be transferred to Christianity. Where I live in Minnesota, Jesus can easily become a Scandinavian, with fair skin and blue eyes, instead of a Middle Eastern Jew. Monoethnicity can warp the gospel. This seduction of being overly identified with a specific culture confronts a growing number of affluent, well-educated, suburban churches and impairs the church's ability to engage outsiders or even see the heart of the Christian message.

In the multiethnic world, pastors, churches, and Christians need to operate under the rules of the early church's mission to the Gentiles. At the church's birth on the day of Pentecost, a diverse crowd from throughout the Mediterranean region experienced the coming of the Holy Spirit. It is clear from the New Testament that God intended the early Christian church to be diverse ethnically, for both theological and practical reasons. While Israel was predominantly a monoethnic nation, God had called them to be a light to the Gentiles. A multiethnic church reflects this heart of God for all people.

Expressions of worship show us one picture of the texture and completeness of multiethnic Christianity. When other cultures express their Christian faith, our faith becomes enriched as we experience it. As an example, the practice of Asian Christianity reminds me of the importance of prayer. African American Christians enrich my life through heartfelt worship, while Hispanic believers teach me about the importance of familial relationships within and without the church.

The multiethnic transition is distinct from the first two changes. Neither the European Enlightenment nor postmodernism significantly influenced Non-Anglo culture in the United States. Because non-Anglo churches never truly adopted the modernist worldview, one of God's wonderful serendipities is that they can provide Anglo churches with helpful models of fruitful ministry in this new world.

Our country's changing ethnic makeup is creating three trends that impact American Christianity. The first trend is the inevitability of more ethnic diversity in the future because of both immigration and birthrates. Figure 10.1 shows that the Hispanic birthrate is almost double the Anglo birthrate.[10] Combined with Asian and Hispanic immigration, it is certain that America will become more multiethnic with every passing year.

The second multiethnic influence on American Christianity is the effect of global Christianity. The Christian church is growing rapidly in the Southern and Eastern hemispheres, and declining in the Northern and Western hemispheres. Philip Jenkins has described this change in *The Next Christendom: The Coming of Global Christianity*. As the power center of

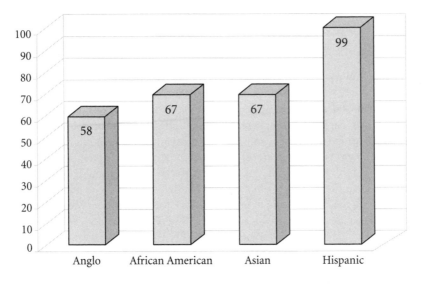

Fig. 10.1 2005 birthrates per 1,000 women.

Christianity moves south and east, the multiethnic church is becoming the normal and natural picture of the new face of Christianity.

The third key influence of multiethnicity is its challenge to power and privilege. In America these qualities have been the domain of Anglos. Jesus presented a countercultural view of these two traits when he challenged the Roman view of power and authority with the model of servanthood. Unfortunately, American Christians have often allowed the world to determine their view of power and privilege, rather than Scripture. This has created an Anglo Christianity that is increasingly affluent, suburban, and educated, yet functionally disconnected from non-Anglo populations. A multiethnic church will bring to American Christianity a new awareness of these issues from a biblical perspective so that the new people of God, the church, may truly reflect the diversity and equality inherent in the gospel.

Living in the New World

To many Christians, these changes are overwhelming. Retreating to the safe world of the past seems enticing. Unfortunately, it does not matter which world we *want* to live in; we can only live in the world that *exists today*. The word for living in a world that no longer exists is *delusion*. If we wish to engage our culture relevantly and meaningfully, we must accept and learn to live with joy in this present world.

This new world has many potential advantages for Christianity. In fact, it may be more receptive to the gospel than was the modern world. This new world is remarkably similar to the Greco-Roman world that the book of Acts describes. Acts 17 tells a remarkable story of the cultural connection the apostle Paul made in the intellectual center of his world, Athens.

> While Paul was waiting for them in Athens, he was greatly distressed to see that the city was full of idols. So he reasoned in the synagogue with both Jews and God-fearing Greeks, as well as in the marketplace day by day with those who happened to be there. A group of Epicurean and Stoic philosophers began to debate with him. Some of them asked, "What is this babbler trying to say?" Others remarked, "He seems to be advocating foreign gods." They said this because Paul was preaching the good news about Jesus and the resurrection. Then they took him and brought him to a meeting of the Areopagus, where they said to him, "May we know what this new teaching is that you are presenting? You are bringing some strange ideas to our ears, and we would like to know what they mean." (vv. 16–20)

Paul wandered around the city, observing its cultural and religious artifacts and engaging in its religious and philosophic dialogue. After discussing theology in the Jewish synagogue, he was invited to address the philosophers and spiritually curious. Here is a slightly imaginative and abbreviated rendition of the story of Jesus that Paul told audiences throughout the Mediterranean world, including the Athenians.[11]

> Paul: I have come to tell you about a prophet from Israel.
> Crowd: You mean that small, insignificant, marginalized vassal state at the east end of the Mediterranean?
> Paul: That prophet is Jesus the Messiah.
> Crowd: What are you talking about? We have never heard the term *Messiah*.
> Paul: Jesus the Messiah was crucified.
> Crowd: Oh, that is impressive. Those nasty Romans got the better of him, eh?
> Paul: But God raised him from the dead.
> Crowd: You expect us to believe that? Resurrection is not an everyday occurrence here in Athens.
> Paul: He has now ascended to the right hand of God as Lord and is appointed as the coming Judge of the world.
> Crowd: Now you have crossed the line. A prophet from the backwater of Israel, judging us, the elite of the world?

This example of the words and actions of the early church's Gentile mission provides us with a model for today's church as we learn how to become a missional church in a secular yet spiritually curious culture. Paul impressively modeled the dance of culture by connecting with both the Stoics and Epicureans in a profound manner, weaving their history and ideas into his sermon. To further the cultural connection, Paul quoted from an altar inscription and later quoted a Greek poet, probably the Stoic philosopher Aratus.

But then he challenged his listeners and their culture in a very profound way with the story of Jesus. In a city filled with temples of stone and sculptured idols, Paul became *countercultural* and challenged them saying, "The God who made the world and everything in it is the Lord of heaven and earth and does not live in temples built by hands. And he is not served by human hands, as if he needed anything. Rather, he himself gives everyone life and breath and everything else" (Acts 17:24–25).

After Paul's cultural connection and countercultural challenge, the remarkable result was the power that the message of Jesus exerted over the Athenians, who had no cultural background to understand the meaning of Paul's sermon. The five statements made by Paul in his typical gospel rendition flew in the face of their experience and reasoning. Yet there was a power in the story of the gospel that broke through to a deeper place in the hearts of many of the listeners. While some scoffed, many others wanted more conversation, and a number of Athenians became followers of Jesus that day, including Dionysius, a member of the Areopagus, and Damaris, a wealthy and influential woman of Athens. A cultural connection, a countercultural force, and the story of Jesus combined to become a powerful vehicle for the work of the Holy Spirit. May this fourfold combination describe the story of the American church in the next generation.

Questions for Reflection and Discussion

1. Do you instinctually react with fear or with hope in the face of cultural change?
2. Which of the three transitions — post-Christian, postmodern, multiethnic — will be most challenging for your church? Why?
3. How can you and your church have an experience of the multiethnic world, carried out with equality of position?
4. By the end of the chapter, were your initial concerns about the American cultural changes intensified or relieved?

Please go to www.theamericanchurch.org/TACIC/Chapter10.htm for updates and additional information and resources for this chapter.

Chapter 11

SOBER REFLECTIONS ON THE FUTURE OF THE AMERICAN CHURCH

In J. R. R. Tolkien's novel *The Fellowship of the Ring*, the Elven queen Galadriel brings the Hobbits Frodo and Sam to a basin of water, the surface of which reveals glimpses of the future.

> At the bottom, upon a low pedestal carved like a branching tree, stood a basin of silver, wide and shallow, and beside it stood a silver ewer. With water from the stream, Galadriel filled the basin to the brim and breathed on it, and when the water was still again, she spoke. "Here is the Mirror of Galadriel," she said. "I have brought you here so that you may look in it, if you will." Many things are revealed in the mirror—the past, the present and things that may yet come to be. But that which is seen, even the Wise cannot always tell.[1]

Prophecy is a dangerous business. The Old Testament contains severe penalties for false prophecy. The true prophets of Yahweh were often disdained and occasionally murdered. Many times seers of the future are famously in error. Consider the British Parliamentary Committee's report on Edison's electric lightbulb, which concluded that his invention was "unworthy of the attention of practical and scientific men." Lord Kelvin, famous British scientist and president of the Royal Society declared in 1883, "X-rays will prove to be a hoax." An 1876 internal Western Union memo stated, "The telephone has too many shortcomings to be seriously considered as a means of communication. The device is inherently of no value to us."[2]

Predictions about the future are not the only risky prognostications, as Princeton University's Bernard Lewis recently recalled from a meeting he attended many years ago in Italy:

> The business of the historian is the past, not the future. I remember being at an international meeting of historians in Rome during which a group of us were sitting and discussing the question: should historians attempt

to predict the future? We batted this back and forth. This was in the days when the Soviet Union was still alive and well. One of our Soviet colleagues finally intervened and said, "In the Soviet Union, the most difficult task of the historian is to predict the past."[3]

While businesses do not prophecy, they do project. When developing sales projections for a product, a business starts with its present sales and then calculates the influence of changing demographics, competitive factors, and internal initiatives to promote the product. In this way a company can decide whether to spend additional resources to develop a product's market share. This chapter will project the future of the American church by extrapolating from its recent history and trends.

What If the Church Continues with Its Present Habits?

The first question to ask when projecting is, "What will happen if the situation remains static, if the organization does not change its practices?" When asked about the future of the church, the question becomes, "If the American church continues to do ministry as it has in recent years, what will be the resulting attendance projections for 2010, 2015, and 2020?" The following estimates use recent attendance trends to model a realistic projection for evangelical, mainline, and Roman Catholic churches.

Projection 1: Overall Church Attendance in 2020

The percentage of the population attending a Christian church on any given weekend will decline from 17.5 percent in 2005 to 14.7 percent in 2020.

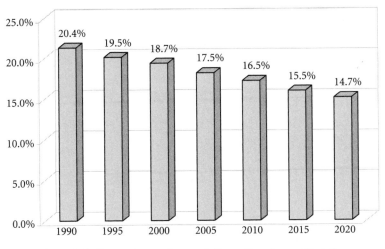

Fig. 11.1. Percentage of population attending a Christian church each weekend.

While numeric church attendance will decline slightly from 52 million in 2005 to 49 million in 2020, the American population will grow from 296 million in 2005 to 336 million in 2020,[4] causing a significant percentage decline.

Projection 2: Closed and Opened Churches by 2020

Approximately 55,000 churches will close between 2005 and 2020, while 60,000 new churches will open, producing a net gain of 4,500 churches. However, to keep pace with population growth, a net gain of 48,000 churches will be needed. In those 15 years the American church will fall short of this mark by almost 43,500 congregations.

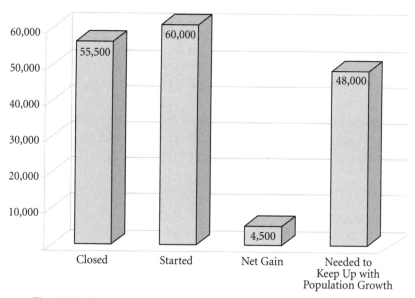

Fig. 11.2. Change in number of Christian churches 2005–2020.

Projection 3: Evangelical Attendance Percentage in 2020

The evangelical church will not keep up with population growth between 2005 and 2020. While evangelical churches almost kept up with population growth from 1990 to 2004, evangelical attendance growth slowed considerably in 2005 and 2006. This has caused a decline in future attendance projections.

The weekend attendance percentage at evangelical churches will fall below 9 percent by 2010 and will be at 8.5 percent in 2020. Evangelical groups that excel at "mammalian" church planting have the potential to grow at two to four times the rate of population growth. Evangelical

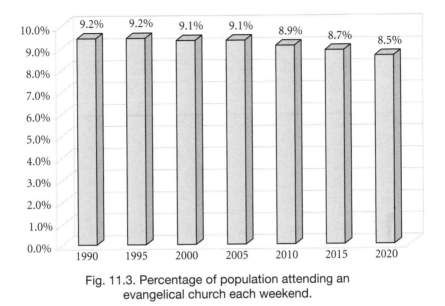

Fig. 11.3. Percentage of population attending an
evangelical church each weekend.

groups that plant churches in a "reptilian" manner will grow numerically
but seldom as fast as population growth. Evangelical groups that start few
new churches and have an underdeveloped church-planting system will
continue to decline. Many established evangelical churches have already
begun to show signs of decline. From 2005 to 2006, attendance at evangelical churches over 40 years old declined by 1.3 percent—a loss of more than
240,000 worshipers in just one year.

Projection 4: Mainline Attendance Percentage in 2020

All mainline denominations are projected to continue to decline, continuing a downward slide that started in 1965.

There are many reasons why the decline will continue. First, established
churches in mainline denominations are declining at a rate of 2 percent per
year, meaning they will shrink by almost 30 percent in attendance from
2005 to 2020. Second, mainline denominations do not start many new
churches and have not done so since 1965. Figure 11.5 shows the dramatic
increase in the 1950s of new mainline churches, then a sharp decline to
the present time. This means there are few replacements for the churches
that close, effectively creating a missing generation of churches. One conse-
quence of the lack of church planting is that mainline denominations lack
the innovation and energy that new churches inject into an organization.

Third, mainline denominations are facing severe financial challenges.
For example, giving in 2005 for the national basic support of the United

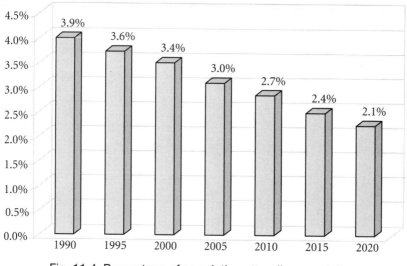

Fig. 11.4. Percentage of population attending a mainline
church each weekend.

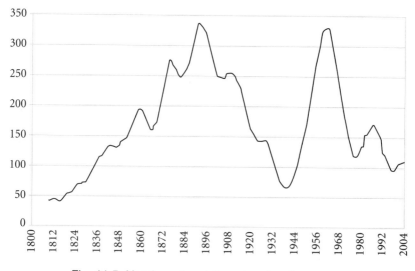

Fig. 11.5. Number of mainline churches by year
founded. Based on start dates of 36,283 churches.

Church of Christ was $10 million, down from $12.5 million in 1995 and
$13.1 million in 1985. Inflation increased by 80 percent in those 20 years,
reducing the value of the 2005 income to $5.6 million in 1985 dollars.[5]

Finally, a significant number of churches are leaving their historic
mainline denominations. Many of these seceding churches are stable

or growing congregations. In 2006 the Pacific Southwest Conference of American Baptist Churches USA voted to leave their denomination. In the United Church of Christ, 250 congregations voted to leave from 2005 to 2007. In 2007 several of the Episcopal Church's largest congregations voted to sever ties with the Episcopal Church in the United States and align with a bishop of the Anglican communion in another part of the world.

Projection 5: Roman Catholic Attendance Percentage in 2020

The Roman Catholic Church will grow in membership because of immigration, but Mass attendance will continue to decline. The drop-off in attendance will continue to be most pronounced in the Northeast and the Midwest, where the Roman Catholic Church was historically strongest. Mass attendance will decline from 7.1 percent in 1990 to 4 percent in 2020.

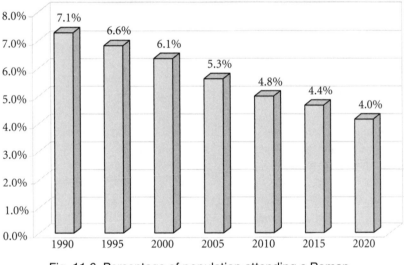

Fig. 11.6. Percentage of population attending a Roman Catholic church each weekend.

The growing priest shortage is already causing consolidation and retrenchment in many parishes, and this will escalate. The current financial stress on the dioceses will continue unabated, reducing the number of new parishes they can start.

A Recap—2020 Attendance Summary

In summary, the future looks grim for the American church. The conditions that produce growth are simply not present. If present trends continue, the church will fall farther behind population growth. Figure 11.7 displays the summary.

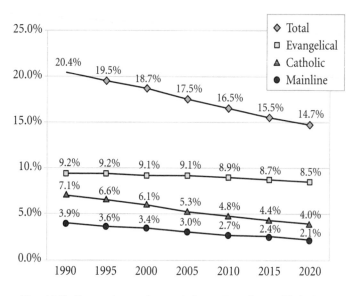

Fig. 11.7. Percentage of population attending a Christian church each weekend.

What Changes Are Necessary for the Church?

Despite the grim outlook, all is not lost for the American church. The redemptive question to ask is, "What changes would the American church have to make to reverse ongoing decline and to keep up with population growth?" The answer is relatively simple, though the solution would realistically take 15 to 20 years to accomplish. Certain prevailing assumptions among churches and denominations need to be reversed, and new pathways for growth need to be developed.

First, all established churches must courageously strive toward both health and growth. Established church attendance is presently declining by between 1 and 2 percent per year. By 2020, that will produce a decline of more than 20 percent in the attendance of established churches. That numerical decline does not even consider the task of keeping up with population growth. Reversing that decline and reestablishing growth will take place only as churches clarify their message and mission, develop healthier internal and external habits, and create pathways for growth. Chapters 8, 10, and 12 – 16 discuss the components needed for this to come to pass.

Second, established churches need to actively parent new churches. Planting a new church should become a part of the long-range outreach plan of established congregations, either through parenting or as a group of partner churches. Does your church have anything of value to pass on to future generations? If so, your church should plant a new church, as church planting is the best method for sustained generational transmission of the Christian faith.

Large churches in particular could produce a major advancement for Christ's church if they devoted resources and energy to planting a series of like-minded churches in their metropolitan region. There are many notable examples of very large churches that are intentionally following this strategy.

Third, denominations must recognize that church planting is essential for their future health. Every denomination needs a turbocharged mammalian structure to effectively plant and resource new congregations. The American church needs to start 2,900 additional new churches every year if it hopes to keep up with population growth. Denominations need to start these new churches with greater intentionality and strength if they are to reach the growing number of Americans who have no connection with the body of Christ. While a denomination can create a strong church-planting system, the parenting help of established and new congregations is critical in the creation of a thriving church-planting movement.

It is five to seven times easier to plant a new church than it is to revitalize an established church. While revitalization is valuable as a growth strategy, church planting should be the dominant missional focus of every denomination.

Breaking the Ice

Early this spring my wife, Shelly, and I went kayaking on the small lake on which we live. It was March 26, and the temperature in Minneapolis shot up to a record 81 degrees — 35 degrees above average. While ice still covered most of the lake, the heat and sun caused the edges to melt. We pulled out our kayaks, life jackets, and paddles and rushed to the lake with our neighbor Dan not far behind. Each year we compete with Dan to see who is first into the lake once the thaw begins, and this year Shelly and I won by five minutes.

Ice still covered two-thirds of the lake, so we navigated through the open water, occasionally venturing close to the edges of the melting ice and paddling through the slush. When our oldest daughter, Erica, joined us, she started crashing into the thicker ice. I soon followed her example. For half an hour we imagined we were Nordic explorers breaking through the polar icecap as the ice became increasingly brittle from the warm air and bright sun. The sound of crackling ice punctuated the silence of the lake. Ice shards sprang up from the water and slid across the sheet of ice. Paddling our kayaks up onto large shelves of ice, six or seven inches thick, we aimed for a thin but visible fault line. Our weight and the edge of the boat's keel slowly split the ice along the fault, freeing a large floe of ice. The risk and anxiety of beaching an unstable kayak on a shelf of ice created excitement and tension as we hoped the ice would give way before the kayak listed and capsized. The rare feeling of exhilaration we felt was unforgettable! Before the next morning's dawn, all the ice had disappeared and our voyage vanished into memory.

A chill wind is blowing in America, affecting the future of Christianity. Most of the basic indicators point downward. Will the ice remain frozen, or will the melting begin? Will the future become a dark night of winter for the church, or will spring break forth and create new life?

In *The Lion, the Witch, and the Wardrobe*, C. S. Lewis created the magical land of Narnia. When the four children enter Narnia through the professor's wardrobe, they come into a land of eternal winter. The White Witch holds an unusual power in Narnia, keeping winter from ending. One of the children, Lucy, says, "She has made a magic so that it is always winter in Narnia—always winter, but it never gets to Christmas."[6]

But something is happening. There is a rumor that Aslan the lion is roaming the land. His very presence is causing a winter-wonderland nightmare for the White Witch: the ice and snow are melting. "This is no thaw," says the dwarf to the White Witch. "This is spring. What are we to do? Your winter has been destroyed, I tell you. This is Aslan's doing!"[7] All around them snow melts, trees bud, and the water in the creeks flows again. Aslan is destroying the witch's power.

Just as the lion Aslan was the hope of Narnia, so the only hope for our world is Jesus, the Lion of Judah. His story has a supernatural power to end winter, bring spring, unleash life, and melt frozen hearts. To this story we now turn.

Ten Necessary Changes for the American Church to Have a Bright Future

1. Christian leaders need to be honest about what is happening in the American church and in their denomination and its churches, and personally lead the church forward with spirituality, chemistry, and strategy.
2. Established churches need to have the courage and commitment to pursue both health and growth. This dedication needs to come from pastoral and lay leaders and from members.
3. Christian leaders and churches need to accept and learn to thrive in the new world that is post-Christian, postmodern, and multiethnic.
4. The best pattern for the mission of the American church is the early church's attitude, model, and mission strategy to the Greco-Roman world.
5. In this new world, pastors need to upgrade their ministry gifts and skills, learning to articulate the message and mission of Jesus with passion, power, and wisdom.
6. Christians must engage their neighbors with a humble and listening attitude, relishing the new opportunities God has made available. A great way to begin is through the recovery of the historic Christian ministry of hospitality.
7. Established churches must embrace church planting as a primary method of passing the faith on to future generations.
8. Denominations need to learn how to develop turbocharged mammalian church planting structures while encouraging the initiative and interest in church planting to come from the grassroots level, both in established and new churches.
9. Pastors and leaders need to devote more energy to raising up and training young leaders in their churches, colleges, and community organizations.
10. The church needs to recognize anew the importance of the Holy Spirit in the life of the church.

Questions for Reflection and Discussion

1. Are you surprised at the future projection of church attendance in the United States? Why or why not?
2. What implications will that decline bring for our culture?
3. Given the projected decline in established churches, how important is it for them to be more intentional about both health and growth?

Please go to www.theamericanchurch.org/TACIC/Chapter11.htm
for updates and additional information and resources for this chapter.

Chapter 12

WHAT IS THE AMERICAN CHURCH TO DO?

As we have explored the state of the American church, have you felt the daunting challenge that the church faces? Almost all of the data indicates that the church is fated to decline in influence every year in the near future. At this point we must ask ourselves, "What is the American church to do?"

Over the last two decades, much of the American church responded to this question with two reactions. The first response was to address the church's irrelevance. The style of the message and music felt outdated. The truth of Scripture needed greater practical applicability to the listeners' lives. The solution was to reshape both the message and music in a way that reflected current cultural practices.

The second response was to refocus the church's vision. The great need was better strategy. Churches were encouraged to create a better plan and purpose for their church. Many churches' ministry plans bore a resemblance to business models. The Christian book market is saturated with how-to books specializing in relevance and strategy.

While I embrace the value of both relevance and strategy, the church faces a more profound problem. The church's critical challenge is to restore Jesus' words and actions to their place of centrality. For the last few years, I have listened carefully to the message churches communicate through their sermons, vision statements, and music to ascertain what they communicate about Jesus. I have discovered that many churches have somehow failed to communicate clearly this most important message.

Much of the church's public discourse about Jesus is secondhand conversation, instead of allowing Jesus' own words and actions to speak. Imagine that someone has never met you but has heard about you from others. Can this person know the "real you" through secondhand information? Not well. He or she would need firsthand experience to truly know you. He or she would need to meet you in the flesh, hear your words, and watch your actions to obtain a sense of your personality, character, and personal presence.

We arrived at this state of affairs because Christendom made it possible for the church to thrive while speaking about Jesus in that secondhand manner. American culture and the church took for granted a common body of knowledge about Jesus. We assumed that everyone understood religious phrases. Secondhand words about Jesus often become trite, assuming the hearer knows what certain theological "code words" mean, whereas the actual words of Jesus have the power to cut deep into a person's heart.

Those assumptions of Christendom are no longer effective in the post-Christian, postmodern, and multiethnic world. In our twenty-first-century American culture, firsthand communication will carry the most weight. People are no longer interested in an abstract and indistinct picture of Jesus. They desire immediacy. In a culture that no longer trusts authority, people desire firsthand personal experience. They need to hear for themselves his words and see for themselves his actions.

The early Christians were constantly retelling firsthand experiences with Jesus, reflecting on what his words and actions meant. Consider how the early church relied on firsthand testimony about Jesus: "That which was from the beginning, which we have heard, which we have seen with our eyes, which we have looked at and our hands have touched—this we proclaim concerning the Word of life. The life appeared; we have seen it and testify to it, and we proclaim to you the eternal life, which was with the Father and has appeared to us" (1 John 1:1–2).

The apostle Paul specifically referred back to Christ more than 50 times in the first three chapters of Ephesians and the first chapter of Colossians. Galatians 1–3 and Philippians 1–2 contain more than 60 additional references to Jesus. Paul was constantly making sure his listeners' eyes, ears, and hearts were focused on Jesus.

Dorothy Sayers was a prominent Christian author and intellectual in mid-twentieth-century England, connected to the literary circle of C. S. Lewis and J. R. R. Tolkien. Her analysis of the state of Christianity in Great Britain in the 1940s was this: "It is fatal to imagine that everybody knows quite well what Christianity is and only needs a little encouragement to practice it. The brutal fact is that in this Christian country, not 1 in 100 has the faintest notion what the church teaches about God, or man, or society or the person of Jesus Christ."[1] Sayers may have overstated her point. Perhaps the number in reality was 2, 3, or 5 in 100. Yet her point is clear. Even in a country considered "Christian," most of its citizens may have a woefully inadequate understanding of basic Christian theology and possess limited knowledge of Jesus.

Is this the case in America? This description seems painfully true of most Americans, whether inside or outside the church. American evangelicalism has often reduced the message of Jesus to practical tips about living life. The Bible then becomes a how-to guide for a successful and happy life. Mainline Christianity has often untethered itself from the historic Christian understanding of Scripture. The Roman Catholic Church has a crisis of insufficient scriptural understanding at the lay level.

Not only do the powerful words and actions of Jesus no longer play a prominent role in the American church today, but we also have allowed a shallow and narrow understanding of the message and mission of Jesus to persist. Rather than the glorious vision of Jesus, the focal point of the church's message is often the fulfilled life of the listener. That message possesses neither the power to transform nor the necessity to worship.

My wife, Shelly, and daughter Andrea enjoy making pottery. When the lump of clay is ready for shaping, the first task of a potter is to place the clay in the very center of the potter's wheel. While the wheel is spinning, the poster uses both hands to gently yet firmly coax the clay into a symmetrical form. Unless the clay is positioned correctly, as the potter raises the walls of the pot, they will become too thick in some places and too thin in others. This causes the piece to become lopsided and weak. When properly centered on the wheel, the pottery possesses a sense of balance and stability. In the same way, when the story of Jesus ceases to be the center point of our message, the church becomes weak and unbalanced.

The Great Awakenings and revivals in the American church originated from the fountainhead of a renewed focus on the person and work of Jesus. The years 1880 to 1910 were a remarkable era in American church development as God's Spirit gave birth to multiple Christian denominations that focused their primary passion on Jesus.[2] The church in America is always most vibrant when its central focus is Jesus. That is the power of Paul's words in 1 Corinthians 3:11: "No one can lay any foundation other than the one already laid, which is Jesus Christ." Yet the American church of today has subtly moved away from that cornerstone.

Why do so many seekers report that they are attracted to Jesus but not to the church? Perhaps the problem is that the church has done a splendid job of concealing the powerful life-giving Jesus. We domesticate him; we make him our servant; we assume that people have more knowledge about him than they do. We are producing Christians who lack the vitality and depth that should mark Christ-followers. To quote John Perkins again, "We have over-evangelized the world too lightly." We have allowed a narrow and limited understanding of Jesus to marginalize and reduce the revolutionary nature of his message and mission.

The Topography of Scripture

For six years, our family lived in the foothills of the Sierra Nevada Mountains above Sacramento, California. Just a few miles from our home began the Mormon Emigrant Trail. Originally created by Mormons returning to Utah following the California Gold Rush, this historic trail led from the California gold discovery site, eastward through the Sierra Nevada Mountains, and on to Salt Lake City. When pioneers and settlers followed that trail back westward from Utah, they passed three small mountain ranges. Then the topography flattened out until they arrived at the breathtaking 1,645-feet-deep Lake Tahoe. At the far west end of the lake, the pioneers were confronted by the perpendicular face of an enormous block of granite that soared thousands of feet upward and extended 350 miles from north to south, forming the spectacular peaks of the Sierra Nevada Mountains. They wound their way up that sheer cliff until they reached the summit. From there, a steady decline brought the travelers gradually down the final 70 miles to Sacramento.

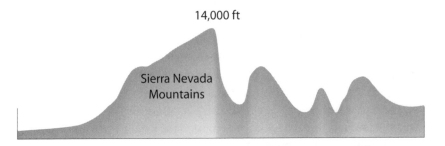

Fig. 12.1. Cross-section of Sierra Nevadas.

Try to imagine the physical topography of their trip as the topography of Scripture, as illustrated in figure 12.1 viewed from right to left. The three small mountain ranges represent the three historic divisions of the Old Testament: the Law, the Writings, and the Prophets. In a sense, the writers of those books stood on those peaks and looked forward to what was coming. They could not clearly see everything that was ahead, yet they were empowered by the Spirit of God to prophesy the end of the exile, the defeat of evil, and the return of the King to Israel: "Concerning this salvation, the prophets, who spoke of the grace that was to come to you, searched intently and with the greatest care, trying to find out the time and circumstances to which the Spirit of Christ in them was pointing when he predicted the sufferings of Christ and the glories that would follow" (1 Peter 1:10–11).

The period of almost 400 years of silence from Malachi onward ended dramatically with John the Baptist's announcement of the arrival of the Lamb of God. In this scriptural topography, the incarnation of Jesus is parallel to the upthrusting Sierras. Jesus is the magnificent climax of Scripture, revealing the glory of God.

When our family traveled from Sacramento to our home, the foothills obscured the Sierra Nevadas to the east. Just before our freeway exit, we would drive over the crest of a small hill and catch our first glimpse of the glorious snow-covered Sierras. Each time I crossed that crest, I would involuntarily exclaim, "Look at those mountains!" It became a point of family humor, as repeatedly my reaction to the beauty and grandeur of the vista would well up in my spirit and need audible expression.

In the same way, Acts and the Epistles function as an outburst of joy and amazement. They look back at the glorious achievement of Christ and reflect on how the story of Jesus fulfilled God's eternal plan of creation and redemption. It is impossible to understand the message of the Epistles until we grasp the fullness of the message and mission of Jesus. For it is in the four Gospels that the story of Jesus and the power of God are most fully revealed. Yet Christians often bypass the Gospels, giving primary attention to the Epistles.

My reaction of awestruck astonishment at the beauty of the Sierras is akin to the original listeners' response to Jesus. In the accounts of Matthew, Mark, Luke, and John, these appear as the five immediate reactions of the original followers of Jesus:

- How great was his love for people, particularly the poor and the outcast.
- How astonishing were his healings, exorcisms, and acts of power.
- How surprising was Jesus' selection of disciples.
- How devastating was the pathos and horror of the crucifixion.
- How astounding was the shock of the resurrection.

The renewal and restoration of the American church must begin with an awe-inspiring encounter with Jesus, the crucified, resurrected, and ascended Messiah and Lord. That central focus on Jesus is critical to the health and growth of missional churches. For that to happen, we need clarity regarding the message and mission of Jesus, and then we need to let his words and actions shape the message and mission of the church. To that story we now turn.

Questions for Reflection and Discussion

1. Do you agree that much of our conversation about Jesus is second-hand? Why or why not?
2. What changes would we need to make to begin talking about Jesus in a first-person manner? What part of Scripture would we need to reference more? What would have to change in your own relationship with Jesus?

Please go to www.theamericanchurch.org/TACIC/Chapter12.htm for updates and additional information and resources for this chapter.

Part 4

ACTION

> *Paul has discovered, through years of actually doing it, that when you announce Jesus as the crucified and risen Lord of the world something* happens: *the new world which was born when Jesus died and rose again comes to fresh life in the hearts, minds and lifestyles of the listeners, or at least some of them. This isn't magic, though it must sometimes have felt like that. It is God's power at work, through the faithful announcement of his Son.*
>
> N. T. Wright[1]

Churches and leaders should begin to initiate the *action* stage after the stages of observation, evaluation, and introspection are accomplished.

This final stage is most profitable when churches align their behaviors and resources with their missional values. Missional churches anticipate how they are to participate in God's plan of creation and redemption for their community and world. When a church's behaviors and resources are disconnected from its missional values, it builds on a foundation of sand, losing its ministry potential. Fruitful action in a church or denomination includes rooting the necessary changes in Scripture, creating understanding and ownership at the grassroots level, then finding and empowering transformational leaders to guide the way forward.

The final four chapters suggest that action does not primarily proceed from relevance or strategy. Instead, the beginning point is the alignment of the church with the story of Scripture, particularly as revealed in the message and mission of Jesus. This becomes the message and mission of the church, which finds its culmination in an act of restoration by the Holy Spirit, so the church might again transform its culture.

Chapter 13

THE MESSAGE OF JESUS

What Is the Gospel?

When I travel and speak in different parts of the country, I ask my audience this simple question: "What is the gospel? How would you explain the message of the Christian faith?" As the listeners try to collect their thoughts in a cogent manner, someone usually says, "The gospel is that Jesus died for my sins so I can go to heaven." This statement is definitely true and of critical importance, but nonetheless reveals a narrow and limited understanding of the gospel. The scope of the gospel is much larger than that abbreviated summary.

So what is the gospel? My journey in answering this question came from a study of the four Gospels and from reading what has been for me the most personally significant and transformative book on Jesus, N. T. Wright's *Jesus and the Victory of God*.[1] As I read, I would stop every few pages, overwhelmed as Wright framed the provocative challenge of Jesus' words and actions in their historic context. I then read Wright's 700-page masterpiece a second time to absorb and integrate his framework for understanding Jesus. After that, I poured over the four Gospels and asked a series of questions:

- What were the most important messages of Jesus in the Gospels?
- What was the background of these messages, and how were they rooted in the Old Testament?
- What were the principal actions that Jesus performed?
- How did Jesus' everyday actions correlate with his greatest actions?

I found the answers to these questions in five central messages of Jesus, which correlate with five missions of Jesus. These create a framework that allows the gospel story to be more fully integrated into your life and the life of your church. While these thoughts are the fruit of my own study, they are in another sense not original with me — they are the historic message and mission of the church throughout the centuries. I simply hope this arrangement will allow Christians to see anew the whole gospel and help the American church return to its core focus and understanding of Jesus.

Message 1: To Forgive Our Sins and Reconcile Us with God

The first message of Jesus is that he came to save people from their sins. Three Old Testament stories of sin and sacrifice are crucial for understanding Jesus' message of forgiveness and reconciliation with God. The first is the story of Abraham, who brought his son Isaac to Mount Moriah as a sacrifice to God. At the last possible moment, God provided a substitute sacrifice for Isaac, in the form of a ram caught in a thicket.

Second is the Passover, which marked the beginning of the exodus from Egypt. The Israelites covered their doorposts and lintel with the blood of a lamb, which caused the angel of death to pass over the Israelites' homes. Every year modern Judaism commemorates this sacrifice that provided deliverance.

Third is the Day of Atonement, when the high priest sent a goat into the wilderness with the past year's sins of the people figuratively placed upon its head. These three images were burned in the Israelites' minds and hearts and reminded them that God required a sacrifice for sin, which the ritual sacrificial system of Israel reinforced daily.

Two prominent forgiveness stories in the ministry of Jesus are woven early into two of the Gospels. Each story reflects a powerful and complex human drama. In Mark 2 a paralyzed man's friends bring him to see Jesus. Because the house is overflowing with people, the friends dig through the roof and lower the paralyzed man to be in the presence of Jesus. The man obviously needs healing, but Jesus chooses first to forgive his sins and then proceeds to heal him.

The account in Luke 7 of the sinful woman who anoints Jesus' feet is a potent narrative in which Jesus interconnects love and forgiveness. The woman experiences deep forgiveness while Jesus reprimands his host, a Pharisee named Simon who looks down on the woman. Jesus uses a parable to illustrate the interrelationship between love and forgiveness, how one cannot survive without the other.

Zechariah's song at the beginning of Luke's gospel sums up the magnitude of forgiveness brought about by Jesus' ministry. Zechariah's son was John the Baptist, who prepared the way for Jesus, who came

> "To give his people the knowledge of salvation
> through the forgiveness of their sins,
> because of the tender mercy of our God,
> by which the rising sun will come to us from heaven

> to shine on those living in darkness
>> and in the shadow of death,
>> to guide our feet into the path of peace." (Luke 1:77–79)

In the book *Faces of Forgiveness*,[2] LeRon Schulz and Steve Sandage point out the necessity of placing forgiveness within the context of both a renewed relationship with God and with other people. Without the restoration of relationships, forgiveness is only a forensic reality—the guilt is gone, but there is no reconciliation in its place.

The church often perceives forgiveness as the only important message of Jesus. Perhaps the reason we most closely connect with forgiveness is that we are so aware of our own human failings and our need for daily pardon. However, the scope of Jesus' message was much greater than forgiveness alone.

Message 2: To Destroy the Power of Satan and Deliver People from Bondage

In Luke's gospel the defining story introducing the ministry of Jesus occurs in chapter 4, when he speaks at the synagogue in Nazareth. He opens the scroll and reads from Isaiah 61, describing the scope and purpose of his ministry with these words:

> "The Spirit of the Lord is on me,
>> because he has anointed me
>> to proclaim good news to the poor.
> He has sent me to proclaim freedom for the prisoners
>> and recovery of sight for the blind,
> to set the oppressed free,
>> to proclaim the year of the Lord's favor." (vv. 18–19)

The book of Isaiah played a principal role in the Jewish expectation of the coming Messiah and in Jesus' own self-definition. Because Israel's story was wrapped up in the history of its captivity in Egypt and Babylon, it was natural that freedom and release would be a theme of the promised Deliverer. The two most controversial actions of Jesus—both then and now—were healings and exorcisms. Both of those acts liberated oppressed people.

The second message of Jesus is to set people free from the power of Satan and deliver them from bondage. In both healing and exorcism, the goal was to restore people back to God's original creation of them. Jesus' words of healing always restored people to health. Lepers become clean. The blind receive sight. Dead people are brought back to life. Exorcism functioned similarly, reversing the evil inflicted upon the tormented.

Philip Jenkins, professor of history at Pennsylvania State University, describes the power of God at work through the second message of Jesus.

> Precious little is left of the New Testament after we purge all mention of angels, demons and spirits. Shorn of healing and miraculous cures, the four gospels would be a slim pamphlet indeed. For the earliest followers of Jesus — and presumably for Jesus himself — healing and exorcism were essential components of proclamation. In his acts of healing, Jesus was not just curing individuals, but trampling diabolical forces underfoot, and the signs and wonders represented visible and material tokens of Christ's victory over the real forces of evil.[3]

In his commentary on Luke, N. T. Wright adds: "Jesus' task is therefore not simply to teach people a new way of life; not simply to offer a new depth of spirituality; not simply to enable them to go to heaven after death. Jesus' task is to defeat Satan, to break his power, to win the decisive victory, which will open the way to God's new creation in which evil, and even death itself will be banished."[4] Jesus understood that there was a problem even deeper than sin, namely, a cosmic rebellion against the almighty God. There are forces of evil who oppose God at every opportunity by corrupting his good creation. Jesus' second message offered freedom and liberation from that oppressive bondage.

Message 3: To Change Hearts of Stone to Hearts of Flesh

Jesus often wrapped his message in the form of parables. Perhaps the most important for the gospel writers was the parable of the sower. Mark places this parable first in his gospel, and Matthew positions it first in his collection of parables in Matthew 13. This crucial placement reveals its importance in the teaching of Jesus. Matthew 13:1 – 9 tells the parable, while verses 18 – 23 reveal the explanation. Sandwiched in the middle is this enigmatic quote from Isaiah 6:9 – 10:

> "Though seeing, they do not see;
> > though hearing, they do not hear or understand....
> For this people's heart has become calloused;
> > they hardly hear with their ears,
> > and they have closed their eyes.
> Otherwise they might see with their eyes,
> > hear with their ears,
> > understand with their hearts
> and turn, and I would heal them." (vv. 13 – 15)[5]

Jesus seems to think that the primary problem with the listeners is that they have defective sensory apparatus. They see, but they cannot attach the right meaning to what they see; they hear, but they cannot interpret its significance. Can you imagine Jesus pleading in frustration, "For this people's heart has become calloused," followed by the impassioned appeal, "Otherwise they might see with their eyes, hear with their ears, understand with their hearts and turn, and I would heal them!"

The prophetic literature of the Old Testament, which looked forward to the end of exile and the coming of the Messiah, was the background for his challenge. "I will give you a new heart and put a new spirit in you; I will remove from you your heart of stone and give you a heart of flesh" (Ezek. 36:26). "This is the covenant I will make with the house of Israel after that time," declares the LORD. "I will put my law in their minds and write it on their hearts. I will be their God, and they will be my people" (Jer. 31:33).

Jesus' third message is that he came to change hearts of stone to hearts of flesh. This became a recurring theme in his teaching. The heart was "the inner life, the center of the personality and the place where God reveals himself."[6] Jesus used this term almost 50 times in the Gospels. People were in need of a heart transplant, as their hearts were spiritually dead. This call for spiritual transformation came as both a warning and an invitation.

How does spiritual formation take place in his followers? Throughout the Gospels, Jesus seems to encourage them to develop three types of hearts. The first is a heart of mercy: "But go and learn what this means: 'I desire mercy, not sacrifice'" (Matt. 9:13). The second is a heart of love: "A new command I give you: Love one another. As I have loved you, so you must love one another" (John 13:34). The third is a heart of faith: "I tell you, I have not found such great faith even in Israel" (Luke 7:9).

Message 4: To Treat People with Compassion and Justice as God's Loved Creation

Jesus interacted with people in a respectful and attentive manner. People were not a means to an end, but themselves had intrinsic value. "He causes his sun to rise on the evil and the good, and sends rain on the righteous and the unrighteous" (Matt. 5:45). The theological basis for this saying rested upon twin teachings from the Torah. Yahweh is revealed as a God who is righteous, is full of compassion, and requires justice. He also is the Creator who made all humans in his image. For Jesus, this understanding was shown in how he loved people, particularly the poor, the outcast, and the unimportant. The time and tenderness with which Jesus cared for the poor, the sick, and the marginalized is striking, showing his heart of mercy.

Jesus treated those he encountered as people created in the image of God, even though sin had cracked and broken that image. Human beings were created to live in fellowship with God and to be his special creation. Because of this, Jesus advocated righteousness, justice, compassion, and mercy for all, extending from our personal relationships to the social contracts that govern how nations treat their people and other nations.

Jesus expressed this clearly in his confrontations with the religious and political powers of his day. Matthew 23 is a compilation of seven statements spoken to the religious leaders, which begin "Woe to you." Here is the fourth woe: "Woe to you, teachers of the law and Pharisees, you hypocrites! You give a tenth of your spices — mint, dill and cumin. But you have neglected the more important matters of the law — justice, mercy and faithfulness. You should have practiced the latter, without neglecting the former" (vv. 23 – 24). The religious leaders were legalistically correct in the small matters but missed the critical relational categories of justice, mercy, and faithfulness.

Jesus also challenged political leaders, albeit in a more restrained manner. His mission was to complete his Father's business, which meant avoiding a premature death such as that of John the Baptist. His political confrontation culminated during Holy Week when Pilate and Herod interrogated Jesus. In both the religious and political confrontations, his righteous indignation came because of the disregard with which they treated others, especially marginalized people. He referred to these outcasts as "the lost sheep of Israel" (Matt. 10:6).

Message 5: To Invite and Summon Followers to Become the New People of God

Jesus welcomes, invites, calls, and summons followers to be the new people of God, to live in intimate connection with Jesus and with each other.[7] Some seem to think that the creation of a loyal community was the last thing on Jesus' mind, but the opposite is true. The calling of the twelve disciples reminded the original listeners of the twelve tribes of Israel and the calling of their nation. Jesus was not a solitary, itinerant teacher; instead, he created a community to embody the kingdom of God on earth. He did this by giving people a threefold call: "Repent ... believe the good news! ... Come, follow me" (Mark 1:15, 17). That call involves being taught by Jesus, learning to live in community, and being sent out to do kingdom work in the name of Jesus.

The motley crew that responded to the call was to be the picture of the new people of God. Social status was irrelevant to Jesus, previous reputation did not concern him, and he certainly was not leading a "men only" club (Luke 8:1 – 3). Jesus created a community that would carry on his message and mission to generation after generation, as was the pattern of Israel's call.

Two qualities were most important to healthy community life. The first was love: "By this everyone will know that you are my disciples, if you love one another" (John 13:35). Love was expressed in the type of people who were called, in the ministry actions of Jesus, and in the tender moments of intimacy, such as during Passover week before his death. "It was just before the Passover Festival. Jesus knew that the hour had come for him to leave this world and go to the Father. Having loved his own who were in the world, he loved them to the end" (John 13:1).

The second quality of Jesus' new community was bold truth. Jesus was very forthright in his speech with the disciples. He used truth to affirm them yet was painfully blunt when rebuke was needed. To Peter he said, "Get behind me, Satan! You do not have in mind the concerns of God, but merely human concerns" (Mark 8:33). This combination of love and bold truth creates the relational dynamics among his followers that produce authentic community and intimate relationships.

Questions for Reflection and Discussion

1. What part of this chapter personally influenced you the most? Why?
2. Has this chapter helped you to articulate the gospel? How?
3. When people primarily hear "secondhand" information about Jesus, how do you think that affects the message? How could Christians and the church use more first-person communication?

Please go to www.theamericanchurch.org/TACIC/Chapter13.htm for updates and additional information and resources for this chapter.

Chapter 14

THE MISSION OF JESUS

While words told the message of Jesus, his actions communicated his mission. The Gospels frequently refer to Jesus as a prophet. In the Old Testament tradition of prophets, their use of symbolic actions was perhaps even more important than their use of words. As a prophet, Jesus lived out each of the five messages through his day-to-day actions, and ultimately through his five decisive eternal actions.

Mission 1: To Be the Sacrifice for the Sins of the Whole World on the Cross

This first mission of Jesus was expressed in his extension of forgiveness to individuals. This forgiveness even included the soldiers who crucified him: "Father, forgive them, for they do not know what they are doing" (Luke 23:34). Moments later Jesus expressed the ultimate action of forgiveness and reconciliation with God by dying on the cross. C. S. Lewis described the ultimate destination this way: "God has paid us the intolerable compliment of loving us, in the deepest, most tragic, most inexorable sense."[1]

The cross is a powerful symbolic reality yet seldom is understood at its deepest level by many American Christians. Paul described the crucifixion this way: "But God chose the foolish things of the world to shame the wise; God chose the weak things of the world to shame the strong. God chose the lowly things of this world and the despised things—and the things that are not—to nullify the things that are, so that no one may boast before him.... For I resolved to know nothing while I was with you except Jesus Christ and him crucified" (1 Cor. 1:27–29; 2:2). In his earthly ministry, Jesus used his power to heal, forgive, and restore people. His ministry was extraordinarily effective, because Jesus possessed all authority and power. The surprise for Paul, though, was that the greatest work of Jesus occurred not in his strength, but in his moment of weakness. Jesus in his death fulfilled the Old Testament vision of the innocent and powerless sacrifice for sin.[2]

This became a theme of Paul's ministry: that God often accomplishes his greatest acts of power through weakness. This was why the crucifixion became the centerpiece of his preaching. Somehow the American church has not grasped this truth and often comes off to the world as triumphalist. We prefer a theology of glory rather than a theology of the cross. The church likes to glory in its power, but seldom does it glory in its weakness.

Mission 2: To Fight the Decisive Battle with Satan, Triumphing through the Grave

While the healings and the exorcisms illustrated the second message of Jesus, the grave was where Jesus' great actions won the victory over death and Satan. What exactly happened during the 39 hours between the death of Jesus at 3:00 p.m. on Good Friday and his resurrection at 6:00 a.m. on Easter morning? Scripture refers clearly to the grave as the time when Jesus dealt a deathblow to Satan, but a precise understanding of the details in those hours is difficult to discern.[3] Yet the Christian creeds and confessions have always affirmed that this was a spiritually critical period of time, when Jesus descended into Hades.

Catholic medieval theologians portrayed Jesus as a human spirit, descending into hell to triumph over Satan and his demons and to announce to them the deliverance of the believers who lived under the old covenant. The Lutheran Formula of Concord states, "It is enough to know that Christ went to hell, destroyed hell for all believers, and has redeemed them from the power of death, of the devil and of eternal damnation of the hellish jaws."[4] John Calvin wrote, "Therefore, by his wrestling hand to hand with the devil's power, with the dread of death, with the pains of hell, he was victorious and triumphed over them, that in death we may not now fear those things which our Prince has swallowed up."[5]

American Christianity's individualistic focus keeps Christians from seeing the larger cosmic significance of the work of Christ. Instead, American Christians often focus only on how that work personally benefits themselves. Yet the apostles' preaching and the whole New Testament reveal that from Jesus' birth until his resurrection, he was locked in a decisive confrontation with Satan. This conflict bookends the Synoptic Gospel narratives, with the temptation of Jesus at the beginning and the travail in the garden of Gethsemane and the betrayal by Judas at the end. Jesus triumphed through the cross and the grave, forever dooming Satan, destroying the power of death, and opening the gates of heaven.

Mission 3: To Be Authenticated as the Son of God through the Resurrection

Jesus challenged hard hearts by reminding listeners that the heart, not mere outward observances, is the gauge of a person's relationship with God. But the ultimate transformation from a heart of stone to a heart of flesh happened at the resurrection of Jesus. God restored Jesus' physical heart, which was dead, to life. The third mission of Jesus was to be physically authenticated as the Son of God through the power of his resurrection. "Who through the Spirit of holiness was appointed the Son of God in power by his resurrection from the dead: Jesus Christ our Lord" (Rom. 1:4).

According to N. T. Wright, the most powerful argument that the resurrection actually occurred was the transformation of the disciples' feelings of grief and hopelessness into their overwhelming need to proclaim the risen Christ. That the resurrection changed the disciples, turning them into bold witnesses of the mighty acts of God, is illustrated in Acts 4. "When they saw the courage of Peter and John and realized that they were unschooled, ordinary men, they were astonished and they took note that these men had been with Jesus" (v. 13).

Lewis expressed the resurrection this way in *The Lion, the Witch, and the Wardrobe*: "When a willing victim who had committed no treachery was killed in a traitor's stead, the table would crack and Death itself would start working backwards."[6] "Death working backwards" means that God was undoing the deadening power of the fall through the life-giving effect of the resurrection, creating new life in those who follow Jesus.

For early Christians, the resurrection confirmed that the words and the mission of Jesus were true. The resurrection is the event that secures and anchors the work of Christ. His resurrection was confirmation that a new world was indeed dawning. Paul used the image of resurrection when describing the new life in Christ. "We were therefore buried with him through baptism into death in order that, just as Christ was raised from the dead through the glory of the Father, we too may live a new life" (Rom. 6:4).

Mission 4: To Challenge Earthly Principalities and Powers through His Ascension

The fourth mission of Jesus is to challenge the earthly principalities and powers, both religious and political, by seeking to incarnate the values of the kingdom of God on earth. Jesus' words and actions paint a powerful picture of the countercultural manner in which Christians are to treat others. Consider the actions these words of Jesus call into being: "Love your enemies, do good to those who hate you, bless those who curse you, pray for those who mistreat you. If someone slaps you on one cheek, turn the other also. If someone takes your coat, do not withhold your shirt. Give to everyone who asks you, and if anyone takes what belongs to you, do not demand it back" (Luke 6:27–30). This response of love is radically different from our natural inclinations.

This fourth mission is critical to the nature of the church, because sin and selfishness cause humans to dominate others in destructive ways. Lewis described the results of that domination: "All that we call human history—money, poverty, ambition, war, prostitution, classes, empires, slavery—[is] the long terrible story of man trying to find something other than God which will make him happy."[7] The drive for happiness necessarily requires a drive for power over others, placing ourselves on the throne that God alone is to inhabit.

The ascension was Jesus' ultimate action of challenge to the earthly powers and principalities. The early church emphasized the ascension much more than does contemporary Christianity. Beginning with Peter's sermon on the day of Pentecost (Acts 2), the enthronement of the Messiah at the right hand of the Father was placed alongside his death, burial, and resurrection as being the critical episodes of the gospel story. The New Testament title of Jesus that is associated with the ascension is "Lord."

That title had a double meaning for early Christians, particularly for those living under the domination of the Roman Empire. Lord is the English translation of the Greek word that was used for "Yahweh," the unspeakable name of God in the Old Testament. In the Roman Empire, beginning with Augustus, the Caesars also used the title Lord to denote their absolute authority. So, when Paul and his companions traveled throughout the Roman Empire saying, "Jesus is Lord," it was not only a phrase reflecting the divinity of Jesus; their message was equally a challenge to the political and religious power of Caesar. In effect, Christians said to Caesar, "Jesus is Lord, and you are not!" When Paul's followers were arrested in Thessalonica, notice the charges against these Christians: "They are all defying Caesar's decrees, saying that there is another king, one called Jesus" (Acts 17:7).

In the New Testament the ascension is related to the future return of Christ in both judgment and final redemption. His return is the Blessed Hope of all Christians, the moment of final and eternal peace, rest, and restoration. The judgment day is the moment of absolute despair for those who chose an existence apart from the presence of the Lord Jesus. They will experience the tragic consequences of a life eternally separated from the love, grace, and mercy of God.

Mission 5: To Establish His Church as the New People of God through the Day of Pentecost

The final mission of Jesus was to call into being the new people of God. This was not to replace the people of God of the Old Testament, but rather to fulfill the Abrahamic covenant, which used faith to mark out the people of God under both the old and new covenants. While Jesus acted this out in his ministry by calling forth a group of disciples and followers, it reached its culmination on the day of Pentecost.

That day was marked by two definite developments for the people of God. First, it happened in a diverse crowd made up of people from throughout the known world. God's church was meant to be a multiethnic people. Second, the day of Pentecost brought the powerful arrival of the promised indwelling Holy Spirit, the one who would, through the church, do the work of God in the world, taking the place of the ascended Jesus.

How Important Are All Five Messages and Missions?

Figure 14.1 is a visual summary of the message and mission of Jesus.

There is an elegant symmetry here — the five messages of Jesus are correlated with the daily actions of Jesus living out each message, and finally by Jesus performing the five "ultimate actions" that eternally changed the world. The messages on the left side of the chart cannot happen without the actions on the right side. We cannot have forgiveness of sins and reconciliation with God without the cross. We cannot be set free from bondage without the work Jesus accomplished in the grave. We cannot live a new life in Christ without experiencing the firstfruits of his resurrection. We cannot truly be advocates for compassion, mercy, and justice without acknowledging that Jesus is Lord. We cannot be the new people of God unless we experience the day of Pentecost.

In the apostolic preaching, all five ultimate actions are frequently mentioned together. For example, in Peter's sermon in Acts 2, the cross, the grave, the resurrection, and the ascension receive meaning within the context of the day of Pentecost. These five ultimate actions of Jesus also parallel the liturgical cycle from Holy Week through Pentecost. The apostles could not stop looking back at Jesus and those great mountains of grace and truth; they could not take their eyes off the achievement of Jesus. In his book *The Freedom of Simplicity*, Richard Foster quotes Mother Teresa of Calcutta, "Pray for me, that I not loosen my grip on the hands of Jesus even under the guise of ministering to the poor." He then comments, "That is our first task: To grip the hands of Jesus with such intensity that we are obliged to follow his lead, to seek first his Kingdom."[8]

The Message The Good News That Jesus Came to Speak	The Mission The Good News That Jesus Came to Act Out	The Ultimate Mission The Eternal Actions of Jesus	The Message and Mission of the Church
He came:	He came:		
1. To forgive our sins and reconcile us with God	1. To be the sacrifice for the sins of the whole world	1. The Cross	1. Evangelism
2. To destroy the power of Satan and deliver people from bondage	2. To personally fight the deciding battle with Satan and triumph through the grave	2. The Grave	2. Ministry
3. To change hearts of stone to hearts of flesh	3. To be authenticated as the Son of God through the resurrection	3. The Resurrection	3. Spiritual Formation
4. To treat people with compassion, mercy, and justice, as God's loved creation	4. To challenge the earthly principalities and powers through his ascension	4. The Ascension	4. Love
5. To invite and summon followers to become the new people of God	5. To establish his church as the new people of God on the day of Pentecost	5. The Day of Pentecost	5. True Community

One of the famous musicians of historic Celtic Christianity was Caedmon. The Venerable Bede (672–735), author of the most important history of the early church in England, commented about him:

> There was in the Monastery of this Abbess a certain brother particularly remarkable for the Grace of God, who was wont to make religious verses, so that whatever was interpreted to him out of Scripture, he soon after put the same into poetical expressions of much sweetness and humility in English, which was his native language. By his verse the minds of many were often excited to despise the world, and to aspire to heaven.[9]

Even though Caedmon was illiterate, he would have someone read to him from Scripture and then spend the night trying to form those thoughts into the words and music of a song that would tell the story of Jesus. Everyone was amazed at the great beauty and power of his songs. The following poem of Caedmon demonstrates the historic church's clarity of focus on Jesus.

Caedmon's Song (Part 1)
Teach us again the greatest story ever told.
In time, the Carpenter began to travel
In every village challenging the people
To leave behind their selfish ways,
Be washed in living water,
And let God be their King.

You plundered death,
And made its jailhouse shudder—
Strode into life
To meet your startled friends.

I have a dream,
That all the world will meet you,
And know you, Jesus, in your living power.
That someday soon all people will hear your story
And hear it in a way they understand.[10]

How will our world meet Jesus? How will they experience his living power? Who will communicate this story? How will they hear it in a way they understand? That is the subject of the next chapter, the message and mission of the church.

Questions for Reflection and Discussion

1. Which mission of Jesus has increased in importance for you? Why?
2. What would it mean for you to act out each of these missions through your personal actions?

3. What would it mean for your church to act out each of these missions through its ministries?
4. Time spent meditating on the actions of Jesus can be a deeply transformative exercise. How can your church balance the emphasis on words with an equal demonstration of actions?

*Please go to www.theamericanchurch.org/TACIC/Chapter14.htm
for updates and additional information and resources for this chapter.*

Chapter 15

THE MESSAGE AND MISSION OF THE CHURCH

As I write this chapter, I am sitting in a coffee shop one block from the Reichstag, looking out at Berlin's Brandenburg Gate. A statue of the Quadriga, with the Greek goddess of peace riding triumphantly on a chariot, sits atop the gate. Two memorable phrases spoken by American presidents at the Brandenburg Gate have become famous. *"Ich bin ein Berliner"* ("I am a Berliner") was the phrase delivered by President John F. Kennedy on June 26, 1963, shortly after East Germany erected the Berlin Wall: "Two thousand years ago the proudest boast was *'civis romanus sum'* ['I am a Roman citizen']. Today, in the world of freedom, the proudest boast is *'Ich bin ein Berliner.'* ... All free men, wherever they may live, are citizens of Berlin, and, therefore, as a free man, I take pride in the words *'Ich bin ein Berliner!'"*

Unfortunately, Kennedy was unaware that a Berliner is also a pastry, specifically a jelly donut. His improper inclusion of the indefinite article *ein* ("a") actually changed the meaning from "I am a Berliner" to "I am a jelly donut," but the crowd understood his intent!

On June 12, 1987, President Ronald Reagan gave his most famous speech at the Brandenburg Gate, insisting, "General Secretary Gorbachev, if you seek peace, if you seek prosperity for the Soviet Union and Eastern Europe, if you seek liberalization: Come here to this gate! Mr. Gorbachev, open this gate! Mr. Gorbachev, tear down this wall!" Two years later, on November 4, 1989, a million protesters gathered in East Berlin, demanding the destruction of the wall, and in five days the wall was breached forever.

Berlin is an iconic epicenter of the two greatest evils of the twentieth century, Nazism and Communism. These two movements were responsible for the deaths of more than 100 million people during those 100 years. As I leave the Brandenburg Gate, I walk past the Reichstag and experience two contrasting impressions. First, I remember the film images of Adolf Hitler addressing the impassioned crowds near where I am now standing. Second, on a wrought iron fence surrounding the grounds of the Reichstag, I see six crosses attached to its bars, honoring martyrs killed trying to escape over the Berlin Wall to freedom. I stroll along the picturesque river walk beyond the Reichstag while listening on an iPod to my friend, Christian musician Lincoln Brewster. Playing is a beautiful instrumental version of the song "Here I Am to Worship," with a heart-wrenching guitar lead, supplemented by strings and a background choir.

My emotions and senses are swirling with the worship of God, the beauty of Berlin in springtime, and the horror of humanity's cruelty, all intermingling. Both of my parents' lives were profoundly affected by events that emanated from this place. I think of my late father, who received a Purple Heart for wounds received in the Battle of the Bulge; I remember my 91-year-old mother, whose first husband was shot down over Germany, captured, and killed during World War II. I wonder, *How can a Christian witness survive in the midst of such iniquity? How does the church speak and act out the gospel in the midst of overwhelming evil?* The mix of beauty, wickedness, and spirituality presses heavily on my spirit.

Yet it is precisely the task of Christ's church to live in the middle of that dissonance. The church is meant to herald the Good News in the midst of the beauty, pain, and suffering of our world. Jesus' message of hope requires a tangible presence, a physical body, to retell and reenact the story. The story requires physical hands and feet and words to translate love from intangible idea to personal touch. The story requires a committed community seeking God's reign on earth as in heaven.

While the projections of the American church found in chapter 11 are discouraging, the church has a history of restoration when confronted with daunting challenges. There is hope — if Christians begin to live out a deeper expression of the gospel, if the church acts out Paul's mission to the Gentile world, and if God performs his work of restoration through the Holy Spirit. This optimism is ultimately based on the defining verse of Romans: "I am not ashamed of the gospel, because it is the power of God that brings salvation to everyone who believes" (1:16).

This powerful gospel cannot and did not come disembodied. Just as the coming of Jesus incarnated the mission of God, so the church is the incarnate people of God continuing that mission. How can the church be rebuilt and restored so that it becomes what God intended his church to be? There is a simple yet profound answer: the message and mission of Jesus must become the message and mission of the church. The words of Jesus must become the words of the church. Jesus' actions must be continually reenacted by the church.

The First Message and Mission of the Church

The church is to proclaim the message of forgiveness in Christ, which produces reconciliation with God. This is called *evangelism*. Evangelism happens publicly and personally when people encounter the love and truth of Jesus.

When a person responds to the call of Christ, both Scripture and Christian experience indicate that new birth takes place. "If anyone is in Christ, the new creation has come: The old has gone, the new is here!" (2 Cor. 5:17). The word *conversion* denotes the reality of sins forgiven and reconciliation with God in the life of the new Christian. The death of Jesus on the cross ended our enmity with God, restoring the possibility of a right relationship with him. "He has rescued us from the dominion of darkness and brought us into the kingdom of the Son he loves, in whom we have redemption, the forgiveness of sins" (Col. 1:13–14). Forgiveness of sins and reconciliation with God can only take place at the invitation of God himself. The saving response is to say yes to God through faith in Christ. A primary task of the church is to proclaim this good news.

God has historically used both public proclamation and intimate conversation to communicate the message of Jesus to people. "How, then, can they call on the one they have not believed in? And how can they believe in the one of whom they have not heard? And how can they hear without someone preaching to them? And how can anyone preach unless they are sent? As it is written: 'How beautiful are the feet of those who bring good news!'" (Rom. 10:14–15). Each church must discover the best way to bring this good news to their community and culture. In the United States, unfortunately, most Christian churches are quite ineffectual at evangelism. Churches that proclaim Christ's message and mission well are marked by loving relationships with those who are not yet Christians, a strong passion to see them experience a changed life. These churches pursue a relentless commitment to experimentation in the search for fruitful pathways of evangelism. This process is always most effective when it occurs through personal relationships, so that conversion can naturally transition into discipleship.

Evangelism is more difficult today than it was 20 years ago. Lon Allison, the director of the Billy Graham Center for Evangelism says, "The distance between pre-Christians and faith in Christ is a much longer distance than it was in previous generations."[1] Yet many churches I work with have seen amazing life-change in response to the proclamation of the gospel.

Throughout this book I have told stories from a wide variety of denominations and backgrounds to illustrate how these ideas come to life

in the American church. In this chapter I will use some of the new churches I have personally worked with to illustrate how the church speaks and acts out its message and mission. Pastor Craig Groeschel of Life Covenant Church (lifechurch.tv) in Edmund, Oklahoma, was an associate pastor at First United

Methodist Church in downtown Oklahoma City at the time of the Oklahoma City bombing. On the morning of April 19, 1995, Craig was away from his office when a truck bomb exploded at 9:02 a.m. across the street at the Murrah Federal Building, killing 156 people. The blast severely damaged the historic First United Methodist Church building, blew out the windows above Craig's desk, and might have critically injured or killed him if he had been there. Feeling that God had spared his life, Craig was encouraged to follow the example of his role model, Billy Graham. Through planting a new church, Craig has used his gift of evangelism to invite others to follow Jesus. Thousands have become Christians in the first 10 years of Life Church's ministry.

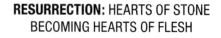

RESURRECTION: HEARTS OF STONE
BECOMING HEARTS OF FLESH

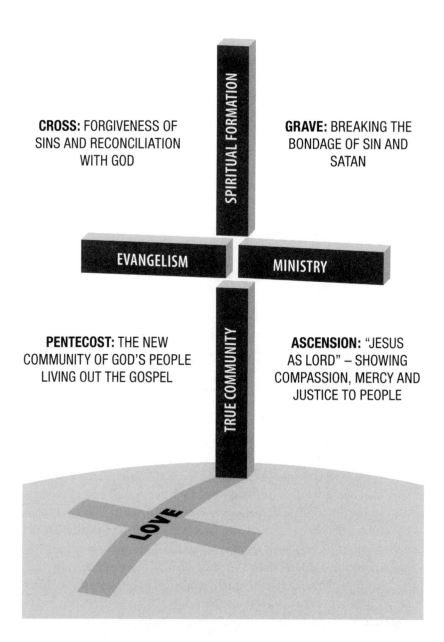

CROSS: FORGIVENESS OF
SINS AND RECONCILIATION
WITH GOD

SPIRITUAL FORMATION

GRAVE: BREAKING THE
BONDAGE OF SIN AND
SATAN

EVANGELISM

MINISTRY

PENTECOST: THE NEW
COMMUNITY OF GOD'S PEOPLE
LIVING OUT THE GOSPEL

TRUE COMMUNITY

ASCENSION: "JESUS
AS LORD" – SHOWING
COMPASSION, MERCY AND
JUSTICE TO PEOPLE

LOVE

The Second Message and Mission of the Church

The church is to help people break the bonds that hold and oppress them, helping restore in them God's original creation. This is called *ministry.* This happens through prayer, healing, and practical help that leads to a restored image of God.

A currently held Christian myth is that when people become Christ-followers, all their problems will disappear. The truth is that the corrosive effects of the sinful aspects of culture, unhealthy family systems, destructive experiences, and the propensity toward sin and selfishness continue after conversion. Ministry is needed both to heal these wounds and to help restore God's original creation in people. This is why Christians pray for each other; this is why we pray for healing, both physical and emotional; this is why people need practical help—wisdom applied to their life challenges. The church exists to help people understand whom God created them to be and to facilitate the restoration of the image of God in them.

Every person needs to receive this kind of ministry, because every person needs to experience freedom and release. All people need to be set free from whatever holds them in bondage, whatever distorts the image of God in them. Liberation is not meant to result in exultation of the self; rather, it allows people to humbly live out their identity as children of God. Paul expresses this in Romans 8:19–21: "The creation waits in eager expectation for the children of God to be revealed. For the creation was subjected to frustration, not by its own choice, but by the will of the one who subjected it, in hope that the creation itself will be liberated from its bondage to decay and brought into the freedom and glory of the children of God."

The biblical word for redemption comes from the slave trade: to redeem slaves was to buy them back from their owners and then set them free. Spiritual redemption took place through the achievement of Jesus in the grave, where he vanquished the power of Satan. Because of this, Christians are "bought back" and set free to live under God, so that God's original image and purpose may be restored in them. The church is to be an agent of that redemption. "Ministry" is the work of the church, customized for each person, to lead them into freedom.

Life House Covenant Church in Longmont, Colorado, is a new church that is especially effective at redemptive ministry. Most attendees have had a caustic experience of Christianity while also being caught in a life of external addictions. Here is the church's vision: "We intend to be the dwelling place of God through whom He offers shelter to the unloved, freedom for the bound, and restoration to the broken, that the world may know that Jesus is Lord." This new church lives out this second message and mission in its day-to-day ministry to those who need healing and liberation.

The Third Message and Mission of the Church

The church is to help people live a new, resurrected life in Christ, through the filling and empowerment of the Holy Spirit. This is called *spiritual formation*. Spiritual formation happens through teaching, Bible study, the spiritual disciplines, and mentoring.

The death of Jesus would have no significance in history without the resurrection. The disciples would not have given their lives for a dead Messiah. This is why Paul says in 1 Corinthians 15:17–19, "If Christ has not been raised, your faith is futile; you are still in your sins. ... If only for this life we have hope in Christ, we are to be pitied more than all others." The resurrection was God's exclamation that a new world was beginning—one that promised life rather than death, hope rather than despair, re-creation rather than decay. The church is to live out that promise of new life, becoming a source of joy, energy, and hope to this world.

Spiritual formation is the resurrected life of Jesus at work inside a Christian, which transforms his or her life. Spiritual formation takes place in many different venues of a church. It occurs through large group, Spirit-inspired teaching and preaching that helps Christians understand how God wants to form their hearts. Small groups can be an equally powerful setting, allowing people to dialogue with each other as they process Scripture and apply it to their lives. The spiritual disciplines use historic Christian practices such as Scripture reading, prayer, and fasting to create habits that slow us down, invite the presence of God, and form us into the image of Christ. Spiritual direction is the process of being spiritually formed under the gentle, prayerful questions and insights offered by a trained mentor.

Spiritual transformation happens through a process of deconstruction followed by reconstruction. We need to dismantle the false and destructive worldviews that we learned from our culture, family of origin, personal experience, selfishness, and sin nature. We need to construct new worldviews and stories based on our new identity as members of the kingdom of God. The reason so many Christians are unchanged by the gospel is that they have not worked through this two-step process in their lives. This is the great void of "cultural" Christianity, in which the message is only absorbed skin-deep and never reaches the deep places of a person's being.

In *Jesus and the Victory of God*, N. T. Wright speaks of the power of parables for spiritual formation:

> The parables functioned the way all (good) stories function, by inviting hearers into the world of the story. They were designed to break open worldviews and to create new ones, encouraging listeners to identify

themselves in terms of the narrative. To see the point of the parable was to make a judgment on oneself.

The parables were therefore, like the apocalyptic genre to which in some senses they belong, subversive stories, told to articulate and bring to birth a new way of being the people of God.[2]

The words and actions of Jesus have the power to deconstruct our natural earthly worldview—first we identify with the narrative, then we come under the judgment of its words and actions. Simultaneously, Jesus' words and actions teach us a new way of living, in which the new values and actions of God's kingdom are incorporated and lived out in our lives. While all parts of Scripture are "God-breathed," the words and actions of Jesus have a special ability to deconstruct and reconstruct the human heart. That the words and actions of the Son of God are this powerful should not be unexpected.

Abbey Way Covenant Church in Minneapolis is a new church plant that uses the historic Rule of St. Benedict to provide a model of life together. They use this monastic model to foster intimate relationships and a commitment to common spiritual practices. The three-hour Sunday service begins with a meal, followed by intergenerational learning activities, and a worship service centered in the sacrament of the Lord's Supper. Among the commitments a family or an individual makes to enter this community is to consistently participate in a "chapter house" (a small group), pray the Divine Hours twice a day (focused Scripture readings and prayer), and be in a spiritual direction group once a month. These habits and rhythms are intended to create true disciples within the context of a committed community.

The Fourth Message and Mission of the Church

The church is to be a compassionate countercultural force in the community, nation, and world. This is called *love*. Love happens locally, regionally, and globally through compassion, mercy, righteousness, and justice.

Christians are to seek and act out creative expressions of compassion for all people. The importance of compassion, mercy, and justice as a part of the gospel is deeply rooted in the history of all four major Christian groups—mainline, Catholic, evangelical, and orthodox. In the United States, Christian organizations founded most hospitals, orphanages, food pantries, and homes for the elderly, homeless, and abused. In the early days of the modern evangelical movement, compassion was an expected part of the church's expression of Christianity. Unfortunately, in the last generation that commitment has diminished among evangelical churches.

The English words *righteousness* and *justice* are translations of the same Greek word, *dikaiosyne*, which speaks of God's faithfulness to his intention for creation as well as his covenant with Abraham. The ascended Jesus, the Lord of that *dikaiosyne*, is to be lived out in this world by the church. We are to be advocates of justice, righteousness, compassion, and mercy for all.

Rodney Stark wrote a powerful book on the social history of early Christianity titled *The Rise of Christianity*. One reviewer of that book commented, "Another important contributor to Christian growth was the role of epidemics, especially the great epidemic ('Plague of Galen') of the second century. Stark suggests that the philosophy the Christians practiced, of selflessness and caring for the sick, created in the Christian community a stronghold of mutual aid, which resulted in a superior survival rate to that of the Greco-Roman pagans."[3] This expression of mercy and compassion was natural for true followers of Jesus, the one who expressed profound concern and love for the sick.

In recent years the evangelical church has primarily used "attractional" strategies of outreach, inviting people to "come and see." This was a method Jesus used in calling his first disciples (John 1:35–51). In the world today, missional churches should utilize "incarnational" outreach as well, demonstrating the gospel by serving people in their community.

The city of Detroit is perhaps the most challenging urban environment in the nation. So when Harvey Carey, the associate pastor of one of the largest African American churches in Chicago, announced that God wanted him to plant a new church in the city of Detroit, everyone was surprised. Citadel of Faith Covenant Church has taken root in a neighborhood that has a median household income of $14,000 a year. Such poverty brings with it hopelessness and a variety of social problems. This new church has a holistic theology that causes it to be an agent for compassion, mercy, righteousness, and justice in the city.[4] This past summer they initiated an urban camping project. Drug houses were identified in the neighborhood, and the men and boys of the church pitched tents in the street outside of those houses, vowing to stay there until the drug dealers left that neighborhood. In a similar manner, Sanctuary Covenant Church in Minneapolis started a Community Development Corporation at the same time as the church was founded, creating a major force for justice and compassion in the economically challenged north side of the city. For both of these churches, their commitment to the gospel message of Christ requires that actions of justice and compassion are central to their ministry.

The Fifth Message and Mission of the Church

The church is to be God's community of broken-yet-healing people that provides love, support, and accountability for each other. This is called *true community*. True community happens through love, worship, fellowship, feasting, and Holy Communion, and multiplies through church planting.

The growth of the early church was intimately connected with the love that emanated from this new community of Christians. Historian John Ferguson described the power of Christian love: "It was … in the way of love revealed, in the witness of community (*koinonia*), in a fellowship which took in Jew and Gentile, slave and free, men and women, and whose solid practicality in their care for the needy won admiration." Love, fellowship, and hospitality to all became a powerful attractor to the early Christian faith.

The power of Christian community is realized when unconditional love and bold truth become the two pillars of community life, creating an irresistible authenticity. In the isolated, individualized lives of Americans, true community fulfills a deeply felt need. Five ingredients seem to contribute most to true community: love, worship, fellowship, feasting, and the celebration of the Lord's Supper.

A recent emphasis of many churches is the recovery of the historic Christian practice of hospitality.[5] What does hospitality mean for your church, and how can each family extend hospitality to their circle of influence? In Middle Eastern culture, food was the center of relational interactions. The natural extension of the Lord's Supper into a common meal exhibited the early Christian's understanding of the power of feasting and hospitality.

In the dominant Roman culture, a person practiced hospitality to gain standing with people of influence. By contrast, in the early history of the church, hospitality was embodied in a simple shared meal. The early church showed hospitality especially to people who did not have influence, who could not repay the gift. It demonstrated God's love for them. Jesus' powerful parables and teachings were the impetus for this profound countercultural behavior. Christian hospitality reveals the difference between self-serving and self-sacrificing motivations.

Church planting is a natural expression of the desire to reproduce irresistible Christian communities. In a local congregation, Christians experience the love of God and the transforming power of community. That transformation inspires them to invite others to experience the power of the whole gospel. The original Christian method for multiplying true community is to start new congregations.

Life Covenant Church in Torrance, California, is a young church that attempts to live out the whole gospel. This objective flows out of its deep commitment to live life together as a community of love and truth. Only a little over two years old, this demographically youthful church of 125 attendees has raised $80,000 above its general budget to help start two new churches in the Los Angeles area. At the same time, they raised an additional $25,000 to provide microeconomic loans in Mozambique. This is not a church of the rich — rather, they have an extraordinary desire to be generous with God's gifts, for the benefit of the world.

Bayside Covenant Church in Granite Bay, California, is a new church that quickly became a megachurch. Instead of focusing only on its own development, they have started six new churches in the greater Sacramento area in the last two years, each targeting a different geographic, cultural/ ethnic, or economic community. These new churches have quickly taken root and grown strong in their communities because of Bayside's ability to support them through coaching and team development. This model is the best example of how a megachurch can expand its influence beyond its own local community, by becoming a diverse group of churches focused on leadership development and missional expansion.

When asked by *Christianity Today* why Bayside had started other churches instead of focusing on becoming a stadium-sized megachurch, pastor Ray Johnston had a simple answer. He said that by starting new churches, Bayside could help more people experience the mission and the message of Jesus. He drew on a comparison to the fast-food industry to make his point: "You can either build one mega-McDonald's or a bunch of small ones," he told *Christianity Today*. "The question is which will feed more people."

How Many Messages and Missions Are Necessary?

Should a Christian incorporate all of the messages and missions in his or her personal life? Should a church incorporate all of the messages and missions in their communal life? Or is it simply natural to focus on one or two to the neglect of the others? My conviction is that each message and mission is at the heart of the gospel. All five were central to Jesus' message, and all were enacted by Jesus in dramatic ways. Likewise, in emulating Christ, all Christians and all churches should understand and live out the whole gospel. These five messages and missions are akin to the five senses. A person can survive with four senses, or even three or two, but fullness of life is best experienced when all five senses are fully engaged. Then the experience of sight, sound, taste, touch, and smell interact to amplify our experiences into a full-orbed expression of life as God intended. In the same way, living out all five messages and missions of Jesus allows Christians and churches to express authentically and completely the good news of God.

Unfortunately, many churches focus on only one message and downplay the importance of the others. For some churches, the message of evangelism is all-important, while the other four go unmentioned. Other churches live out the spiritual formation message but give little attention to the other messages. The whole gospel encompasses all five messages and missions, and the power of the gospel is found in living out all five together. When the church practices all five together, the result is accelerated spiritual growth in each member's personal life and greater completeness in the church's ministry.

Living out the five messages and missions holistically can also serve as a response to the emerging generation's critique of American Christianity. Younger Christians look at contemporary Christianity and make these observations about the shortcomings of our current religious practices:

- Your Christianity is too "plastic." Christians pretend to live fault-less lives; we need more authenticity.
- Your Christianity is too focused on the practical; we need deeper spirituality.
- Your Christianity is too individualistic; we need to learn to live in community.
- Your Christianity is too self-serving, focusing all your time and money on fulfilling your own needs. We need Christians who will live, love, and give for the last, the least, and the lost.

These critiques reflect the younger generation's intuition that we need a holistic return to the fullness of the gospel. The recovery of the spiritual power of the Christian church will come when we take their critique seriously. We are to daily live in forgiveness and reconciliation with God and to spread that message of the achievement of Jesus to all who have not experienced new birth. We are to let God set us free from the habits that hold us in bondage and minister to people who need that touch of re-creation. We are to experience new life in Christ, manifested by a renewed heart of mercy, faith, and love, empowered by the Holy Spirit. We are to be leaders in the struggle for justice, righteousness, mercy, and compassion for all. We are to live these out in a local community of Christ, which we call the church, learning to live in love and truth as we seek to expand the kingdom of God both spiritually and physically.

Paul summarized the connection between Christ and the church in Ephesians 1:22–23: "God placed all things under his feet and appointed him to be head over everything for the church, which is his body, the fullness of him who fills everything in every way."

The Wineskins of the Gospel

How should the church be structured to most effectively live out these messages and missions? While this chapter cannot fully answer this question, the gospel narratives give a clue through the teaching of Jesus about wineskins: "Neither do people pour new wine into old wineskins. If they do, the skins will burst; the wine will run out, and the wineskins will be ruined. No, they pour new wine into new wineskins, and both are preserved" (Matt. 9:17).

A wineskin protects and preserves the precious wine. The wineskin is nothing in itself—the wine is everything—yet the wine cannot be kept or transported without the outward physical container. In the same way, the structure of each church needs to be a flexible and supple wineskin, protecting and preserving its contents, the good wine, which is Jesus.

Over the centuries, people have been understandably frustrated with church structures that become overly institutionalized, bureaucratic, and calcified. Sometimes the extreme reaction to institutionalism is to reject all structure. Yet if a church is to last for generations, it will need to create a strong, flexible wineskin for itself. The challenge is not to allow the structure to overshadow or detract from the precious wine of the gospel.

When I work with a new church, I ask them two questions: (1) How can your church exude the very life of Jesus through your life together and in your community? and (2) How can this new church be started in such a manner that its ministry will last 100 years, changing lives in your community for generations? A church needs to dwell continually within a resilient wineskin that will remain flexible and reveal and preserve the precious wine.

These last four chapters have dealt with how the church may be rebuilt. However, one critical ingredient remains if God's work is to be complete. That ingredient is akin to the role of yeast in the baking of bread. That final element is *restoration*, the spiritual and supernatural work of God. When the story of Jesus is told and lived out, and when the church is creating pathways for fruitful ministry, then the stage is set for the movement of the Holy Spirit to breathe new life into his church.

Questions for Reflection and Discussion

1. Which of the five messages and missions of the church resonates with you? Which one has the least emotional connection?
2. Do you think a church should try to live out all five messages and missions? What would that mean for your church?

Please go to www.theamericanchurch.org/TACIC/Chapter15.htm for updates and additional information and resources for this chapter.

Chapter 16

THE RESTORATION OF THE AMERICAN CHURCH

The American church needs to be "forever building." Building is the church's response to God's missional promptings. But the greatest need of the church is "being restored," which is a spiritual and supernatural act of God.

The story of Moses, Joshua, and Caleb provides us with the model of observation, evaluation, introspection, and action. Unfortunately, the faithless response of Israel in the introspection stage kept the action stage from occurring. The Pentateuch ends with the poignant picture of Moses ascending Mount Nebo in Deuteronomy 34. As he reaches the summit and fixes his eyes beyond the Jordan River, he sees the Promised Land for the first time. God then says to him, "I have let you see it with your eyes, but you will not cross over into it" (v. 4). And so Moses, the greatest prophet of Israel (v. 10) until the one who would come from Nazareth, dies on Mount Nebo, never to place his feet on the Promised Land.

Joshua is chosen to replace Moses and is anointed to lead Israel into the final stage of action, the entering of the Promised Land. The pivotal point of the book of Joshua comes after the Jordan River is crossed, but precedes the fall of Jericho.

> Now when Joshua was near Jericho, he looked up and saw a man standing in front of him with a drawn sword. Joshua went up to him and asked, "Are you for us or for our enemies?"
>
> "Neither," he replied, "but as commander of the army of the Lord I have now come." Then Joshua fell facedown to the floor in reverence, and asked him, "What message does my Lord have for his servant?" The commander of the Lord's army replied, "Take off your sandals, for the place where you are standing is holy." And Joshua did so. (5:13–15)

In this theophany,[1] the commander of the Lord's army gives a shocking response to Joshua's question. His reply, "neither," is unexpected and reveals that the presence of God is not to aid the Israelites or the Canaanites, but rather to accomplish God's overarching purpose and story in our world. In the midst of Joshua's action, God sends a divine interruption. The presence of God renders him prostrate before the Almighty. For the rest of his life this encounter reminds Joshua that he is not just engaged in human activity, but was participating in the very work of God. Only that powerful presence of God can restore the American church.

Ezekiel 37 contains an equally compelling story, that of the spiritual and supernatural action of God's restoration of his people. God showed the prophet Ezekiel a valley of dry bones. While in Berlin, in many ways a place of spiritual desolation, I heard the following Scripture slowly read aloud in a worship service as an electric guitar created the aural sensation of being in the valley of dry bones.

> The hand of the LORD was on me, and he brought me out by the Spirit of the Lord and set me in the middle of a valley; it was full of bones. He led me back and forth among them, and I saw a great many bones on the floor of the valley, bones that were very dry. He asked me, "Son of Man, can these bones live?"
>
> I said, "Sovereign LORD, you alone know."
>
> Then he said to me, "Prophesy to these bones and say to them, 'Dry bones, hear the word of the LORD! This is what the Sovereign LORD says to these bones: I will make breath enter you, and you will come to life. I will attach tendons to you and make flesh come upon you and cover you with skin; I will put breath in you, and you will come to life. Then you will know that I am the LORD.'"
>
> So I prophesied as I was commanded.... "'Come, breath, from the four winds and breathe into these slain, that they may live.'"... and breath entered them; they came to life and stood up on their feet—a vast army. (vv. 1–10)

In Germany, in Canada, and in the United States and all around the world, God's heart is to resurrect and restore a vast multitude of people, transformed by the message and mission of Jesus to minister to and serve our world. While the future of Western Christianity at the present looks bleak, the gospel always offers the hope of restoration and resurrection.

Poet E. B. White wrote the introduction for *Onward and Upward in the Garden*, a collection of columns by his late wife, Katherine S. White. He described her October ritual as she neared the end of her life:

> [She] would open dozens of brown paper packages of new bulbs and a basketful of old ones, ready for the intricate interment.... The small, hunched-over figure, her studied absorption in the implausible notion that there would be yet another spring, oblivious to the ending of her own days, which she knew perfectly well was near at hand, sitting there with

her detailed chart under those dark skies in the dying October, calmly plotting the resurrection.[2]

She lovingly planted each bulb, knowing she would never see them bloom into their springtime glory. By faith she knew that her work would one day produce a miracle of God. Her labor stands as a testimony to the hope of God's life-giving power. The desire for God's infusion of life is found in this historic cry of the church:

> Most powerful Holy Spirit,
> come down upon us and subdue us.
> From heaven,
> where the ordinary is made glorious
> and glory seems but ordinary,
> bathe us with the brilliance of your light,
> like dew.[3]

A Final Memory

My time in Berlin was coming to an end. I was there as an observer at a church planting conference of the European Federation of Free Evangelical Churches. Before we were to fly home, two colleagues and I spent the weekend exploring downtown Berlin. Between our hotel and the Brandenburg Gate was the Memorial to the Murdered Jews of Europe, located on the former site of the Reichministerial Gardens and the air raid bunker of Nazi minister of propaganda Joseph Goebbels. Designed by New York architect Peter Eisenman, the memorial was built with 2,711 blocks of dark gray concrete, the surface of each three by eight feet, each appearing to be the same height, in rows resembling gravestones. The view from

the edge of the memorial is unimpressive at first and evokes little feeling. As I began to walk into the sea of pillars, I unexpectedly discovered that the ground gradually descended. The gray blocks towered above me and a feeling of deep sadness overcame me as I contemplated the murder of 6 million innocent Jews.

After darkness fell late Sunday night, I returned once more to walk through the memorial. My earlier feelings intensified as the shadows enveloped me. I experienced a sense of oppressiveness and fear of what might lurk around the next corner. The monument drew me into the emotion of past events. As well as the Holocaust, I thought of the passion of Jesus on Good Friday, also a Jew, also condemned to an unjust death. As he died on the cross, something forever changed in our world, symbolized by the earthquake and the rending of the temple curtain. Jesus lived in the beauty of the world he created, but also tasted the pain, suffering, and death of fallen humanity. He personally carried the pain and suffering of the cross and the grave.

Early the next morning before leaving for the airport, I walked one last time through the memorial. The sun had just risen above the horizon to the east. Everything was the same as the night before, but the pale golden light cast upon the top of the blocks birthed in me a new feeling. The previous night's response of sorrow and pain over the sin and brutality of humanity did not leave, but now a feeling of hope mingled with the sorrow. What occurred on the cross and in the grave were not the final actions of Jesus. His resurrection and ascension were the visible expressions of the beauty of the new world that Jesus is creating in the midst of our fallen world, which will one day be fully consummated in the Revelation 21 vision of a new heaven and a new earth.

The book of Acts tells the early church's experience of a new hope, a new reality, a new world. Luke's two-volume story of Jesus and the church (Luke-Acts) reaches its final crescendo in its last chapter, Acts 28. The gospel that announces this new hope has journeyed from the backwater of Nazareth, through Jerusalem, and finally to Rome, the power center of the known world. Although the apostle Paul has arrived in chains, his bonds cannot bind the unstoppable power of the gospel.

Luke concludes the book of Acts with these words: "He [Paul] proclaimed the kingdom of God and taught about the Lord Jesus Christ—with all boldness and without hindrance!" (v. 31). Luke's final words should be the call and cry of the American church. We are to herald God's good news in the midst of the pain and suffering of this world. Our focal point is the story of Jesus, forever alive through the power of the resurrection. Our prayer is that the kingdom of God will break in upon this world like the new day's dawning of the sun, as the people of God courageously speak and live out the Good News. God bestows on the church the awesome privilege of reenacting the story of Jesus in our day, as we write with boldness and joy the twenty-ninth chapter of Acts.

Caedmon's Song (Part 2)
I have a dream,
That all the world will meet you,
And know you, Jesus, in your living power.
That someday soon all people will hear your story
And hear it in a way they understand.

So many who have heard forget to tell the story.
Here I am, Jesus: teach me.
I cannot speak, unless you loose my tongue;
I only stammer and I speak uncertainly;
But if you touch my mouth, my Lord,
Then I will sing the story of your wonders.[4]

Questions for Reflection and Discussion

1. Restoration is the work of God. What can a church do to invite or be prepared for that act of restoration?
2. How can your church become the living embodiment of Acts 29?

Please go to www.theamericanchurch.org/TACIC/Chapter16.htm for updates and additional information and resources for this chapter.

NOTES

Introduction: Why Examine the American Church?

1. Abe Levy, "Megachurches Growing in Number and Size," Associated Press, *Yahoo! News*, February 3, 2006, as found at http://news.yahoo.com/s/ap/20060204/ap_on_re_us/mega_churches.

2. John N. Vaughan, "The 100 Fastest-Growing U.S. Churches," *Outreach Magazine* (July 2006): 55–56.

3. These are primarily African American or totally independent churches.

4. This research project studies only "orthodox" Christian churches. It does not consider non-Christian religions or nonorthodox Christian churches, such as the Church of Jesus Christ of Latter-day Saints; Jehovah's Witnesses; Unitarian Universalist churches; Church of Christ, Scientist; and a few other small groups. For a more detailed description of the research methodology, see www.theamericanchurch.org/ResearchMethodology.

5. T. S. Eliot, *The Complete Poems and Plays, 1909–1963* (New York: Harcourt Brace, 1963), 153.

6. Lionel Basney, "Immanuel's Ground," *The American Scholar* 68, no. 3 (Summer 1999).

7. Ibid.

Part 1: Observation

1. David Edmonds and John Eidinow, *Wittgenstein's Poker* (New York: HarperCollins, 2001), 11.

Chapter 1: How Many People Really Attend Church?

1. Definition as quoted on the PBS broadcast "Affluenza," 15 September 1997, www.pbs.org/kets/affluenza/home.html.

2. Greg Easterbrook, *The Progress Paradox: How Life Gets Better While People Feel Worse* (New York: Random House, 2003).

3. Jerry Adler, "'The Secret': Does Self-Help Book Really Help?" *Newsweek* (March 5, 2007), as found at www.msnbc.msn.com/id/17314883/site/newsweek.

4. Lionel Basney, "Immanuel's Ground," *The American Scholar* 68, no. 3 (Summer 1999), emphasis added.

5. George Barna, as found at www.outreachtraining.com/documents/Attendance.pdf.

6. Ibid. As we will see, church attendance numbers remain remarkably stable year after year, with a very small yearly percentage change, not the 16 percent change in one year that Barna reports. Barna, and later Gallup, comment on their numbers as if the study's confidence interval did not exist.

7. George H. Gallup Jr., in *National Catholic Reporter*, January 9, 2004, at http://findarticles.com/p/articles/mi_m1141/is_10_40/ai_112450677.

8. A 10 percent increase of the 65 million Catholics in the United States.

9. Michael Paulson, "1 in 6 Go to Mass, Data Show," *Boston Globe* (February 7, 2004), as found at www.boston.com/news/local/massachusetts/articles/2004/01/30/1_in_6_go_to_mass_data_show/. The archdiocese has a baptized membership of 2,084,000.

10. As found in the 2006 Composite Data Report, *Catholic News* (January 2, 2004): 62, at www.archdiocese-chgo.org/departments/research_planning/pdf/data_composite_book_06.pdf.

11. George Barna, at www.barna.org/FlexPage.aspx?Page=BarnaUpdate&BarnaUpdate. The American Church Research Project shows that Protestant churches have an average attendance of 124 adults and children. The median attendance of a Protestant church is 70.

12. Bob Smietana, "Statistical Illusion: New Study Confirms That We Go to Church Much Less Than We Say," *Christianity Today* (April 2006): 85–88.

13. Penny Long Marler and C. Kirk Hadaway, "Testing the Attendance Gap in a Conservative Church," *Sociology of Religion* (Summer 1999): 175–86, as found at http://findarticles.com/p/articles/mi_m0SOR/is_2_60/ai_55208518.

14. Stanley Presser and Linda Stinson, "Data Collection Mode and Social Desirability Bias in Self-Reported Religious Attendance," *American Sociological Review* 63, no. 1 (February 1998): 137–45.

15. Ron Inglehart, Institute for Social Research, 1990–95 data based on a world values survey, as found at www.umich.edu/newsinfo/Releases/1997/Dec97/r121097a.html.

16. C. Kirk Hadaway and Penny Long Marler, "How Many Americans Attend Worship Each Week? An Alternative Approach to Measurement," *Journal for the Scientific Study of Religion* 44, no. 3 (September 2005): 307–22.

17. The division into evangelical, mainline, and Roman Catholic denominations is based on the typology found in the Glenmary Religious Congregations and Membership Study. Mainline denominations are the older historic denominations that tend to espouse more liberal theology. In general, evangelical denominations are more conservative in theology and more conversionist in practice than mainline denominations. All African American denominations are considered evangelical in this typology. Eastern Orthodox churches are included in the "Total" column but are too small in attendance to receive their own column. The classifications can be found with the Association of Religious Data Archives at www.thearda.com/mapsReports/reports.

18. Marler and Hadaway, "Testing the Attendance Gap in a Conservative Church."

19. The statistical model looked at a variety of combinations of attendance ratios, such as weekly, three of four weeks, every other week, only Christmas and Easter, etc. By adjusting the model to try out different possibilities, the regular participant number was between 25 percent and 35 percent higher than weekly attendance.

20. Quoted in Rebecca Barnes and Lindy Lowry, "7 Startling Facts," *Outreach Magazine* (May/June 2006), as found at www.christianitytoday.com/outreach/articles/americanchurchcrisis.html.

21. Some groups also call these "resident members" or "active members."

22. Some groups also call these "members" or "baptized members."

Chapter 2: The Trajectory of the American Church

1. See http://themeparks.about.com/od/coasterridereviews/fr/KingdaKa.htm.

2. "She's One in 300,000,000," *Chicago Sun-Times* (October 18, 2006), as found at www.chicagoist.com/archives/2006/10/18/chicago_gives_birth_to_300_millionth_american_maybe.php.

3. "Now We Are 300,000,000," *The Economist* (U.S.), (October 14, 2006).

4. The differences between straight numerical growth and percentage growth can seem complicated. In most cases, the research in this book is more interested in percentage growth or decline, because that factors in population growth.

5. Rodney Stark, *Cities of God* (San Francisco: HarperSanFrancisco, 2006), 67.

6. Ibid., 65.

7. Rodney Stark, "Reconstructing the Rise of Christianity: The Role of Women," *Sociology of Religion* (September 22, 1995), as found at http://findarticles.com/p/articles/mi_m0SOR/is_v56/ai_17612365.

8. Samuel Shoemaker, "I Stand by the Door," available at www.FaithAtWork.com. Used by permission.

Chapter 3: The Millennium Effect

1. Based on 2000 U.S. Census data for per capita income. See "Hey, Big Spenders," *Marin Independent Journal* (March 9, 2007): sec. 1, 1.

2. Ibid.

3. Anne Lamott, *Traveling Mercies* (New York: Anchor, 2000), 9.

4. This excludes two counties in Utah with more than 60,000 residents. The American church research includes only orthodox Christian churches and does not include non-orthodox Christian churches such as the Mormon church.

5. Personal email from Art Greco.

6. See http://cara.georgetown.edu/.

7. See, e.g., *Catholic News Service* (May 10, 2006), as found at www.catholicnews.com/data/briefs/cns/20060510.htm#head2.

8. William D'Antonio, quoted in Cathy Lynn Grossman and Anthony DeBarros, "Church Struggles with Change," *USA Today* (November 11, 2004), as found at www.usatoday.com/news/religion/2004-11-07-church-main_x.htm.

9. Michael Paulson, "65 Parishes to Be Closed: News Brings Despair, Relief," *Boston Globe* (May 26, 2004).

10. Quoted in Marcella Bombardieri and Erica Noonan, "The Waiting Ends with a Letter: Emotions High at Local Parishes," *Boston Globe* (May 26, 2004).

11. Bella English, "Asleep in the Pews: St. Albert's Parishioners Hold 'Eternal Prayer Vigil' to Keep Church Open," *Boston Globe* (September 9, 2004).

12. American Religious Identification Survey, as found at www.gc.cuny.edu/faculty/research_briefs/aris/key_findings.htm. The PDF is at www.gc.cuny.edu/faculty/research_briefs/aris.pdf.

13. Joseph Jenkins, at http://fatherjoe.wordpress.com/eucharist/mass-attendance-catholic-identity.

14. Helen Osman, "Here in Central Texas, the Church Is Experiencing a Few Growing Pains," at www.austindiocese.org/dept/bishops_office/ar_growing_pains.php.

15. Bear in mind that the population from 1990 to 2000 increased by 13.2 percent, meaning that the percentage of the population attending mainline churches decreased by 15.4 percent in the 1990s.

16. American Religious Identification Survey. This survey is based on self-identification. For this chart, I assigned their denominational categories to evangelical or mainline based on the primary composition of each category. The complete PDF is at www.gc.cuny.edu/faculty/research_briefs/aris.pdf.

17. See Michael Hout, Andrew Greeley, and Melissa J. Wilde, "Birth Dearth," *Christian Century* (October 4, 2005): 24–27. The journal article on which the *Christian Century* article is based is "The Demographic Imperative in Religious Change in the United States," *American Journal of Sociology* 107 (September 2001): 468–500.

18. Ibid. In the journal article, mainline membership grew faster than their demographic (birthrate) model suggested from the mid-1940s to 1958, and then declined faster than predicted by the model from 1958 to 1973. The data fit better with strong mainline new church development from 1945 to 1955 and its subsequent decline from 1957 to 1970, rather than birthrates. Research by the American Church Research Project shows that while 1990–2000 mainline and Roman Catholic attendance mirrored the birthrate of their county, evangelical attendance growth was stronger in low-birthrate counties than in high-birthrate counties. For more information, see www.theamericanchurch.org/birthrates.

19. Statement from the Alliance of African Anglican churches, quoted in Philip Jenkins, "The Global South," *First Things* (December 2006): 14.

20. C. Kirk Hadaway, quoted in "The Advocate July–August 2006," at www.diolex.org/artman/publish/2006julyaugust/article060706.shtml.

21. William R. Coats, "Who (or What) Caused the Decline in Membership in the Episcopal Church," as found at www.rci.rutgers.edu/~lcrew/dojustice/j325.html.

22. More information on the effect of church size is found in chapter 5.

23. This data is taken from the American Religious Identification Survey, a survey based on self-identification. I assigned each group to either an evangelical or mainline category, based on its primary composition. The complete PDF is at www.gc.cuny.edu/faculty/research_briefs/aris.pdf.

24. Ibid.

25. Center for Millennial Studies at Boston University, Richard Landes, director, at www.mille.org/.

Chapter 4: The Church's Remarkable Regional Landscape

1. Roger Finke, "Innovative Returns to Tradition: Using Core Teachings as the Foundation for Innovative Accommodation," *Journal for the Scientific Study of Religion* (November 30, 2003).

2. "Francis Asbury: Methodist on Horseback," *Christian History and Biography*, at www.christianitytoday.com/history/special/131christians/asbury.html.

3. Finke, "Innovative Returns to Tradition."

4. Garrison Keillor, *Lake Wobegon Days* (New York: Penguin, 1990), quoted as The New York Times Quotation of the Day, June 14, 1987. See also http.//prairie home.publicradio.org/about/podcast/.

5. The "Other" category in the pie charts represents all other Christian churches that do not fit into a denominational family category.

6. "Other evangelicals" refers to a group of 12 smaller evangelical denominations. See chapter 7 for information about their composition.

7. "The Parish Church of Christ the King," www.cathedralparish.org/archi tecture.htm.

8. Tom Haroldson, "Episcopal Cathedral Sold; Unnamed Buyer to Pay $1.275M for 38-Year-Old Landmark," *Kalamazoo Gazette* (April 30, 2007).

Chapter 5: "Poor, Uneducated, and Easy to Command"

1. Michael Weisskopf, "Energized by Public or Passion, the Public Is Calling," *Washington Post* (February 1, 2, and 6, 1993): sec. A.

2. Jon Meacham, "What the Religious Right Can Teach the New Democrats," *Washington Monthly* (April 1993), as found at http://findarticles.com/p/articles/ mi_m1316/is_n4_v25/ai_13618596.

3. "Lake Forest, California," at www.thearbor.info/pdf/2005%20Economic%20Profile.pdf.

4. "MuniNetGuide: South Barrington, Illinois," at www.muninetguide.com/ states/illinois/municipality/South_Barrington.php.

5. Michael S. Hamilton, "We're in the Money! How Did Evangelicals Get So Wealthy, and What Has It Done to Us?" *Christianity Today* (June 12, 2000): 43.

6. "Aging Body," Merck, at www.merck.com/mmhe/sec01/ch003/ch003a.html.

7. The data on this chart was derived from a sample of more than 75,000 Protestant churches, balanced proportionately between mainline and evangelical.

8. www.AndretheGiant.com.

9. www.nccbuscc.org/vocations/schwietz.shtml.

10. Tim Cherry, "Young Clergy Forge Bonds among Peers, Seek Church's Respect," Episcopal News Service, June 24, 1998, as found at http://andromeda. rutgers.edu/~lcrew/under35.html.

11. James D. Davidson, "American Catholics and American Catholicism: An Inventory of Facts, Trends and Influences," at www.bc.edu/bc_org/research/rapl/ church-in-america/davidson.html.

12. "Aging Body."

13. This study did not include new churches under 10 years old, so as to minimize the influence of church planting.

14. David Murrow, *Why Men Hate Going to Church* (Nashville: Nelson, 2005), quoted in Holly Pivec, "The Feminization of the Church: Why Its Music, Messages and Ministries Are Driving Men Away," in *Connections*, as found at www.biola.edu/admin/connections/articles/06spring/feminization.cfm. See also

Kristen Campbell and Adelle M. Banks, "Empty Pews: Where Did All the Men Go?" *Washington Post* (June 10, 2006).

15. Paul Vernon, "Beliefwatch: God's Girls," *Newsweek* (July 3–10, 2006), at www.msnbc.msn.com/id/13529122/site/newsweek. A Duke University study of congregational life found that the typical adult audience at a U.S. congregation is 61 percent female (see www.decaturdaily.com/decaturdaily/religion/060701/church.shtml). The U.S. Congregational Life Survey (based in Louisville, KY) also reported 61 percent female, 39 percent male (see www.uscongregations.org).

16. Dalia Sussman, "Who Goes to Church? Older Southern Women Do; Many Catholic Men Don't," at www.abcnews.go.com/sections/us/DailyNews/church_poll020301.html.

17. James Twitchell, *Branded Nation* (New York: Simon & Schuster, 2004), as found at www.motherjones.com/news/feature/2005/03/megachurches-3.html.

18. Werner Haug and Phillipe Warner, *The Demographic Characteristics of the Linguistic and Religious Groups in Switzerland*, quoted in Richard Egan, "Church Attendance: The Family, Feminism and the Declining Role of Fatherhood," AD2000, as found at www.ad2000.com.au/articles/2002/sep2002p8_1115.html.

19. John Ferguson, *Religions of the Roman Empire* (Ithaca, N.Y.: Cornell University Press, 1970), 125ff, quoted at www.christian-thinktank.com/urbxctt.html.

Chapter 6: Denominational Winners and Losers

1. Christian Churches belong to the evangelical family. Churches of Christ are evangelical and noninstrumental, which means they do not use musical instruments and are often outstanding at a cappella singing. Author Max Lucado is a minister in the Church of Christ. The Disciples of Christ (Christian Church) are part of the mainline branch.

2. I regularly find churches that claim to be independent on their website, but further investigation reveals they are a member of a denomination, something many of their members and even some of their staff do not know.

Part 2: Evaluation

1. Jack L. Griggs, *All the Birds of North America*, American Bird Conservatory's Field Guide (New York: Harper Perennial, 1997), preface.

Chapter 7: The Survival of the Species

1. Figure 7.1. is based on Roelant Savery's 1626 painting of a stuffed specimen —note that the Dodo has two left feet (see http://en.wikipedia.org/wiki/Extinct_birds).

2. "Brinkley, Ark., Embraces 'The Lord God Bird,'" NPR website, at www.npr.org/templates/story/story.php?storyId=4721675.

3. Jack L. Griggs, *All the Birds of North America*, American Bird Conservatory's Field Guide (New York: Harper Perennial, 1997), preface.

4. Fortunately, the rumor is becoming less common on the Internet, but it still appears, such as at www.newchurches.com/public/resources/read

ing/docs/ChurchPlantingManualbyJohnIuliano.pdf; www.healthychurches. org/Nov_06_Connection.pdf; and http://yourjourney.org/waterNew/default. asp?T=502907&DID=1189.

5. H. G. Parsa, "Restaurant Failure Rate Much Lower Than Commonly Assumed, Study Finds," Ohio State Research News, at http://researchnews.osu. edu/archive/restfail.htm.

6. This number reflects those that are started and last long enough to report an attendance figure.

7. Having this net gain would keep the ratio of people per church constant.

8. Lewis Wilkins, "Plumbing the Heart of God's People," at www.pcusa.org/ research/compstats/cs2005/wilkins_article.pdf.

9. Based on a 2 percent church-planting rate with an 80 percent survival rate (16 percent) for the first ten years and a 1 percent closure rate over the next three decades (21 percent).

10. These two denominations were chosen because they are old and historic. Older denominations do not actually have a disadvantage reaching these benchmark compared to younger denominations. Usually the challenge only reflects a lack of energy for new births. It is no more difficult for an older denomination to plant 2 percent new churches than it is for a newer denomination.

11. "The Story: The Search for the Ivory-bill," Big Woods Conservation Partnership, at www.ivorybill.org/story.html.

12. Ibid.

13. Ibid.

Chapter 8: Why Established Churches Thrive or Decline

1. This "Three Tree" model was developed by colleagues at the Department of Church Growth and Evangelism of the Evangelical Covenant Church.

2. By definition, established churches are those over 10 years old. However, the research in this chapter looks at churches either over 20 years old, so as to eliminate the residual growth effect of newer churches in the sample, or over 40 years old, which mark the significant milestone of entering its second generation of life.

3. Mark I. Pinsky, "As Downtown Is Reborn, So Are Its Churches: Orlando's Rapid Residential Revival Creates the Possibility of a Religious Resurrection," Orlando Sentinel (March 18, 2007), at www.orlandosentinel.com/news/ orl-revival1807mar18,0,7276683.story?coll=orl-news-headlines.

4. "Aging Body," Merck, at www.merck.com/mmhe/sec01/ch003/ch003a.html.

5. David Yonke, "Upon Entering a New Era: Church Revived By McKinstry Is Building a New Facility," Toledo Blade (April 28, 2007).

6. Presented at an Alban Institute seminar, "Leading Change in the Congregation," in Atlanta, March 5–7, 2007.

7. C. S. Lewis, On Stories and Other Essays on Literature, ed. Walter Hooper (New York: Harcourt Brace Jovanovich, 1982), xiii.

8. Diana Butler Bass, "Vital Signs: Congregations Find Passion and Purpose by Blending Ancient Traditions and Contemporary Action," Sojourners (December 2005), at www.sojo.net/index.cfm?action=magazine.article&issue=soj0512&article=051210.

9. Cathy Lynn Grossman, "Some Protestant Churches Feeling 'Mainline 'Again," *USA Today* (November 1, 2006), at www.usatoday.com/news/religion/2006-10-31-protestant-cover_x.htm.

Chapter 9: In the Birthing Room of the American Church

1. The Covenant Assessment Center, started in 1993, is a four-day intensive evaluation of pastors and spouses who are considering planting a new Covenant church.

2. "First Covenant Church: Seattle: History," at www.seattlefirstcovenant.org/history.html.

3. Ibid.

4. George Barna reported in 2006 that his polling showed 9 percent of Americans (27 million) attended a house church each week, and 75 million attended at least once a month. If true, the 27 million figure is the same as attend all 200,000 evangelical churches in the United States! The actual number is only a fraction of that. Reliable estimates are difficult to come by, but in all probability weekly attendance at house churches is between 100,000 and 300,000. As of 2007, it was a growing movement (see www.barna.org/FlexPage.aspx?Page=BarnaUpdateNarrow&BarnaUpdateID=241).

5. While the number of churches planted is an important indicator, equally significant is how well they are started.

6. Michael S. Hamilton and Jennifer McKinney, "Turning the Mainline Around: New Sociological Studies Show That Evangelicals May Well Succeed at Renewing Wayward Protestantism," *Christianity Today* (August 1, 2003), at http://ctlibrary.com/16902.

7. Luke 9:24.

8. See http://cleave.blogs.com/pomomusings/2005/11/brians–lecture–.html.

9. *Sunset Western Garden Book* (Menlo Park, CA: Sunset Publishing, 1988), 82.

10. Pioneer church plants are new churches started in a community without a parent church or other supporting churches and without preexisting networks of relationships. This is sometimes called the parachute method. The process of parenting well is greatly facilitated by coaching and experience. Help can be found at www.theamericanchurch.org/parenting.

11. More information on genuine multiethnic churches can be found at www.theamericanchurch.org/Multiethnic.

12. Documented by *Guinness Book of Records*, as found at http://en.wikipedia.org/wiki/Elizabeth_Bolden and http://www.cbsnews.com/stories/2006/12/11/national/main2249442.shtml?source=RSSattr=U.S._2249442.

Part 3: Introspection

1. Matthew Arnold, "Dover Beach," in *New Poems* (London: Macmillan, 1867).

Chapter 10: Cultural Change in America

1. J. R. R. Tolkien, *The Fellowship of the Ring* (Boston and New York: Houghton Mifflin, 2002), 772.

2. "Historic Buildings of NMSU," New Mexico State University, at www.nmsu. edu/General/Maps/historic.html.

3. Elsa Brenner, "Westchester; A Softer Look for a Dark Campus," *New York Times* (July 24, 2005), at http://query.nytimes.com/gst/fullpage.html?res=9D05E 7D9173FF937A15754C0A9639C8B63&partner=rssnyt&emc=rss.

4. What follows is a vast simplification of much more complex patterns, but hopefully will help in understanding the complementary and adversarial interaction between Christianity and the changing culture.

5. The United States is usually 40 years slower than Europe in adopting these new worldviews. Canada seems to be halfway between the United States and Europe.

6. "I sent you to reap what you have not worked for. Others have done the hard work, and you have reaped the benefits of their labor."

7. A strange and unexpected phenomenon happened among many mainline churches. The more a church accommodated to the increasingly secular culture, the more the church declined in numbers, much to their chagrin.

8. Europe entered this phase in 1965, but because of the inability of the state churches to adapt and the weakness of the free churches, very few churches became effectively missional. There are some encouraging recent signs, however, and a growing interest in church planting.

9. Personal email from Art Greco.

10. "Birth and Fertility Rates," Child Trends Data Bank, at www.childtrends databank.org/pdf/79_PDF.pdf.

11. Some fundamentalists consider the Athens episode the greatest failure of Paul's ministry because he apparently didn't persuade the philosophers of the supremacy of Christ and didn't draw as many converts as elsewhere. Luke certainly does not view this episode as such.

Chapter 11: Sober Reflections on the Future of the American Church

1. J. R. R. Tolkien, *The Fellowship of the Ring* (Boston: Houghton Mifflin, 2002), 321.

2. Arthur C. Clarke, *Greetings, Carbon-Based Bipeds! Collected Essays, 1934–1998* (New York: St. Martin's Griffin, 2001), as quoted in "Famous False Predictions," at www.paulbenger.net/2004/08/famous-false-predictions.html.

3. Bernard Lewis, "The 2007 Irving Kristol Lecture by Bernard Lewis," at the American Enterprise Institute Annual Dinner, March 7, 2007, as found at www. aei.org/publications/filter.all,pubID.25815/pub_detail.asp.

4. U.S. Census Bureau estimate, at www.census.gov/ipc/www/idb/ranks. html.

5. The United Church of Christ, at ws.ucc.org/index.php?option=com_conte nt&task=view&id=551&Itemid=54.

6. C. S. Lewis, *The Lion, the Witch, and the Wardrobe* (New York: Collier, 1970), 16.

7. Ibid., 118.

Chapter 12: What Is the American Church to Do?

1. Dorothy Sayers, "Creed or Chaos," in *The Whimsical Christian* (New York: Collier, 1978), 35 (speaking about England during World War II).

2. E.g., the Christian and Missionary Alliance, the Church of God (Anderson), the Evangelical Free Church, the Assemblies of God, the Church of the Nazarene, the Foursquare denomination, the Evangelical Covenant Church, the Baptist General Conference, and numerous others.

Part 4: Action

1. Tom Wright, *Paul for Everyone*: *Romans*, pt. 1 (Louisville: Westminster John Knox, 2004), 11–12.

Chapter 13: The Message of Jesus

1. N. T. Wright, *Jesus and the Victory of God* (Minneapolis: Fortress, 1996). Wright is a noted British New Testament scholar and bishop of Durham, England.

2. LeRon Schulz and Steve Sandage, *Faces of Forgiveness* (Grand Rapids: Baker, 2003).

3. Philip Jenkins, "Believing in the Global South," *First Things* (December 2006): 16.

4. Tom Wright, *Luke for Everyone* (Westminster John Knox, 2001), 124. Tom Wright is the pen name for N. T. Wright in these popular commentaries.

5. Matthew uses the Septuagint translation in 13:15.

6. Colin Brown, ed., *Dictionary of New Testament Theology*, vol. 2 (Grand Rapids: Zondervan, 1976), 180.

7. *Welcome, invite, call,* and *summon* are four words that N. T. Wright uses to describe Jesus' call to his followers. See Wright, *Jesus and the Victory of God*, 244–319.

Chapter 14: The Mission of Jesus

1. C. S. Lewis, *The Problem of Pain* (New York: Macmillan, 1950), 29.

2. See the book of Hebrews for more about the sacrifice of Jesus.

3. E.g., see 1 Peter 3:18–22.

4. Formula of Concord IX.4.

5. John Calvin, *Institutes of the Christian Religion*, www.reformed.org/master/index.html?mainframe=/documents/Christ_in_hell.

6. C. S. Lewis, *The Lion, the Witch, and the Wardrobe* (New York: Macmillan, 1951), 185.

7. C. S. Lewis, *Mere Christianity* (New York: Doubleday, 1943), 53–54.

8. Richard Foster, *The Freedom of Simplicity* (San Francisco: HarperSanFrancisco, 2005), 97.

9. Bede, *Historia Ecclesiastica Gentis Anglorum* (Church History of the English People), IV.24.

10. Northumbria Community, *Celtic Daily Prayer* (New York: HarperCollins, 2002), 199–202. Used by permission.

Chapter 15: The Message and Mission of the Church

1. Lon Allison, "Rethinking Public Evangelism," Billy Graham Center, http://64.233.167.104/search?q=cache:eKT3eT4PzHIJ:bgc.gospelcom.net/ise/RTpapers/Papers04/allisonpdf.pdf+lon+allison+RETHINKING+PUBLIC+EVANGELISM&hl=en&ct=clnk&cd=2&gl=us.

2. N. T. Wright, *Jesus and the Victory of God* (Minneapolis: Fortress Press, 1996), 181.

3. Mark W. Durm, "The Rise of Christianity: A Sociologist Reconsiders History," *Skeptical Inquirer* (July 1999), reviewing Rodney Stark's *The Rise of Christianity* (Princeton, NJ: Princeton University Press, 1996).

4. This is Citadel of Faith Covenant Church's vision statement: "To build a ministry where all of the hurting, distressed, confused, rich or poor, of all races and cultures, will come to seek answers from the word of God that are relevant to the issues of their lives. In order to attract those who are in need of God's manifest power in their lives, we will reflect the light of God through sincere and consistent connection and service to those in our community. As we develop genuine relationships, and serve one another, our works will connect those individuals to God. And as the life of God awakens in each individual blessed by our ministry, a community will begin to grow in which people can see the power of God change and bless their lives, their families, their communities, and their world."

5. An excellent book on hospitality is Christine Pohl, *Making Room: A Guide to Christian Hospitality* (Grand Rapids: Eerdmans, 1999).

Chapter 16: The Restoration of the American Church

1. A theophany is a visible manifestation of God.

2. Katherine S. White, *Onward and Upward in the Garden* (Boston: Beacon Press, 2002), introduction.

3. Northumbria Community, *Celtic Daily Prayer* (New York: HarperCollins, 2002), 3.

4. Ibid., 199–202. Used by permission.